Malebranche and Ideas

Malebranche and Ideas

Steven Nadler

New York   Oxford
OXFORD UNIVERSITY PRESS
1992

Oxford University Press

Oxford New York Toronto
Delhi Bombay Calcutta Madras Karachi
Kuala Lumpur Singapore Hong Kong Tokyo
Nairobi Dar es Salaam Cape Town
Melbourne Auckland

and associated companies in
Berlin Ibadan

Copyright © 1992 by Steven Nadler

Published by Oxford University Press, Inc.,
200 Madison Avenue, New York, New York 10016

Oxford is a registered trademark of Oxford University Press

Library of Congress Cataloging-in-Publication Data
Nadler, Steven M., 1958–
Malebranche and ideas / Steven Nadler.
p. cm. Includes bibliographical references and index.
ISBN 0-19-507724-5
1. Malebranche, Nicolas, 1638–1715. I. Title.
B1897.N33 1993 194—dc20
92-3797

9 8 7 6 5 4 3 2 1

Printed in the United States of America
on acid-free paper

For Rose
and
for my parents

Acknowledgments

In the course of writing this book, I have received invaluable advice and suggestions (and lessons) from a number of people. I would especially like to thank Monte Cook, Nicholas Jolley, Tom Lennon, Don Rutherford, Red Watson, and John Yolton for taking the time to read the complete manuscript and for their extensive and helpful comments, as well as Angela Blackburn of Oxford University Press for her efforts in bringing this work to publication. Much of the work for this book was supported by a number of summer research grants from the Graduate School of the University of Wisconsin–Madison, and I am grateful for their assistance. I owe the greatest debt to my wife, Jane, whose love, patience, and encouragement made it possible for me to continue working. Finally, I dedicate this book to our daughter, Rose, for the love and beauty she has brought into our lives, and to my parents, Arch and Nancy Nadler, for the support they have always provided.

Contents

Abbreviations

The following list includes works cited frequently in the text and notes. Full references may be found in the bibliography. Unless an English translation is cited, the translations of French and Latin sources are my own.

Works by Malebranche

OC   *Oeuvres complètes de Malebranche* (referred to by volume number:page number).

Search   *De la recherche de la vérité* (1st ed., 1674–75).

LO   *The Search After Truth*, English translation of *Recherche* by T. M. Lennon and P. Olscamp, based on sixth (1712) edition.

Préface   *Préface contre le livre de Foucher* (included in vol. 2 of 1st ed. of *Recherche*).

Réponse   *Réponse de l'auteur De la Recherche de la Vérité au livre de M. Arnauld des vrayes et des fausses idées* (1684).

TL   *Trois Lettres de l'auteur De la Recherche de la Vérité, Touchant la Défense de M. Arnauld contre la Réponse au livre des vrayes et des fausses idées* (1685).

Dialogues   *Entretiens sur la métaphysique* (1688).

D   *Dialogues on Metaphysics*, English translation of *Entretiens* by W. Doney.

RLA   *Réponse du Père Malebranche, Prêtre de l'oratoire à la troisième lettre de M. Arnauld Docteur de Sorbonne, touchant les Idées & les Plaisirs* (1699).

Works by Descartes

AT   *Oeuvres de Descartes* (referred to by volume number:page number).

CSM   *The Philosophical Writings of Descartes*, translated by J. Cottingham, R. Stoothoff, and D. Murdoch (referred to by volume number:page number).

Works by Arnauld

VFI   *Des vraies et des fausses idées* (1683) (in *Oeuvres de Messire Antoine Arnauld*, vol. 38).

Défense   *Défense de M. Arnauld, contre la réponse au livre des vraies et des fausses idées* (1684) (in *Oeuvres*, vol. 38).

Works by Foucher

Critique   *Critique de la Recherche de la vérité* (1675).

RCP   *Réponse pour la Critique à la Préface du second volume de la Recherche de la vérité* (1676).

Works by Locke

"Examination"   "An Examination of P. Malebranche's Opinion of Seeing All Things in God" (in *The Works of John Locke*, vol. 9).

Malebranche and Ideas

At a certain point everyone looks at the books. The numbers don't lie. They read the numbers, they see what. only makes sense. It's like numbers are language, like all the letters in the language are turned into numbers, and so it's something that everyone understands the same way. You lose the sounds of the letters and whether they click or pop or touch the palate, or go *ooh* or *aah*, and anything that can be misread or con you with its music or the pictures it puts in your mind, all of that is gone, along with the accent, and you have a new understanding entirely, a language of numbers, and everything becomes as clear to everyone as the writing on the wall. So as I say there comes a certain time for the reading of the numbers. Do you see what I'm getting at?

Abbadabba Berman in
E. L. Doctorow's *Billy Bathgate*

1

Introduction

It should be clear to anyone who reads carefully the *Search After Truth*, the *Treatise on Nature and Grace*, and other works by Nicolas Malebranche that he is a profoundly good philosopher. To be sure, he does not possess the analytical rigor and lightning-quick wit of Arnauld, or the sheer natural brilliance of Leibniz, or even the grace and style of Descartes. And yet he was recognized by his contemporaries (most of whom disagreed with him) as an important and influential thinker, one with a wide-ranging and penetrating intellect. He was a systematizer who sought to develop, within a neo-Cartesian framework, an epistemology and metaphysics which were firmly rooted in a proper theological foundation. It is somewhat surprising, given Malebranche's importance for the study of early modern philosophy—he should certainly be of great interest to those working on Descartes, Leibniz, Berkeley, or Hume—that he has received so little attention in the anglophonic philosophical world, and that so few have taken the time and effort to work through his philosophical writings.[1]

This, as one would expect, has led to great misunderstandings and gross caricatures of Malebranche's doctrines. The most glaring example concerns the theory of causation for which Malebranche is perhaps best known. There is a certain textbook mythology regarding the genesis and significance of occasionalism that still enjoys widespread credibility. According to the usual narrative, occasionalism—the view that finite created beings have no causal efficacy whatsoever, and that God is the only true causal agent—

---

1. French scholars, on the other hand, have honored him with numerous studies, most importantly those of Alquié, Dreyfus, Gouhier, Gueroult, Robinet, and Rodis-Lewis.

develops out of a perceived failure on the part of Cartesian dualism to be able to accommodate mind–body interaction. If unextended thinking substance and extended matter are so radically different, then it seems inconceivable that they can become causally engaged and that one can bring about effects in the other. The ubiquitous causal activity of God, the story runs, is thus called upon to explain why mental states follow upon certain physical occasions (as pain follows pinprick) and why appropriate bodily motions follow certain mental events (as the rising of the arm follows the volition to raise it). On this view, then, occasionalism is simply an ad hoc attempt by later Cartesians to make their metaphysical system more consistent.[2]

We can now dispense with this unhistorical and incorrect reading. In the first place, occasionalism is not simply an explanation of the apparent correspondence between mental states and bodily states. It is just as much an account of body–body "interaction" as it is of mind–body "interaction." God is responsible not only for affecting minds when certain brain states occur but also for moving bodies when they collide.[3] In fact, it can be argued that Malebranche and other occasionalists do not even recognize a "mind–body problem" such as we understand it today. For them, whatever problem there may be about mind–body interaction results not from dualism per se but from certain principles about causation in general, principles which rule out real causal interaction among finite created substances (whether they be mental or material).[4]

In the second place, a more than superficial reading of Malebranche's texts on causation and physics reveals that his occasionalism is really intended, at least in part, to supplement a perceived incompleteness in the mechanical philosophy to which he is committed. Material substances, as parcels of pure extension alone, cannot be genuine causes. Cartesian bodies are inert and passive entities and therefore cannot be the source of either their own

2. See, for example, Copleston, *A History of Philosophy*, vol. 4, pp. 176ff.; and Boas, *Dominant Themes of Modern Philosophy*, p. 103. This myth is also found in recent scholarly work on Malebranche; see Radner, *Malebranche*, pp. 10–12, and Balz, *Cartesian Studies*, p. 213.
3. For a good discussion of occasionalism from this point of view, see Lennon, "Philosophical Commentary," LO 810ff.
4. See Nadler, "Occasionalism and the Mind–Body Problem."

motions or the motions of other bodies. What occasionalism provides is a metaphysical framework within which mechanical explanation can be saved by ultimately being grounded in something higher than mere extension, a framework in which motion and force are given a true causal foundation outside the limits of physics proper, namely, in the infinite, omnipotent will of God.[5]

I have discussed occasionalism at length not only to demonstrate the kind of distortion and oversimplification to which Malebranche's philosophy has been subjected—even by those seventeenth-century critics who read him carefully—but also to provide the reader with an idea of the way (more sophisticated than is usually recognized) in which Malebranche's theological and philosophical/ scientific concerns are woven together. And what is true in both these respects for occasionalism applies as well to his theory of ideas.

It is a central thesis of this book that Malebranche's vision in God does for epistemology precisely what occasionalism does for physics. As the causal theory places the mechanical philosophy in its proper theologico-metaphysical context, so the vision in God demonstrates the ultimate dependence we as knowers have upon God. Our conceptual and perceptual processes are fundamentally grounded in the divine understanding, just as events in nature are grounded in the divine will. Conception or "pure intellection," as well as perception, demand concepts, or what Malebranche calls "representative ideas." But, he claims, the general concepts or ideas we employ in intellection and perception are not abstracted from particulars; in fact, they are not empirically acquired at all. Nor are they innate in the mind, provided to us preformed at birth and ready to be brought into consciousness. Rather, the ideas which function in *our* cognitive activities are in the divine understanding; that is, "our" ideas are God's ideas[6] (or, as Malebranche prefers to

5. However, particular explanations at the level of physics remain purely mechanical, without recourse to God; see *Search*, Elucidation XV: OC 3:213; LO 662. For a discussion of occasionalism and its relationship to mechanism, see Clark, *Occult Powers and Hypotheses,* chapter 4.
6. In using this expression I do not intend to beg the question whether for Malebranche there is a multitude of discrete ideas in God. Malebranche, in fact, is ambiguous on this question in the first edition of the *Search* and is forced to reconsider the issue in the *Elucidations* added to the third edition (1677–78); see chapter 2 in the present study.

put it, "our ideas are in God"), and they become accessible to us only because God wills them to be present to our minds. The vision in God is thus a theologization of cognition and refers us back to the divine source of the clear and distinct contents of our thoughts.

Malebranche first presents the vision in God in the *Search After Truth*, by far his most important work. It is a monumental opus, covering not just knowledge and truth, but also psychology, sense physiology, moral philosophy, physics, metaphysics, even theology. He was, at the time of its publication, thirty-six years old and a priest of the Congregation of the Oratory (an order founded in 1611 by Cardinal Bérulle, later an admirer of Descartes). When writing the *Search*, Malebranche was already a devotee of Cartesian philosophy, having been deeply moved by reading Descartes's *Traité de l'homme* in 1664, and a devotee as well of the thought of St. Augustine, whose writings were studied in the Oratory. Upon its publication, the *Search* made an immediate impact. Simon Foucher (1644–96), a chaplain in Paris and a skeptical critic of Cartesian philosophy, became the first in a long line of critics (and defenders) of Malebranche's system.[7] He was soon followed by Arnauld, Malebranche's most famous adversary, who objected primarily to the doctrine of grace presented in the *Treatise on Nature and Grace* (1680) and saw the *Search* mainly as a philosophical prolegomenon to the more properly theological work. Arnauld's attack began a long period of public polemic, during which Malebranche was constantly engaged in explaining his views and defending them against philosophers and theologians, Cartesians and anti-Cartesians, Catholics and Protestants. In these debates Malebranche was forced to expand and develop his ideas, and he eventually wrote the *Dialogues on Metaphysics* (1688) as an attempt to present his doctrines—particularly the vision in God—in their mature form.

Malebranche's theory of ideas has never been fully understood, much less appreciated. This is partly Malebranche's fault. Owing to certain ambiguities in his presentation of the theory, it readily lends itself—like his occasionalism—to various kinds of misreadings. Thus he speaks both of perceiving *bodies* and of perceiving *ideas*, without telling us whether or not different senses of 'perceive' are at

---

7. In fact, Foucher's *Critique* appeared even before the publication of the second volume of the *Search* in 1675.

work. In fact, as I argue in chapter 5, our purely intellectual apprehension or "perception" of ideas is one element in our (ordinary) perception of bodies; but ideas themselves are not objects of (ordinary) perception. We can (intellectually) perceive ideas alone, but this is understanding or conception, not perception.

Encouraged by such ambiguities, Malebranche's harsher critics certainly have a tendency toward caricature in interpreting his thought on ideas. He is often portrayed by them as enclosing the mind in a "palace of ideas," forever cut off from any kind of cognitive or perceptual contact with the material world. Malebranchian ideas, in the hands of his critics, thus become immaterial sensory objects, much like the sense data of recent representative theories of perception; we directly (and ordinarily) perceive these ideal entities instead of the bodies in the material world that they represent. This is how Arnauld and Locke read him, and I examine their version in detail in chapter 5. But even those critics who nonetheless admire, and even borrow elements from, Malebranche's system fail truly to comprehend the nature and role of ideas therein. Leibniz, for example, thinks Malebranche a profound thinker, and believes that his view of ideas as objects of thought is preferable to Arnauld's view of them as mental acts. But while Leibniz finds "many lovely thoughts" in the *Search*, he ultimately considers the vision in God, however "useful" it may be for demonstrating our dependence on God, rather too mystical for his own taste.[8] On Malebranche's view, as he reads it, "assuming that God annihilates all the beings he has created . . . and assuming further that God presents to our minds the same ideas presented to our minds in the presence of objects, we would see the same beautiful things as we see at present. Therefore, the beautiful things we see are not material, but intelligible beautiful things"; it is clear that 'see' refers here to ordinary perception.[9] Although somewhat gentler in his critique, Leibniz apparently shares with Arnauld and

8. See the letter of 4 November 1715 to Rémond, in Robinet, *Malebranche et Leibniz*, p. 481. Leibniz here provides his own understanding of how it can be said that "nous voyons tout en Dieu." See also Leibniz's *New Essays on Human Understanding* II.1, p. 109.

9. *Conversation of Philarète and Ariste*, in *Philosophische Schriften*, vol. 6, p. 591 (translation by Garber and Ariew in *Leibniz: Philosophical Essays*, p. 266). For a discussion of Malebranche and Leibniz, see Jolley, *The Light of the Soul*.

Locke a rather fanciful and distorted image of the role Malebranche's ideas play in knowledge and perception.

Berkeley, while clearly influenced by Malebranche's views on causation and the vision in God, nonetheless sees in Malebranche a perfect instance of the kind of materialist philosophy against which he is arguing. On this "absurd" view, there is, beyond the ideas we immediately (and, again, ordinarily and sensibly) perceive, an inert, "useless" material world, itself unknowable and unperceivable. This, Berkeley believes, can only lead to skepticism and atheism. Malebranche's philosophy, he derisively asserts, is nothing more than an "enthusiasm," and insists (somewhat incredibly) that "there are no principles more fundamentally opposite than his and mine."[10]

Finally, Thomas Reid considers Malebranche's theory a paradigmatic instance of the "philosophers' view" of ideas and perception. "Their opinion is, that we do not really perceive the external object, but the internal only. . . . The way in which philosophers speak of ideas, seems to imply that they are the only objects of perception."[11] In Malebranche's case, according to Reid, all we ever see are divine ideas—a rather "visionary" system, he adds. Nonetheless, he does give Malebranche, a man of "penetrating intellect" and "great genius," credit for discerning and honestly acknowledging the full consequences and difficulties—epistemological and ontological—of holding such a theory.

Thus Arnauld, Locke, Leibniz, Berkeley, and Reid (and most recent commentators as well) all share a reading of Malebranche's theory of ideas according to which ideas are visual-like data, immaterial sensory objects ordinarily perceived. Moreover, they (at least in their more generous moments) consistently attribute to him a rather unorthodox version of the representative theory of perception.

It is part of my thesis here that this reading of Malebranche's theory of ideas is wrong. For Malebranche, ideas are logical con-

---

10. See *Three Dialogues Between Hylas and Philonous*, Dialogue II, *Works*, vol. 2, p. 214. For studies of Malebranche and Berkeley, see Luce, *Berkeley and Malebranche*, and McCracken, *Malebranche and British Philosophy*, chapter 6.

11. *Essays on the Intellectual Powers of Man*, Essay II, p. 125. For a discussion of Malebranche and Reid, see McCracken, *Malebranche and British Philosophy*, chapter 8.

cepts or essences, not visual-like images; our "perception" of them is intellectual, not sensory; and his theory of perception is not a representative theory at all. Furthermore, I argue that the central epistemological role of ideas in Malebranche's system is in his account of pure, abstract knowledge, not in his theory of sense perception. To miss this and to emphasize the role of ideas in our ordinary perceptual acquaintance with the material world is precisely what leads to the kind of misinterpretation and distortion just surveyed.

Most of the criticism (and ridicule) leveled at Malebranche's theory of ideas (with the exception of Reid's remarks) is directed not so much at the epistemological role he grants ideas, but rather at the modifications he introduces into the tradition often called the "way of ideas." For seventeenth-century philosophers as diverse as Descartes, Spinoza, Leibniz, Arnauld, Locke, and others, it is a given that *ideas*, or immaterial representative images,[12] mediate both abstract conceptual knowledge and perceptual acquaintance with the material world. The differences among these thinkers usually concern the nature and function of these representations. For some, ideas are mental acts, or perceptions modifying a thinking substance. Descartes, for example, notes that when considered "materially," that is, in regard to its actual or "formal" mode of being, an idea is simply an operation of the intellect (*operatio intellectus*).[13] And Spinoza, in the *Ethics*, insists that an idea is not "some dumb thing like a picture on a tablet," but "a mode of thinking, to wit, the very act of understanding."[14] For others, ideas are not acts but *objects* of thought—mental images toward which the mind's operations are directed. This appears, on occasion, to be Locke's view: "I must here in the entrance beg pardon of my reader for the frequent use of the word 'idea' which he will find in the following treatise. It being that term which, I think, serves best to stand for whatever is the object of the understanding when a man

---

12. My use of the term 'images" should not be taken to imply that ideas are picture images; see chapter 2 in this volume.
13. *Meditations*, Preface: AT 7:8; CSM 2:7.
14. *Ethics*, Part II, Proposition 43, scholium. See also Arnauld: "I take the perception and the idea to be the same thing" (VFI 198).

thinks."[15] Finally, Leibniz claims that an idea is not a mental act, nor an object apprehended by the mind, but rather a disposition to think of some object: "An idea consists, not in some act, but in the faculty of thinking, and we are said to have an idea of a thing even if we do not think of it, if only, on a given occasion, we can think of it."[16]

In all three of these accounts, whatever differences there may be among them, ideas are in some way or another *mental* items, properties or modifications of the soul. Whether ideas are mental acts, mental objects, or mental dispositions, they are nonetheless in the mind. Now Malebranche's ideas are, in one sense, of the second variety; that is, they are *objects* apprehended by the mind. But his crucial ontological innovation, as I show in chapter 2, is to move ideas outside the human mind and into the divine understanding.[17] And this view, in spite of its fine Augustianian pedigree, is to his critics' minds philosophically (and theologically) unacceptable. Truly, some claim, Malebranche has transported us into an otherworldly realm where the only objects we know and perceive are divine immaterial beings. Moreover, ideas in God's understanding, others claim, would certainly be as external to our minds as material bodies. How, then, can they be the direct and immediate objects of the mind, while bodies cannot? Malebranche, for his part, simply sees himself as a traditionalist on the matter of ideas, upholding the original (i.e., Platonic) philosophical understanding of the term.

Malebranche's theory of ideas is the centerpiece of his epistemology, essential to his project in the *Search After Truth*. That project, as he describes it, is to discern the sources of error, deliver the mind from its prejudices, and lead it toward the discovery of truth. And

---

15. *An Essay Concerning Human Understanding* I.1.viii. Recently this traditional view of Locke as holding an object theory of ideas has been contested. See for example Yolton, *Perceptual Acquaintance*, chapter 5; and Stewart, "Locke's Mental Atomism and the Classification of Ideas."

16. "What Is an Idea? [*Quid sit idea?*]," *Philosophischen Schriften*, vol. 3, p. 263. For a general discussion of the various theories of ideas in the seventeenth century, see McRae, "'Idea' as a Philosophical Term in the Seventeenth Century"; and Yolton, "Ideas and Knowledge in Seventeenth-Century Philosophy."

17. Jolley offers a fine discussion of what he calls Malebranche's "anti-psychologism" regarding ideas; see *The Light of the Soul*.

for avoiding error and attaining truth, he insists, nothing is more necessary than "reasoning only upon clear and evident ideas" (*Search*: OC 2:451; LO 528). Ideas are grasped in a nonsensory manner by the pure intellect, and reveal to us with absolute evidence eternal essences and the necessary truths based on them. The senses, on the other hand, only distract us from the contemplation of truth and lead us astray in our quest for knowledge.

> The mind becomes purer, more luminous, stronger, and of greater scope as its union with God increases, because this union constitutes its entire perfection. It becomes corrupted, blind, weakened, and restricted as its union with its body is increased and strengthened, because this union constitutes all its imperfection. Thus, a man who judges all things by his senses, who follows the impulses of his passions in all things, who perceives only what he senses and loves only what flatters him, is in the most wretched state of mind possible. In this state he is infinitely removed from the truth and from his good. But when a man judges things only according to the mind's pure ideas, when he carefully avoids the noisy confusion of creatures, and, when entering into himself, he listens to his sovereign master with his senses and passions silent, it is impossible for him to fall into error. (*Search*, Preface: OC 1:15-16; LO xxiii)

Ideas "instruct us in the truth" about mathematics, moral law, and even the material world. They thus provide a solid foundation for all the sciences, for systems of true and evident propositions. In this general respect Malebranche's project is a Cartesian one. Descartes's epistemological goal, in the *Meditations* and elsewhere, is to "draw my readers' minds away from the senses as far as possible," eliminate the unwarranted confidence we place in our preconceived opinions, and further the search for truth by demonstrating the importance of relying only on clear and distinct ideas in our reasoning.[18]

Now there is certainly a theological dimension to Descartes's epistemology. We can be assured that our clear and distinct conceptions are not just subjectively certain but also objectively true, because our reasoning faculty is given to us by a nondeceiving, infinitely good and powerful God. If we use that faculty properly, we will not be led astray. But this divine guarantee is a rather

---

18. See *Meditations*, Dedicatory Letter and Preface; and the *Discourse on Method*.

extraneous one. The ideas and powers we employ are our own, and as created knowers we are epistemologically independent of God.[19] With Malebranche, on the other hand, the theologization of knowledge is thoroughgoing. The contemplation of divine ideas informs our most basic cognitive processes and represents, for Malebranche, our proper activity—our *eudaimonia*, even—and a "conversion and return to God." The pursuit of knowledge becomes more than an endeavor to be practiced in one's spare time, or something worthy merely for its own sake or for the worldly benefits it may confer on us. Rather, it is our absolute duty, an obligation we owe to God and to ourselves, as well as a necessary condition for our happiness: "It is evident that God can act only for Himself, that He can create minds only to know and love Him, and that He can endow them with no knowledge or love that is not for Him or that does not tend toward Him. . . . Hence, the relation that minds have to God is natural, necessary, and absolutely indispensable" (*Search*, Preface: OC 1:10; LO xx).

Another way of looking at this—one which informs this book—is to bear in mind that Malebranche's theory of ideas is an amalgam of Cartesianism and Augustinianism. From Descartes, Malebranche inherits a commitment to mind–body dualism and the exhaustive ontology of substance and modification, as well as his views on the epistemological role of clear and distinct ideas. From St. Augustine, on the other hand, he takes a rather broadly interpreted theory of divine illumination, one that explains not just our knowledge of eternal truths, but even our most ordinary perceptual apprehension of the world. The mixture of Cartesianism and Augustinianism is not always a harmonious and consistent one, and, as I argue, it results in certain tensions in Malebranche's system.

Malebranche's doctrine of ideas and the vision in God is primarily a theory of knowledge and understanding. It is an account of our rational apprehension of universals (including the essences of material things), mathematical and moral truths, "common notions," and other nonsensory cognitions. As I show in chapter 2, ideas themselves are abstract logical concepts, not pictorial images. They

---

19. However, as *beings* we are not ontologically independent of God, since we require him to sustain us in existence; see *Meditations* III.

are the proper objects of human knowledge (la science), not of perception. But Malebranche's doctrine *does* play a role in his account of our perceptual acquaintance with the world. Ideas contribute the epistemic component he deems essential for perception. In chapter 3 I examine the various arguments Malebranche offers for the claim that ideas are required in conception and perception. In chapters 4 and 5, respectively, I turn to the vision in God and untangle the various elements in his account of knowledge and perception. The resulting interpretation of Malebranche's account is a rather unorthodox one. Yet it makes good sense of much of what he says about ideas and their role in thinking and perceiving. It also has the further advantage of ascribing to Malebranche a much more sophisticated and philosophically tenable theory than critics and commentators traditionally accuse him of holding—a theory, in fact, worthy of a philosopher of his stature.

2

Representative Ideas

Any examination of the nature and role of ideas in Malebranche's system must begin with the important distinction he draws between ideas (idées) and sensations (les sensations, les sentiments). The distinction has its immediate roots in the Cartesian picture of the mind (which Malebranche accepts, with some important modifications) and the mechanistic account of nature, while its late ancestors include Galileo's doctrine of explanation, and its more remote ancestors, ancient atomist theories. It is the same bifurcation that appears in its best-known form in Locke as the distinction between ideas of primary qualities and ideas of secondary qualities.[1]

Malebranche's crucial (and controversial) innovation is to take what was generally considered to be a purely epistemological difference among our ideas (whereby some ideas truly represent and make known properties of objects in the external world, while other ideas do not) and transform it into an ontological difference as well. Ideas, for Malebranche, provide us with clear and true knowledge, and are located in the understanding of God, ontologically independent of (yet present to) the human mind. Sensations, on the other hand, are properties of the soul, and tell us nothing about the external world beyond what effects material objects occasion in us. Ideas alone function in conception or "pure intellection," while both ideas and sensations are necessary elements in perception, with ideas contributing the cognitive component and sensations its sensuous character.

---

1. See *An Essay Concerning Human Understanding*, II.23.ix. Locke, however, finds much to criticize in Malebranche's understanding of the distinction; see "Examination," p. 232f., 236.

Primary Qualities and Sensory Effects

Ancient atomists such as Democritus, Epicurus, and Lucretius appear to be the first to separate those intrinsic qualities which really and inseparably belong to material objects (size, shape, motion) from the sensory effects which they produce in the mind (color, pain, pleasure, heat, taste, etc.), which sensory effects bear no resemblance whatsoever to the properties of the atomic particles in motion which cause them.[2] In the modern period it is Galileo who first systematically introduces a distinction between what he calls "primary" or "real" qualities and mere "sensations." Body or corporeal substance is nothing more than a bounded, shaped parcel of solid matter having a particular size, place, relations to other bodies, and a degree of motion or rest. Tastes, colors, odors, sounds, and other sensuous qualities do not really belong to bodies: "[They] are no more than mere names so far as the object in which we place them is concerned, and . . . they reside only in the consciousness." Heat, pain, pleasure, and sweetness belong only to the perceiving mind, and, unlike those other qualities which we conceive of as inseparable from body, "have no real existence save in us."[3] What this means is that among our sense perceptions we can distinguish between those which bear an element of truth about the external world and represent the real qualities of objects, and those which are radically dissimilar from anything outside the mind and, hence, are incapable of providing knowledge about the nature of material bodies. Our perception of heat, for example, is caused by a multitude of minute particles having certain shapes and sizes and moving with various velocities. When these particles come into contact with our body, their impact or penetration causes in the mind the painful or pleasant sensation which we call "heat."[4] But the hot or warm sensation itself reveals nothing of the underlying mechanistic processes which cause it. Thus while the distinction Galileo is primarily concerned with is an ontological one regarding the real properties essentially belonging to bodies, its epistemologi-

2. See for example Lucretius, *De rerum natura*, Book IV.
3. Galileo, *The Assayer* (1623), in Drake, trans., *Discoveries and Opinions of Galileo*, pp. 274–77.
4. Ibid., pp. 277–78.

cal consequences are evident, although Galileo himself does not actually draw them.

Descartes's epistemological and scientific projects, on the other hand, clearly involve distinguishing explicitly between those of our perceptions or ideas which clearly and distinctly represent real properties of external material bodies, and those which are merely the confused and obscure mental effects of the action of those bodies upon the body to which the mind is joined. His physics shares with Galileo's the picture of an external world devoid of any nonquantifiable, nongeometric properties. Matter, for Descartes, is pure extension in three dimensions, and bodies are composed solely of "various differently shaped and variously moving parts" (*Principles of Philosophy* II.1: AT 8-1:40–41; CSM 1:223). A body, then, has only those properties which can be modifications of extension: shape, size, figure, number, and motion. Tastes, colors, pains, pleasures, sounds, smells, and so on have no place in the material world. "All the properties which we clearly perceive in [matter] are reducible to its divisibility and consequent mobility in respect of its parts, and its resulting capacity to be affected in all the ways which we perceive as being derivable from the movement of the parts" (*Principles of Philosophy* II.23: AT 8-1:52; CSM 1:232). The mode of being of sensuous qualities is a purely mental one.

The Cartesian account of the material world entails that it is possible, from the mind's point of view, to identify two distinct kinds of ideas or mental images (*imagines*)[5]: those which display or present (*exhibet*) to the mind geometrical and motive realities (extension and its modifications); and, on the other hand, those which present a purely sensuous content (colors, tastes, pains, pleasures, etc.). The former are "clear and distinct [*clara et distincta*]" and

---

5. The use of the term 'image' here does not imply that ideas are mental *pictures* for Descartes. As he insists, all ideas are *tanquam rerum imagines* (*Meditations* III: AT 7:37); that is, they are all representations exhibiting a certain content (or "objective reality") to the mind. But his denoting them *imagines* does not necessarily commit him to a pictorial mode of representing for ideas. See Wilson, *Descartes*, pp. 100–119; and Costa, "What Cartesian Ideas Are Not." Costa argues that Descartes's ideas are not "immaterial images," although he seems to understand by this simply that they are not pictures.

truly represent properties in bodies.[6] The latter are "confused and obscure," and are simply mental effects of matter in motion; they represent and make known nothing external to the mind.

> For if I scrutinize [my ideas of corporeal things] thoroughly and examine them one by one, in the way in which I examined the idea of the wax yesterday, I notice that the things which I perceive clearly and distinctly in them are very few in number. The list comprises size, or extension in length, breadth, and depth; shape, which is a function of the boundaries of this extension; position, which is a relation between various items possessing shape; and motion, or change of position; to these may be added substance, duration, and number. But as for all the rest, including light and colors, sounds, smells, tastes, heat and cold and the other tactile qualities, I think of these only in a very confused and obscure way. (*Meditations* III: AT 7:43; CSM 2:29–30)

All ideas, for Descartes, are on the same *ontological* plane (or, in Cartesian terms, are alike in terms of their "formal" reality): they are all modifications or properties of thinking substance, the mind existing in such and such a manner. There is, however, an essential *epistemological* difference between those ideas which are clear and distinct, and sensations. Clear and distinct ideas inform us as to "the essential nature of the bodies located outside us" (although we are not assured of this until clear and distinct perception itself has been validated through the omnipotence and benevolence of God), and allow us to know them "in so far as they are the subject matter of pure mathematics"—that is, in so far as they are conceived in terms of pure extension and its modifications (*Meditations* VI: AT 7:72; CSM 2:50). Consequently, clear and distinct ideas provide a reliable (and divinely guaranteed) foundation for a geometrized science of nature (*Meditations* V: AT 7:71; CSM 2:49).

Sensations, on the other hand, do not in any way resemble (*non esse simile*) real properties in objects. "Sensory perception does not

---

6. Not all ideas that present primary qualities are, for Descartes, clear and distinct. We do have ideas of primary qualities that are sensory and hence not clear and distinct (for example, my sensory idea of the sun's size as compared to my "astronomical" idea of its size; see *Meditations* III: AT 7:39; CSM 2:27).

show us what really exists in things, but merely shows us what is beneficial or harmful to man's composite nature" (*Principles of Philosophy* II.3: AT 8-1:41; CSM 1:224). If clear and distinct ideas represent and make known the *essential* (geometric) properties of bodies, sensations at best inform us in an obscure way about certain limited *relational* properties bodies may possess (for example, that a particular body causes such and such modifications in the human body, hence occasioning such and such modifications—particularly the sensations themselves—in the soul). Their value as representations is minimal (in contrast to the maximal representative value of our ideas of bodies qua extended), and they often furnish the mind with material for error (*materiam erroris* [*Meditations* III: AT 7:234; CSM 2:163–64]).

While Malebranche's theory of ideas and his distinction between ideas and sensations are indeed, in many crucial respects, similar to Descartes's, the modifications Malebranche makes are sufficiently unorthodox (and problematic) as to attract the objections of Cartesians and non-Cartesians alike.

Ideas and Sensations

Malebranche's doctrine of ideas suffers from ambiguities as soon as it is introduced in the beginning of the *Search After Truth*. In Book I, chapter 1, the term 'idea' is used explicitly to refer to two kinds of immaterial entities present to the mind: those which represent objects external to the mind and allow us to understand their properties, and "sensations," which are merely modifications of the mind and do not represent anything in the external world. This ambiguity is particularly evident in the first four editions (1674–88).

> It can be said that the soul's ideas are of two kinds, if we take the term 'idea' generally to mean everything which the mind perceives immediately. Those of the first kind represent to us something external to us, such as a square, a triangle, etc. [such as a square, a house, etc. (3rd and 4th eds.)]; and those of the second kind only represent to us that which takes place within us, such as our sensations, pain, pleasure, etc. For it will be seen later on that sensations are nothing

but modes of the mind, and it is for this reason that I call them modifications of the mind. (OC 1:42)[7]

Here, both representative entities (êtres représentatifs) and sensible impressions are "ideas." Elsewhere in the work, however, Malebranche draws a strict distinction between ideas proper and sensations. In Book I, chapter 18, for example, he notes that sensations often distract the mind from its contemplation of ideas and lead it away from the truth.[8] In Book III, part 2, chapter vi, Malebranche enumerates the two elements composing perceptual awareness:

> When we perceive something sensible, two things are found in our perception: *sensation* and *pure idea*. The sensation is a modification of our soul, and it is God who causes it in us. He can cause this modification even though he does not have it Himself, because He sees in the Idea He has of our soul that is capable of it. As for the idea found in conjunction with the sensation, it is in God, and we see it because it pleases God to reveal it to us. God joins the sensation to the idea when objects are present so that we may believe them to be present and that we may have all the feelings and passions that we should have in relation to them. (OC 1:445; LO 234)

Malebranche's critics were quick to point out the inconsistency. Arnauld, for example, claims that Malebranche simply contradicts himself when discussing the nature of ideas, and insists that he has trouble understanding just what Malebranche intends by the word 'idea'. After quoting the passage that I cite from *Search* I.1, he complains that Malebranche uses 'idea' (idée) to denote both a genus and one species within the genus (l'être représentatif), but not

---

7. In the fifth through seventh editions (1700–1712), Malebranche changes this as follows:

> We can say that the soul's perceptions of ideas are of two kinds. The first, which are called pure perceptions, are, as it were, accidental to the soul: they do not make an impression on it and do not sensibly modify it. The second, which are called sensible, make a more or less vivid impression on it. Such are pleasure and pain, light and colors, tastes, odors, and so on. For it will be seen later on that sensations are nothing but modes of the mind, and it is for this reason that I call them *modifications* of the mind. (OC 1:42; LO 2)

The ambiguity, however, remains: the term 'idea' refers both to the objects of the mind's pure perceptions, and to its own sensations.

8. OC 1:176–77; LO 79–80.

the other species (la sensation). "The definitions of words are arbitrary [*libres*]. Nonetheless, it is troublesome to give the name of the genus to one species and not to give it to the other species; this might prevent us from considering this other species as belonging to the notion of the genus" (VFI 187).[9]

Locke, too, finds it difficult to understand Malebranche's distinction between 'idea' and 'sentiment' if, as Malebranche insists, ideas generally are simply that which the mind perceives immediately.

> The distinction he makes . . . between "sentiment" and "idea," does not at all clear to me, but cloud, his doctrine. . . . [If] the figure of the violet be to be taken for an "idea," but its "colour" and "smell" for sentiments: I confess it puzzles me to know by what rule it is, that in a violet the purple colour, whereof whilst I write this I seem to have as clear an idea as the figure of it; especially, since he tells me in the first chapter here, which is concerning the nature of ideas, that, "by this word idea he understands nothing else, but what is the immediate or nearest object of the mind when it perceives anything."[10]

Malebranche himself is aware of the ambiguity:

> The word *idea* is equivocal. Sometimes I take it as anything that represents some object to the mind, whether clearly or confusedly. More generally I take it for anything that is the immediate object of the mind. But I also take it in the most precise and restricted sense, that is, as anything that represents things to the mind in a way so clear that we can discover by a simple perception whether such and such modifications belong to them. (*Search*, Elucidation III: OC 3:44; LO 561)

The apparent inconsistency in Malebranche's account thus stems from several different senses of 'idea':

(A) When taken in the broadest sense, it means "tout que l'esprit aperçoit immédiatement" and clearly includes both pure representations and sensations, both of which are apprehended by the mind immediately (in spite of the ontological difference between the two, which I discuss).

9. Arnauld was probably working from the fourth (1678) edition of the *Search* (*Des vraies et des fausses idées* was written in 1684; see OC 1:xxvii, n. 4). Perhaps his criticism here led Malebranche to modify the passage as of the fifth (1700) edition (see n. 7).

10. "Examination," pp. 232–34.

(B) There is another broad sense of 'idea' according to which it signifies "anything that represents some object to the mind, whether clearly or confusedly [*tout ce qui representent à l'esprit quelque objet, soit clairement, soit confusement*]." That is, whatever presents the mind with a representational content, however minimal and obscure, can be called an "idea" in this second sense.

(C) Finally, in the *strict* sense of 'idea' ("le sens le plus précis et le plus réservé"), only that which represents in a clear and distinct manner is an idea.

While sensations can be called "ideas" according to (A), it is not clear whether they qualify as "ideas" according to (B), since Malebranche's account of the representational character and value of sensations contains its own ambiguities. There seem to be three possibilities that need to be distinguished here: (1) sensation as a certain kind of natural, unconscious judgment about the size, figure, and distance of a body (that is, its extension); (2) sensation as a complex involving both a "passion de l'âme" and an accompanying involuntary judgment projecting that *passion* onto the body; and (3) the *passion* or sensuous quality itself.

In the *Search*, Book I, chapter 7, Malebranche identifies our sensory awareness (l'idée sensible, la sensation) of extension (i.e., of the figure, shape, and size of an object) with a certain *jugement naturel* that is, in effect, a mental modification or correction of corporeal images located in the fundus of the eye. The sensation is simply that unconscious judgment which, for example, in the sense perception of a cube, allows one to perceive a three-dimensional object with all its angles and sides equal on the occasion of a two-dimensional image with unequal angles and sides occurring on the retinal nerve (*Search* I.7.iv: OC 1:96–97; LO 34). The mind is here subliminally following the rules of perspectival geometry and finds itself with a "corrected" sensory experience of the size and figure of the object (one sees a round penny, not an oval one). Malebranche calls this natural judgment a "compound sensation [*sensation composé•*]" because it depends on two or more simultaneous impressions occurring in the eyes—for example, an impression of shape and an impression of distance. The sensation in which these corporeal images are brought together and compared is, in effect, a "judgment" as to what the true shape and size of the external object are.

> When I look at a man walking toward me, for example, it is certain
> that, as he approaches, the image or impression of his height traced
> in the fundus of my eyes continuously increases and is finally
> doubled as he moves from ten to five feet away. But because the
> impression of distance decreases in the same proportion as the other
> increases, *I see him as always having the same size.* Thus, *the sensa-
> tion I have of the man* always depends on two different impressions.
> (*Search* I.7.iv: OC 1:97; LO 34; emphasis added)

Note that I *sense* the size of the man (and his shape and motion and
distance from me). The correction of the bodily impressions, as a
product in the mind, is a sensation, but one which involves a kind of
judgment concerning those impressions. "What is in us is but a
sensation [which] can be considered in relation to the Author of
Nature who excites it in us as a kind of [*comme une espèce de*]
judgment" (OC 1:97; LO 34).[11]

By identifying the corrective judgment as a *sensation*, Malebranche gives this species of sensation, namely, the sensory awareness of the properties of a body qua extended, a representational
content. Moreover, the content possessed by these sensations bears
a modicum of truth regarding the external world: it seems generally
to tell us something about what is happening in external space,
something about the real properties of extended bodies. This applies, however, *only* to such judgment-sensations regarding figure,
size, and distance. For sensuous qualities such as pleasures, pains,
and colors there is nothing even remotely similar to them outside
the mind (as I discuss).

> It must be agreed that [the judgments we form on the testimony of
> our eyes concerning extension, figure, and motion] are not altogether
> false: they include at least this truth, that outside us there are figures,
> motion, and extension. . . . We can be assured that ordinarily exten-
> sion, figure, and motion are external to us when we see them. These
> things are not merely imaginary; they are real, and we are not

11. In my discussion I follow the account of natural judgment in the second and all
later editions of the *Search*. This seems, however, to be a modification of the account
in the first edition. For a discussion of natural judgment in Malebranche, and of the
apparent change between editions, see Robinet, *Système et existence dans l'oeuvre de
Malebranche*, pp. 305–15; Alquié, *Le Cartésianisme de Malebranche*, pp. 167–73;
Lennon, "Philosophical Commentary," LO 773–81; and Bréhier, "Les 'jugements
naturels' chez Malebranche."

mistaken in believing that they have a real existence, independent of our mind. . . . It is certain, then, that the judgements we make concerning extension, figure, and motion of bodies include some measure of truth. But the same is not true of those concerning light, colors, tastes, odors, and all the other sensible qualities, for truth is never encountered here. (*Search* I.10: OC 1:121–22; LO 48)

However, while our sensations of extension do have a somewhat veridical representational content, it is not one that is clear and distinct. In fact, "they can still be occasions for error for us. . . . [T]hese natural judgements deceive us not only with regard to the size and distance of objects but also by making us see their figures other than as they are" (*Search* I.7: OC 1:97–98; LO 35–36). The information they provide about these properties of bodies is entirely relative to the perceiver's own body, and is limited by the laws of perspective and the physiology of optics and of the tactile sense organs. Moreover, the sensuous geometry employed by these judgment-sensations is certainly less clear, complete, and precise, and thus less true (vraie), than the geometry based on the pure perception of (eternal) representative ideas in God.[12] Thus sensations in this sense are "ideas" according to definition (B), but not according to definition (C).

With regard to sensations such as light, colors, heat, tastes, sounds, odors, pain, and pleasure, another ambiguity appears. Malebranche distinguishes between the sensation proper and a sensation/judgment complex. Sensation proper is "the passion, sensation, or perception of the soul, i.e. what each of us feels when near the fire" (*Search* I.10.vi: OC 1:129; LO 52). What Malebranche has in mind here is the sensuous phenomenon itself, or what he calls the *qualité sensible*. These sensations proper possess no representational content, and contain no element of truth regarding the external world. They are only what happen in the mind on the occasion of certain bodily (brain) motions. Thus according to definitions (B)

12. It is crucial to distinguish this *sensory* awareness of extension from the *intellectual* apprehension of intelligible extension in God. This distinction is similar to, but not identical with, Descartes's distinction between the two ideas of the sun: the (adventitious) sensory idea and the astronomical/intellectual idea (derived from innate notions); see *Meditations* III: AT 7:39; CSM 2:27. In chapter 5 I show how this distinction supports my interpretation of the role ideas play in perception for Malebranche.

and (C) of 'idea', sensations proper are absolutely distinct from ideas.

Malebranche notes, however, that every sensation (e.g., pain, heat) is accompanied by an involuntary *jugement naturel* that, for example, "what [the soul] perceives is in the hand and in the fire" (*Search* I.10.vi: OC 1:130; LO 52). The spontaneous judgment that the sensation (la passion) which modifies the mind is in the sense organ ("the pain is in my hand") or in the external object itself ("the fire is hot") so closely and constantly accompanies the sensation that it is often "confounded" with the sensation proper and the two are taken for one and the same thing (*Search* I.14.ii: OC 1:157; LO 68–69). This natural judgment (which must be distinguished from, but is often followed by, an explicit "voluntary judgment" to the same effect) is always false (*Search* I.14.i: OC 1:156; LO 67). The sensation/judgment compound is itself often called a *sensation* by Malebranche (*Search* I.10.vi: OC 1:130; LO 52) and clearly possesses a representational content of some kind, however false and obscure. The judgment, in a sense, attaches a content to the sensation proper, to the *qualité sensible*, thereby making it an intentional or object-directed phenomenon (e.g., "this pain is in that hand"). With this extended notion of *sensation*, sensations might be called "ideas" according to definition (B): they "representent à l'esprit confusement."

Thus according to the broad definition (A) of 'idea', all sensations might be called "ideas," since they are all immediately perceived by the mind. And according to the somewhat less broad definition (B), there are two cases in which sensations are "ideas" (i.e., in which they represent something to the mind): sensation qua natural judgment concerning shape, size, and figure (our sensory awareness of extension); and sensation qua *passion*/judgment complex. But in neither case do sensations represent in a way which is "so clear that one can discover, from an ordinary survey, whether such and such modifications belong [to the object]." Thus they fail to qualify as "ideas" according to the "strict and precise" definition (C). And sensations proper—that is, 'sensation' in the strict sense of the term, the "passion de l'ame" which forms part of the *passion*/judgment complex, such as heat, pain, and pleasure—do not purport to represent anything at all. In the strictest sense of 'idea', then, and in the strictest sense of 'sensation', the two are distinguished, first of all, on epistemological grounds. (In my discussion henceforth, I use the term 'sensation' only in this strict sense.)

Sensations are no more than modifications of the soul that occur in relation to what takes place in the body with which that soul is united. "I feel pain, for example, when a thorn pricks my finger; but the hole it makes is not the pain. The hole is in the finger . . . and the pain is in the soul, for the soul senses it keenly and is disagreeably modified by it" (*Search* I.10.i: OC 1:123; LO 49). More specifically these modifications, these sensuous events, are (in accordance with Malebranche's occasionalist account of causation) caused by God, who acts on the occasion of an external body being present to and "affecting" (also by occasional causation) the human body. Pleasures, pains, heat, sadness, colors, our "passions and natural inclinations" are all "modalitez ou modifications de l'âme" (*Réponse* VI, OC 6:55). Since they are simply modes of being of the mind itself, they are perceived solely by "inner sensation [*sentiment intérieur*]." They are, as Malebranche puts it, "nothing but the soul itself existing in this or that way."[13] It follows from this, and from the principles of mind–body dualism, he believes, that sensations cannot represent anything external to the mind. Our perceptions of heat, color, and so forth, do not represent anything real in the external object. Since the soul is unextended thinking, it is inconceivable to Malebranche how a modification or property of the soul could be representative of anything material (extended) external to it.[14] While sensations

13. Malebranche acknowledges Descartes as his source on the nature of sensations as simply modes of the soul; see TL I (OC 6:201). In fact, his apparent debt to Descartes on the matter of sensation generally is even greater. For example, Malebranche distinguishes "four things we confuse in each sensation": the action of the object against the body; the agitation of the sense organ; the *passion* or sensation itself in the soul; and the natural judgment projecting the sensation onto the human body or external object (*Search* I.10.vi). This corresponds almost exactly with Descartes's "three grades of sensory response" (Descartes's account combines the external object's action on the body and the agitation of the sense organ): the immediate stimulation of the body; the "immediate effects produced in the mind as a result of its being united to a bodily organ which is affected in this way"; and the resulting "judgements about things outside us"—e.g., that a stick is colored. See Sixth Replies, AT 7:437; CSM 2:294–95.

14. See *Réponse* X, OC 6:86. This is the essence of Malebranche's argument against Arnauld's *perceptions représentatifs*, operations of the soul or mental acts that represent external things.

can inform us as to which objects are pleasant and to be pursued, and which are painful and to be avoided as harmful to the body (that is, while they can inform us as to certain relational properties of objects), they really tell us less about the world than about the mind itself—that it is capable of such and such modifications. In an important sense, sensations for Malebranche are epistemically empty. They are merely "confused and obscure" mental events which the mind perceives in itself,[15] and tend to distract the mind from its contemplation of ideas.

Representative Ideas

Ideas proper are not modifications of the human soul but are in God (see chapter 4). Thus they differ ontologically from sensations. And as definition (C) above suggests, the epistemological difference between ideas and sensations consists in the fact that ideas represent in a clear and distinct manner, while sensations (in the strict sense) do not have any representational content at all. That is, ideas present a content to the mind, one that is characterized by Malebranche, in various contexts, as "perfect," "complete," "evident," "clear," and "true." What this claim involves, and the resulting epistemic value of ideas, is the subject of this section.

Unlike sensations, which (while we can clearly distinguish one from another) are representationally "blank" events in the mind as such and carry no external reference (although the mind is led by a natural judgment to project them outside itself), ideas purport to be about something—they are "presentational" phenomena and thus have intentionality.[16] Every idea displays a certain determinate content, exhibits characters and relations among characters which

---

15. See *Réponse* XIII, OC 6:98.
16. This difference between ideas and sensations could be compared to a similar kind of difference that may exist among paintings. On the one hand, there are portraits, landscapes, still lifes, etc., all of which are presentations of an object or a set of objects and purport to be "about" them. On the other hand, one might simply cover each of a number of canvases with a single, undifferentiated pigment (a black canvas, a red canvas, etc.). While the painter may intend the all-black canvas to "represent" despair or life in New York City, it is not a "presentation" of any object and does not, in itself, purport to be about some thing.

are accessible to an inspection by the mind. Thus ideas have what Malebranche (following Descartes) refers to as "objective reality."[17] There is something about each idea itself which makes it the idea *of* (or the presentation *of*) one object rather than another.

Moreover, the manner in which ideas represent provides absolutely clear and evident knowledge about the idea's *representatum*. As Malebranche insists, when we see things by way of ideas, "we always see them in a perfect fashion [*d'une manière très parfaite*]. . . . Through their ideas, we perceive bodies and their properties, and for this reason the knowledge we have of them is quite perfect" (*Search* III.2.vii: OC 1:450; LO 237).[18] In fact, from the idea of an object (or a state of affairs), it is possible to determine, with the utmost evidence, four things: the actual nonrelational properties of the object; all the possible or compatible nonrelational properties of the object; what properties are incompatible with the object; and in what relations it does, can, and cannot stand to other things.

First, the idea of an object allows us to see "through simple perception what it contains and what it excludes." The idea of a right triangle, for example, tells us that it is composed of three sides enclosing a space; that it has three angles the sum of which is equal to two right angles; that one of those angles is a right angle; that the square on the hypoteneuse is equal to the sum of the squares on the other two sides; and so on. And it tells us that the right triangle does not have all its sides equal and that it is not equiangular. An idea informs as to all the properties actually possessed by its object, all

17. For Descartes, the objective reality of an idea is simply its representational content, what it "displays" (*exhibet*) to the mind. See *Meditations* III (AT 7:40; CSM 2:28). Malebranche self-consciously departs from Descartes's position on ideas. Nonetheless, he is aware of at least a certain continuity in calling the content of an idea its "objective reality"; see TL I, OC 6:217. For Malebranche, however, the objective reality exhausts the being of the idea. Speaking of Descartes, he insists that "he does not take the word 'idea', as I do, to signify uniquely the objective reality" (ibid.). Thus it might be more accurate to say that, for Malebranche, ideas *are* objective realities.

18. It should not be inferred from this quote that the *representatum* of an idea is necessarily material. In fact, the content of Malebranche's ideas is primarily geometrical, although it is precisely their geometrical nature that allows ideas to represent material bodies (when they do). Thus in the following discussion the 'object' or 'state of affairs' presented by the idea is mathematical.

its characteristics and "internal" relations.[19] It thus also provides a basis for determining what properties do not belong to the object. What Malebranche notes with respect to the idea of extension in general—that "every question about what does or does not belong to extension can be answered immediately, and boldly, merely by considering the idea representing it" (*Search*, Elucidation XI: OC 3:165; LO 634)—applies as well to the idea of any particular extension.

Second, at a more general level, the idea tells us not only what actually belongs to a thing, but also what *can* belong to it—what are the possible properties that an object of that kind can possess. "[The mind] sees things through illumination when it has a clear idea of them, and when by consulting this idea it can discover all the properties of which these things are capable" (*Search*, Elucidation X: OC 3:141; LO 627). The idea of extension, for example, "suffices to inform us of all the properties of which extension is capable"— that it is figurable and divisible, and thus can become round or square, large or small, and so forth (*Search*, Elucidation XI: OC 3:165; LO 634). Similarly, the idea of the parallelogram tells us that it can be square or rectangular. And if we had an idea of the soul, Malebranche insists, we would know a priori, from that idea alone, what modifications the soul is capable of, what kinds of thoughts or perceptions it can possibly have, without needing to consult experience and the actual modifications which we undergo as thinking things.[20]

Third, if the idea of a thing tells us all the properties which that thing *can* have, it also thereby tells us what properties a thing *cannot* have and what is incompatible with its nature.

> We discover by simple perception, then, without any reasoning and merely by applying the mind to the idea of extension, that roundness

19. This is not to say that the idea informs one as to the *existence* of its object. Geometric objects, which do not actually (i.e., materially) exist, still have actual or occurrent properties. The Pythagorean proportion, for example, is an *actual* property of the right triangle.

20. Note that all this is different from telling us the actual properties of the object (e.g., that a parallelogram is a quadrilateral figure having two sets of parallel sides). Perhaps this difference is more clearly framed if it is described in terms of *essential* and *accidental* properties. The idea tells us, then, what are the essential properties of its object, as well as what accidental properties it can have.

and every other figure is a modification belonging to body, and that pleasure, pain, heat, and all other sensible qualities are not modifications of body. . . . Those who say that matter can think do not believe that it has this faculty because it is extended; they agree that extension, taken precisely as such, cannot think. (*Search*, Elucidation XI: OC 3:165; LO 634)

Once we perceive the idea of extension (or the idea of a particular extended body), all questions as to what can and cannot belong to it can be answered; compatibilities and incompatibilities between subject and property are immediately evident, and we know directly that heat or color cannot be a mode of extended substance. Malebranche elsewhere insists that since we have no such clear idea of the soul, there is no agreement on what should be believed about the soul and its modifications—no agreement as to what can and cannot belong to the mind.[21]

This applies not just to general properties but also, as Malebranche claims, to an infinite number of particular properties. We see, for example, that extension has certain *proprietez générales*: it is figurable, mobile, divisible, and so on. But we see also that it can assume an infinite number of particular properties: it can, in the category of figure, become triangular, square, hook-shaped, and so on. And we understand that a triangular extended figure can itself be modified in an infinite number of particular ways regarding size, proportion, angularity, and so on.

I know extension; and if by 'extension' is meant body, then I know the nature of body in general by its idea. For in contemplating the idea of extension, I see that it is divisible and mobile; and, consequently, that body is capable of all kinds of figures. I see, in addition, that it is only capable of this: since the idea of extension . . . excludes all thought, all sensation, pain, color, taste, etc. Thus, in considering the idea of extension, I see, or I can see by a simple view its general properties. I see what it contains and what it excludes; for it excludes everything which it does not contain. I can even discover an infinity of particular properties, by examining the diverse figures with which this idea furnishes me. (*Réponse* XXIII, OC 6:161)

Finally, the idea of a thing informs us in a determinate and exact manner about all the relations in which that thing stands to other

---

21. See *Search*, Elucidation XI: OC 3:165; LO 634.

things known by idea. That is, equalities, differences, proportions, and other kinds of quantitative comparisons are immediately evident when investigated by means of clear ideas. From my idea of a right triangle and my idea of a square whose side is equal to one of the sides of the triangle, for example, I can come to a definite (and true) conclusion as to the ratio of their areas. On the other hand, while I can compare two shades of red and determine which shade is darker, my grasp of the difference between the two shades is "obscure and confused" and not expressible in any exact terms. And we have no way of comparing sensations that are conveyed by different sense organs.

> Can we compare heat with taste or smell with color? Do we know the relation between red and green, or even between two shades of green? Such is not the case with different figures, which we can compare with each other; we know their relations exactly, we know precisely that the square of the diagonal of a square is double that square. What relation is there between these intelligible figures, which are very clear ideas, and our soul's modifications, which are but confused sensations? (*Search*, Elucidation X: OC 3:150; LO 625)

In this way, ideas provide the foundation for the sciences, for systems of true propositions whose logical or other relations are readily accessible to the attentive mind. Truths, for Malebranche, are simply relations within and between clear ideas and, as such, are "nothing real" (*Search* III.2.vi: OC 2:444; LO 234). But since the ideas and relations that constitute them are clear, eternal, and immutable, so the truths themselves partake of these qualities.

> I know the parts of extension clearly because I can see their relations evidently. I see clearly that similar triangles have proportional sides, that there is no plane triangle the three angles of which are not equal to two right angles. I see these truths or relations clearly in the idea or archetype of extension. For that idea is so luminous that contemplating it is what makes Geometers and good Physicists, and it is so fertile in truths that all minds together will never exhaust it. (*Dialogues* III.6: OC 12:66–67; D 59–60)[22]

Thus a clear and distinct idea gives us complete and well-defined knowledge of its object. Moreover, it does so with perfect evidence,

---

22. See also TL I, OC 6:199; and RLA, OC 8:933.

allowing no room for doubt as to the properties and relations—actual or possible—included or excluded by its content, and providing impeccable grounds for true judgment. "Truth is almost never found except with evidence, and evidence consists only in the clear and distinct perception of all the constituents and relations of the object necessary to support a well-founded judgement" (*Search* I.2: OC 1:54–55; LO 10). As Aristes says in the fifth of the *Dialogues on Metaphysics*, when he finally makes some progress toward the Malebranchian position, the ideas of things "make known to us their nature, their properties, the relations they have, or can have, to one another, in short, the truth" (OC 12:113; D 107).

Malebranche's understanding of the nature of a clear and distinct idea is a genuinely Cartesian one. For Descartes, clarity of conception is a matter of forcefulness and vivacity, whereby an idea strikes the mind with an unmistakable and unignorable (and, when it comes to making a judgment based on it, irresistible) vigor. "I call a perception clear when it is present and accessible to the attentive mind—just as we say that we see something clearly when it is present to the eye's gaze and stimulates it with a sufficient degree of strength and accessibility" (*Principles of Philosophy* I.45: AT 8-1:22; CSM 1:207). Distinctness, on the other hand, is a matter of discreteness, whereby the "boundaries" or limits of an idea (what exactly it represents and what it excludes) are readily determined, and the idea is not easily confused with another. An idea is distinct when it is "so sharply separated from all other perceptions that it contains within itself only what is clear" (AT 8-1:22; CSM 1:208). This property of the idea is clearly a function of the fullness and determinateness of its representational content. A conception is distinct because we can distinguish accurately what it comprehends from all other notions (*Principles of Philosophy* I.63: AT 8-1:31; CSM 1: 215).

In three important respects, however, Malebranche departs from Descartes's views on ideas. First, for Malebranche *all* ideas are essentially and necessarily clear and distinct. I have already shown that, in the strict sense of the term, an "idea" is definitionally that which represents to the mind in a clear and distinct manner. Descartes, on the other hand, divides our ideas into those that are clear and distinct and those that are obscure and confused (i.e., "materially false"). The task is then to ensure that our judgments are based only on clear and distinct ideas (*Meditations* III: AT 7:43–44; CSM 2:29–30).

Second, Malebranche identifies the clear and distinct idea of a thing with the true idea of it by placing ideas in the mind of God (see chapter 4). God's ideas of mathematical and other abstract objects are the essences themselves of such things. Thus our clear and distinct idea of a triangle is, in fact, the true and immutable essence of the triangle in God's mind. And since God is the creator of the world, God's ideas serve as intelligible archetypes for all created beings. Hence their representational value (or truth) regarding things in the world is guaranteed. By identifying in this way 'clear and distinct idea' with 'true idea', Malebranche definitionally combines notions that, for Descartes, are distinct until proven otherwise. It seems, then, that certain skeptical problems that Descartes finds it necessary to deal with by proving God's existence and benevolence are hereby circumvented.[23] For example, Descartes's "evil genius" of Meditation I impugns the reliability of the clear and distinct conception of mathematical truths. Clarity and distinctness of perception, on this radical skeptical hypothesis, may not be a reliable guide to truth. Malebranche's approach, on the other hand, disarms the "evil genius" hypothesis from the start: the clear and distinct conception of a thing is necessarily a true one.[24]

Third, Malebranche's ideas provide not just clear and distinct knowledge of their objects, but "adequate" or comprehensive knowledge as well. The idea of extension tells us everything we could want to know about extension, if we exercise the proper degree of attention. Descartes, on the other hand, insists that it is quite possible to have a clear and distinct idea of a thing without that idea being adequate as well. He notes that "if a piece of knowledge is to be adequate [*adaequata*] it must contain absolutely all the properties which are in the thing which is the object of

23. To counter the skeptic, however, Malebranche must still prove that God exists and that the ideas we know are in God.
24. It might be claimed that Descartes's clear and distinct ideas are only *contingently* true: God could have given us a reasoning faculty of such a nature that our clear and distinct ideas are false, and true ideas exhibit some other phenomenological characteristics. For Malebranche, however, clear and distinct ideas (in God) can in no conceivable way be false, given God's omniscience and omnipotence.

knowledge" (Fourth Replies, AT 7:220; CSM 2:155).[25] While this is precisely the case with ideas as Malebranche understands them, Descartes believes that our ideas regularly fall short of this ideal. It should be clear from the foregoing that the kind of knowledge afforded by Malebranche's ideas is mainly[26] of a purely *quantitative* nature: numbers and their relations (pure arithmetic), and extension and its properties (pure geometry). In general, it involves mathematical essences and truths, for only information of this kind is capable of being displayed in the absolutely clear and distinct manner characteristic of ideas. Moreover, since the external world is composed solely of extension and motion, ideas also inform us about the true properties of material bodies (if they exist), and make possible the kind of geometrized physics upon which Cartesians insist.[27] But note that ideas represent only the geometrical features of things, the quantifiable properties that belong to bodies qua extended. Any other elements that may enter into our perceptual (and conceptual) awareness of the external world (heat, pain, colors, tastes, etc.) are introduced not by means of clear ideas, but by sensations.

Thus Malebranche's idea/sensation distinction is, in effect, identical to the epistemological distinction with which this chapter began—the distinction, that is, between those of our perceptions that provide us with clear knowledge as to the true properties of external material bodies (or alternately, those ideas that represent their real qualities), and those that are merely sensuous phenomena in the mind and resemble nothing in the world. Malebranche's innovation, however, is to take what in Descartes is only an epistemological difference among our ideas and ground it in an ontologi-

25. See also Second Replies, AT 7:140; CSM 2:100.
26. In a different sphere, Malebranche insists that our access to the ideas in God also affords us moral knowledge, absolute certainty as to what Malebranche calls "immutable order"—the commands of justice and the dictates of divine wisdom. See for example *Search*, Elucidation X; and *Dialogues* III. For a discussion of this aspect of Malebranche's theory of ideas, particularly as it appears in the *Traité de morale*, see Riley, *The General Will Before Rousseau*, pp. 102–13 (as well as his more general discussion in chapter 1).
27. "Thus, for physics it is necessary to admit only notions common to all men, i.e. the axioms of geometers and the clear ideas of extension, figure, motion, and rest, and others as clear as those, if there are any" (*Search*, VI.2.vi: OC 2:376–77; LO 484).

cal difference between ideas and sensations. Descartes's ideas are *all* modifications of the mind, properties of the human soul. They are thinking substance realizing itself in various thought modes. Moreover, every idea for Descartes has some degree of representational content/objective reality. Some ideas are, with regard to their content, clear and distinct, and represent real qualities of material bodies and other objects of thought (particularly important here, for Descartes's purposes, are the ideas of God, matter, and the soul). Other ideas (*sensus*) are obscure and confused and present to the mind the sensible qualities that result from its union with a body (Descartes calls these ideas "materially false," since their representational content is so unclear that they often lead us to error in our judgments about what it is they purport to represent.[28]) Thus all Descartes's ideas have the same ontological status, the same "formal reality"—all are mental acts or events, properties of the mental substance, mind—and are distinguished into types solely by the nature of their representational content/objective reality.

Malebranche's representative ideas (corresponding to Descartes's *ideae clarae et distinctae*), while certainly "present to" the human mind, are not modes thereof but are in God. Sensations, on the other hand, are properties of the mind, modify it—as on Descartes's view, they are simply the mind itself existing in such and such a manner.[29] Moreover, for Malebranche, only ideas have representational content (or as he puts it, "are objective realities"), and the content possessed by an idea is necessarily clear and distinct. Sensations, on his view, are devoid of any representational content whatsoever.

Part of Malebranche's motivation for deviating from Cartesian orthodoxy here and introducing this ontological distinction between modes (or *perceptions*) of the human mind and representative ideas is, in fact, to be able to account for the epistemological distinction. If ideas are to succeed in their essential function as

---

28. See *Meditations* III: AT 7:43–44; CSM 2:30.
29. It should be noted that even in the case of representative ideas, a modification of the mind, a *perception*, is necessary if the idea itself is to be apprehended; see *Réponse* VI, OC 6:60. For a comparative discussion of sensations and ideas in Descartes and Malebranche, see Alquié, *Le Cartésianisme de Malebranche*, pp. 152–59.

representations and perform the kind of cognitive work he wants them to perform, they cannot be properties of the mind itself.

First, when something is perceived through an idea, it is experienced clearly as something independent of the mind. When I perceive a triangle, for example, I perceive it as a "true and immutable nature" the being and truth of which is in no way dependent upon my thought. It is not merely an *ens rationis*, but comes across as having a certain degree of objectivity. Moreover, the real qualities of external bodies that we perceive by idea are perceived as "outside and distinct from ourselves." But if ideas were simply modifications of our being, Malebranche argues, how could "we clearly conceive that the extension we see is something distinct from ourselves . . . [and] see clearly and perceive distinctly that this sun is something distinct from us"?[30] Mental modes cannot represent things as being external to the mind; modes can be apprehended only as modifications of the (mental) substance to which they belong (*Réponse* VI, OC 6:60).

Second, it is clear that we have ideas of infinites. I know, for example, that triangles can have an infinite number of sizes and angularities. Thus my idea of the class of triangles is infinite. And Malebranche believes that the idea of extension to which I have access is infinite. But the human mind is only a finite and limited substance. It is incapable, then, of having a modification that is infinite.

> We cannot see the infinite in the soul or in its finite modes . . . to be able to represent the infinite is not merely to be able to perceive it, or to be able to have a very slight or infinitely limited perception of it, such as we have; it is to be able to perceive it in itself, and consequently to contain it, so to speak. . . . It is clear, then, that the soul,

---

30. *Search*, Elucidation X: OC 3:149–50; LO 625. See also *Réponse* VI, OC 6:57–60, where he argues that modifications of the mind cannot represent objects as being external to the mind: "When I see a centaur . . . I see it, but as a being distinct from myself [*comme un être distingué de moi*]. Thus, it is not a modification of my substance [that I see]"; and *Réponse* X, OC 6:86. But does not this prove only that the centaur is not a modification of my mind, and *not* that the idea representative of a centaur is not a mental mode? Malebranche appears to be conflating formal and objective reality (material being and representational content) here, and saying that only an idea which is itself actually *F* can represent an object that is *F*. I return to this issue in my discussion of what representation is for Malebranche.

its modes, or anything finite, cannot represent the infinite. (*Search* IV.11: OC 2:100; LO 321)[31]

Likewise, we do not have ideas just of particular things, but general ideas as well—for example, the idea of a triangle in general.[32] But the soul is a particular being with particular modifications. It cannot have modifications which themselves are general.

> It is evident that no modality of a particular being can be general. Now I think of a circle in general—the objective reality of my thought is a circle in general. Thus, the objective reality, or the idea of this circle, cannot be a particular modality of my mind. (*Réponse* VI, OC 6:60)

> How could we perceive in one species of being all species of being, or in a finite and particular being a triangle in general and infinite triangles? For the soul indeed perceives a triangle or circle in general, while it is a contradiction that the soul should be able to have a modification in general. . . . [N]o modification of a particular being can be general. (*Search*, Elucidation X: OC 3:149; LO 625)[33]

Thus if ideas are to convey knowledge that is general in nature, or if they are to represent to us the infinite, they cannot be modes of a particular, finite being such as the human mind.

Does Malebranche's argument establish the *general* claim that representative ideas are not modes of the human mind? I do not see

---

31. As Malebranche succinctly puts it to Régis, "notre esprit est fini, et l'idée de l'étendue est infinie. Donc, cette idée ne peut pas être une modification de notre esprit" (*Réponse à Régis*, OC 17-1:283). See also *Réponse* VI, OC 6:58–59; and RLA, OC 9:947. It is important to note here that Malebranche is speaking only of "particular infinites [*tel ou tel infini*]," such as the infinite class of triangles or numbers, or our idea of extension ("l'idée de l'étendue que nous sçavons être infinie") (RLA, OC 9:949). He is not talking about the absolute infinite itself (i.e., God), of which *no* idea is or can be representative; see *Search* III.2.vii: OC 1:449–50; LO 236–37.

32. Strictly speaking, *all* pure ideas for Malebranche are general—as representations of the essences of things—and only become "particular" through sensation.

33. See also *Dialogues* II: OC 12:59–60; D 53: "Any modification of a particular being, such as our minds, can only be particular. It can never rise to the generality which exists in ideas"; and the *Réponse à Régis*, OC 17-1:302: "Toutes les modalitez d'un être particulier, tel qu'est notre ame, sont necessairement particulières. Or quand on pense à un cercle en general, l'idée ou l'objet immédiat le l'ame, n'est rien de particulier. Donc, l'idée du cercle en general n'est point une modalité de l'ame."

that it does, unless he is also working with an unstated premise denying that some representative ideas (those with finite and particular contents) can be modes of the mind while others (infinite and general ideas) are not. On this assumption, all representative ideas must have the same ontological status, whatever it may turn out to be. Without such a premise, Malebranche proves only that *some* representative ideas—infinite and general ones—are not modes of the soul, thus leaving open the possibility that ideas as finite and particular modes of the soul can at least represent finite and particular beings. And it is not clear that this premise can be justified without begging the question as to the ontological status of ideas in general.

I do not see any explicit evidence that Malebranche accepts the assumption in question, although he may certainly be using it implicitly. But there is another, easier way for Malebranche to supplement his argument so that it establishes the ontological claim for ideas generally. For Malebranche, there is a sense in which *all* pure ideas are general: Malebranchian representative ideas are of *kinds* of things, because they are all abstract essences. Even the idea of a particular geometric figure (e.g., the right triangle) is really the idea of a kind of figure. With this premise in hand, Malebranche can then argue that *no* ideas are modes of the soul.[34]

These considerations regarding infinitude and generality are mainly of an epistemological nature. Malebranche certainly seems to feel that the arguments are sufficient to establish the negative claim regarding the ontological status of ideas. There is, however, a more fundamental (and primarily historical) motivation lurking behind these arguments and behind Malebranche's position. In the Platonic–Augustinian tradition to which Malebranche so clearly belongs, "ideas" are not properties or modifications of any finite thinking substance. For Plato, of course, Ideas or Forms are essences that are ontologically distinct from and independent of any

---

34. R. A. Watson has suggested to me that behind the explicit arguments employing infinitude and generality there is an additional, implicit argument which relies on the assumption that representation requires resemblance. Hence ideas that represent material bodies cannot possibly be modes of the mind, for the same reason that ideas that represent infinites cannot be modes of a finite substance, viz., lack of resemblance. This resemblance requirement would also give Malebranche's argument the generality it needs.

particular, created things—especially from the knowing mind that cognizes them. Similarly for Augustine, Ideas (*Ideae*), which the mind contemplates and knows, are unchangeable "realities" located outside the human mind (for Augustine—and, following him, for Malebranche—they are in God; see chapter 4); they are not properties of the mind. Malebranche's use of the term 'idea' to refer to an *extra*mental intelligible reality is simply a reflection of his Augustinian persuasions, a natural demonstration of his fealty to the conceptual apparatus of a pre-Cartesian tradition.[35]

I should note that, while I have been presenting Malebranche's position on the ontological status of ideas as a departure from Descartes, Malebranche himself does not always see things this way. When Arnauld insists that his own position (whereby ideas are mental acts that represent) is simply a faithful rendering of the correct Cartesian view, Malebranche is skeptical that Descartes actually held ideas to be "modalitez de l'âme." He prefers to believe either that Descartes just was not clear on the matter,[36] or that he never really examined in a serious way the nature of ideas in the first place.[37] Occasionally, however, Malebranche insists that Descartes's considered view, were he to spell it out in the proper terms, would be closer to his own position than to Arnauld's.

Malebranche's twofold distinction (on both ontological and epistemological grounds) between ideas and sensations did not sit well with his critics. Foucher at first misunderstands Malebranche to be claiming both that ideas and sensations are equally modifications of

35. As Malebranche notes, "it is principally [St. Augustine's] authority which has given me the desire to press the new Philosophy of ideas" (*Réponse*, OC 6:79–80). Leibniz recognizes that the motivation for Malebranche's departure from the Cartesian view here is a higher commitment to Augustine; see his letter to Rémond, 4 November 1715, in Robinet, *Malebranche et Leibniz*, p. 481.

Harry Bracken identifies another possible motivation for Malebranche's insistence that ideas lie outside the mind. Malebranche, according to Bracken, is committed to the epistemological principle that objects of *knowledge* must be independent of the knowing mind: "the 'things' or entities we can properly be said to know must be ontologically independent of our knowing them"; see "Berkeley and Malebranche on Ideas," pp. 1–9.

36. *Réponse* XXIV, OC 6:172.

37. TL I, OC 6:214–18. For Arnauld's remarks aligning Descartes's theory of ideas with his own, see especially VFI 205–6 (although it is a constant theme throughout all his correspondence with Malebranche).

the mind, and that only ideas represent objects external to the mind. This, Foucher thinks, is an untenable claim: on what basis could such an epistemological difference be maintained, if "both sorts of ideas equally belong to us, and properly speaking are nothing but our soul disposed in such and such a manner?"[38] When an annoyed Malebranche enlightens him as to the true ontological difference between ideas and sensations ("It seems to me that when one criticizes a book, one ought to read it first" [*Preface*, OC 2:496])[39] and thus as to the ground for the epistemological distinction, Foucher admits his mistake (although he blames it on the same ambiguity in Malebranche complained of by Arnauld and Locke). He does, however, raise a new objection: if ideas are not modes of the soul, then in what sense are they "received in the soul"? Moreover, how can both sensations and ideas be *immediately* perceived by the mind, if only the former but not the latter are mental modifications? If sensations belong to the mind but ideas are in God, then ideas are external to the mind and cannot be immediately apprehended as sensations and other mental modes are.[40]

Locke, like Foucher, finds Malebranche's distinction puzzling. Not only does he have trouble understanding what explanatory advantage is to be gained by the use of the term 'modification' to describe how sensations are in the mind,[41] but he sees no reason why "sentiments" should be in us and why what Malebranche calls "ideas" are not. Locke, of course, has no problems with an epistemological dualism among our ideas or perceptions. He himself distinguishes between our ideas of primary qualities, which "resemble" and make known real properties of bodies, and our ideas of secondary qualities, "[which] have no resemblance to them at all."[42]

---

38. *Critique*, p. 45. See Radner, *Malebranche*, pp. 101–4; and Watson, *The Breakdown of Cartesian Metaphysics*, pp. 66, 72.
39. In fact, Foucher wrote his *Critique* after having read only the first volume of the *Search* (which was published alone, before the second volume, and which Foucher took to be a completed work), in which the ontological status of ideas is somewhat ambiguous. The best account of Foucher's exchange with Malebranche is in Watson, *The Breakdown of Cartesian Metaphysics*, chapter 5.
40. RCP, pp. 103–8.
41. "Examination," pp. 234–35. Locke's complaint here raises the question whether for Locke himself ideas are "modifications" or properties of the mind.
42. *An Essay Concerning Human Understanding* II.8.xv.

But he is puzzled as to why for Malebranche this epistemological difference should give rise to an ontological one, particularly since both primary quality ideas and secondary quality ideas (sensations) are equally "the immediate or nearest object of the mind when it perceives anything. . . . The colour of the marigold I now think of, is as much 'the immediate object of my mind' as its figure."[43] Malebranche's sensations and ideas must be found in the same place, must have the same ontological status, whether they are in God (an unlikely and unhelpful hypothesis) or in the human mind.[44]

Arnauld objects to Malebranche's arguments as to why representative ideas cannot be modes of the mind. Malebranche, he insists, has simply misunderstood the way in which the idea of the infinite is infinite, or the way in which a general idea is general. Clearly, the idea of the infinite is itself no more actually infinite than the idea of a circle is itself circular. That is, ideas are not infinite or circular "formally," *in essendo*. Rather, it is a quesiton of representational content—the idea of the infinite is infinite only *in repraesentando*. A *singular* thought or perception ("une modification singulière de mon esprit") can represent a general being ("a triangle in general") without being itself either triangular or general.[45] In a letter to Malebranche of 22 May 1694, he insists that

> [i]t is not true that a modality of our soul, which is finite, cannot represent an infinite thing; and it is true, on the contrary, that however finite our perceptions may be, there are some which must be considered in the sense that they represent the infinite. This is what M. Régis has correctly maintained to you, and what he meant when he said that they are finite *in essendo*, and infinite *in repraesentando*. You are not happy with this distinction. So much the worse for you.[46]

43. "Examination," p. 236. Perhaps Locke is here failing to distinguish in Malebranche's account the sensible "idea" of a body's extension from the true idea of its extension that we perceive in God. In the *Essay* Locke appears on occasion to treat ideas generally as sensible.
44. "Examination," p. 233. For Locke, all ideas are "in the mind"; see *Essay* I.1.viii.
45. *Dissertation sur le prétendu bonheur des plaisirs des sens* (1687), in *Oeuvres*, vol. 40, p. 90.
46. *Oeuvres*, vol. 40, pp. 88–89. Arnauld is emphasizing a point made by Régis in his *Système général* II.1.xviii (Vol. 1, p. 194). For Malebranche's direct response to Régis, see OC 17-1:302–3.

Malebranche responds to Arnauld (and Régis) by essentially denying the legitimacy of their distinction. Only that which is actually
infinite or actually general can represent to the mind an infinite or
general nature. And that which is actually infinite cannot be a
modification of a finite mind.

> That which is finite in itself *in essendo* cannot be infinite *in reprae-
> sentando*. . . . Thus, since [the modalities of our soul] are finite, we
> cannot find the infinite therein, since nothingness is not visible, and
> one cannot perceive in the soul what is not there. Similarly, from the
> fact that I perceive in the circle an infinity of equal diameters, or
> rather, from the fact that there are equal diameters therein *in reprae-
> sentando*, I must conclude that they are really there *in essendo*. For,
> in effect, a circle contains the reality of an infinity of diameters. In
> order, then, for a reality to be present to the mind, for it to affect the
> mind, for the mind to perceive or receive it, it necessarily must really
> be there. (RLA, OC 9:954)

One basis for Malebranche's claim here is his often-used principle
that nothingness cannot be seen—"voir rien, voir le néant, c'est ne
point voir." (I later examine the role this principle plays in Malebranche's arguments for the necessity of ideas in knowledge and
perception.) One can see only as much reality as is actually present
before the mind and no more. If it is not there, it cannot be seen.
Thus, if *per impossibile* the mind were to perceive an infinite in a
finite modality, it would be perceiving more than was actually there,
hence it would be perceiving, above and beyond the present finite
reality, nothing.[47]

But does not Malebranche's response, then, deny the representative relation altogether? He appears, prima facie, to be claiming
that only something which actually or "formally" has the property
F can be representative of *F*; that if we are to see either a thing or a
property or feature of reality by representation, what is apprehended by the mind (i.e., the *representans*) must either actually be
that thing or formally possess that property or feature. But then
what we are talking about is not representation at all, but some
kind of direct presentation of the thing or property itself (this is
precisely Arnauld's point). Malebranche's response, if understood

47. See *Search* IV.11: OC 2:99–100; LO 320–21.

in this way, also appears to have some philosophically and theologically unsound consequences. For example, if the idea of extension is to be representative of extension, to be extension *in repraesentando*, then it must really be extended. But since the idea of extension is in God, this would be to admit extension "formally" in God, to allow that God is really extended.[48] Moreover, it would imply that a painting which represents "drunkenness" (allegorically or otherwise) must actually be inebriated to do so, which of course is absurd. Has Malebranche so misunderstood the nature of representation?

I do not think so. It is clear that Malebranche's remarks on having a property *in essendo* in order to have it *in repraesentando* are intended to apply only to two possible features of ideas: infinitude and generality. Malebranche is not mistaking the representative relation for some other. He is *not* making the more general claim that for *any* property F, if an idea is to represent F, it must really be F. In fact, he explicitly says that an idea representing the properties of an extended body need not itself have those properties: "Matter is nothing but extension in length, width, and depth: but I have never taught that the idea of length, width, and depth was long, wide, and deep" (TL I, OC 6:242). The idea of extension is not itself extended in three dimensions. But an idea has to be infinite and general itself (*in essendo*) in order to represent an infinite or something general.

What, then, is the difference between the two cases? Why is it that while something immaterial can represent material bodies, nothing finite or particular can represent an infinite or general nature? Malebranche's point seems to be that a finite or particular *representans* just would not have the requisite capacity for an infinite or general *representatum*. To represent an infinite is to represent the infinite extension of a particular class at one and the same time and by one and the same means—for example, the pure idea of extension represents the infinite number of possible extended figures. And this is to have a content that is without bounds in the relevant respects. But a finite mental mode (and all modifications of the human mind are necessarily finite), if it *could* represent, could only

48. It is on precisely this point that Arnauld focuses much of his attack on Malebranche's intelligible extension; see VFI, chapter 14.

represent a limited and determinate number of things or aspects of things—that is, its content must necessarily also be finite and limited (in all respects). Likewise, a general idea represents several things at once: the general idea of extension represents *all* extended bodies. Its content is such that it represents objects and properties which, in fact, are opposites or mutually incompatible (for example, a square and a circle). But the content of a particular idea (that is, an idea that is a mode of the human mind), Malebranche is saying, would have to be exclusionary: if it represents one particular kind of extended object (a square), it would thereby be precluded from representing another kind of extended object (a circle).[49] In other words, an infinite (or general) idea must contain or represent an infinite number of things (or many things) at once. But something that is particular and finite cannot do this job, since it can only take on a certain determinate, limited, and particular form or content. Hence it can be only particular and finite in its representative capacity as well. It is, then, the special requirements of infinitude and generality in representation which will not allow something finite or particular *in essendo* to be infinite or general *in repraesentando*.

Moreover, since Malebranche's argument against something finite *in essendo* representing an infinite is premised on his principle that one cannot see more reality than is actually there ("le néant n'est pas visible"), one gets the impression that what is relevantly special about the cases of the infinite and the general is just their "quantitative" excess over the finite and particular. A modification of the soul is finite, and thus simply and necessarily falls short of infinitude in terms of the amount of reality it can present to the mind. Since "what is not in the soul cannot be perceived therein [*on ne peut appercevoir dans l'ame ce qui n'y est pas*]," one cannot perceive in the soul's modifications what is beyond the finite.

> We cannot see three realities where there are only two, since we would see a nothingness, a reality that would not be. We cannot see a hundred real things where there are only forty, for we would see sixty real things that would not be at all. Therefore, we cannot see the

49. Radner puts this point quite nicely; see *Malebranche*, p. 116. In fact, I am indebted to her whole discussion of the *in repraesentando* vs. *in essendo* issue (pp. 107–8, 110–18), although our readings of Malebranche are different.

infinite in the soul or in its finite modes, for we would see an infinite that would not exist. Now, nothingness is neither perceptible nor intelligible; therefore, the soul cannot see in its substance or its modes an infinite reality. (*Search* IV.11: OC 2:100; LO 321)

Now this kind of consideration, while it is supposed to establish the general claim that representative ideas are not modes of the human mind, does not require that, in order for something to represent the material, it must itself be material. An immaterial x has as much reality as a material x—namely, the reality of x. Thus we could see a material x in an immaterial x.[50] In this and other cases, there is enough reality in the *representans* before the mind to cover what is being represented. But in the case of the infinite, only something which is infinite *in essendo* would have enough reality to represent it. The representation or idea we have of extension or matter is infinite and general. Therefore it cannot be a modality of the finite and particular human mind. But none of the reasons which preclude it from being in the human mind precludes it from being unextended and immaterial.

One question can now be put off no longer: namely, the general question of representation. What *is* a representation for Malebranche? Since I am concerned here particularly with Malebranche's theory of ideas, I consider the more specific question, how do *ideas* represent? What does it mean, for example, to say that an intelligible and immaterial entity, an idea in the divine understanding, is a representation of some material body? What is it about an idea that makes it an *être représentatif*? This central and important issue in Malebranche's theory is also, in fact, one of the most difficult to resolve. There is very little agreement among Malebranche's critics and commentators, both in the seventeenth century and today, on

---

50. Descartes's discussion in the Third Meditation (and the First Replies) is very helpful here. His point is that a thing can exist either formally (actual existence) or "objectively" (i.e., in the mind as something thought). In either case, whether it is a matter of its formal or objective existence, the thing has the same degree of reality in virtue of what it is. Thus the idea of a rock (what Malebranche might call an "immaterial rock") contains as much reality objectively as an existing material rock contains formally. See AT 7:41–42; CSM 2:28–29 (and AT 7:102–4; CSM 2:74–76).

just what makes an idea "representative," and very little in the texts themselves to help decide the issue.[51]

The first possibility is that representation involves resemblance. In order for an idea of *x* to be a representation of *x*, it must resemble or be similar to *x* in at least *some* specifiable respects (where the specification is a function of the ontological nature of the representation and/or the purpose the representation is to serve). When we say that an accurate, figurative painting of Napoleon *represents* Napoleon, we mean, at least in part, that the painting resembles him in respect to his appearance. This allows the painting to re-present Napoleon, or "make Napoleon present." There are certain structural, qualitative, and other similarities between the *representans* and the *representatum* (outline, shape, color, relationships between parts—eyes to nose to mouth to hairline to shoulders, etc.), even though resemblance is not complete and exhaustive. Foucher seems to be the most outspoken defender of this view of representation in the seventeenth century, and criticizes Malebranche for deviating from such an obvious truism. "I speak of the resemblance which our ideas have to that which they represent, and I find fault with the author [Malebranche] for supposing that it is not necessary for them to be similar [*semblable*] to objects to represent them."[52] Resemblance, for Foucher, is essential to the relationship of representation.[53] If there were no resemblance between idea and object, he insists, then either any single idea could

51. Malebranche is not alone in this regard. In fact, this seems to be a general (and frustrating) problem facing anyone studying seventeenth-century epistemology. The notion of 'representation', particularly as applied to ideas, is central in Descartes, Arnauld, Régis, and others. Yet they tell us next to nothing about what they mean by the term. Negative examples are plentiful (Arnauld constantly tells us that an idea is not like a painting or a mirror), but very few positive contributions are to be found.
52. *Critique*, p. 50.
53. He uses this as a self-evident premise in his argument against Cartesian ontological dualism. If mind and matter are so radically unlike each other, and resemblance between mental event and physical thing is ruled out, then how can mind know matter?—how can ideas represent (i.e., resemble) corporeal beings? See *Critique*, pp. 50–61. Foucher sometimes speaks as if representation *means* resemblance. At other times, resemblance appears simply to be a necessary condition for representation: for idea *y* to represent object *x* is for *y* to cause in the mind the same or similar effect as *x* would, if it were itself present therein; and for *y* to do this it must resemble *x* (pp. 52–54).

represent any object whatsoever, or many different (or even *all*) ideas, no matter how different from one another, could represent one and the same object. In fact, what makes an idea representative of one object rather than another is its resemblance to that object and its lack of resemblance to others.[54]

Now as far as I know, there is not a single Cartesian in the seventeenth century who opts for the resemblance view of representation. And there are good reasons for this. If one is committed to Descartes's ontological dualism, where there is no likeness whatsoever between mind and matter—neither essentially, nor in the kinds of modifications of which each is capable—and if one is committed to the view that ideas in the mind do represent material objects, then one is not going to hold that representation can be explicated in terms of resemblance.[55]

But Malebranche is not your ordinary, run-of-the-mill Cartesian. Recall that his ideas are not in the human mind, but in God. Does Malebranche, then, allow that ideas represent their objects by resembling them? Occasionally one finds Malebranche speaking in this way: "The difficulty lies in knowing whether the ideas representing something outside the soul and *resembling* them to some extent [*qui leur ressemble en quelque façon*]—such as the ideas of the sun, of a house, a river, etc.—are merely modifications of the soul" (*Search* III.2.v: OC 1:433; LO 228; emphasis added). In the *Méditations sur l'humilité et la pénitence*, he describes God as containing "les idées ou les ressemblances de tous les êtres" (OC 17-1:393).[56]

---

54. Yolton suggests that the seventeenth-century notion of idea-images as *resemblances* of objects has a possible source in the consideration of perception in visual and optical (rather than cognitive) terms; see *Perceptual Acquaintance*, chapter 7. (Yet he does not think that, for Foucher, representation is a matter of resemblance; see pp. 68–69.)

55. See Watson, *The Breakdown of Cartesian Metaphysics*, pp. 79–99.

56. There is also the following ambiguous evidence. When Foucher accuses Malebranche of "supposing that it is not necessary that [ideas] resemble objects to represent them" (*Critique*, p. 50), Malebranche responds only that Foucher "has no understanding whatsoever of my opinion on this matter. He does not even seem to have read what I have written on it" (*Préface*, OC 2:496), and distances himself from Descartes, for whom representation does *not* involve resemblance. If Watson is right, then an "epistemological likeness principle", i.e., representation as resemblance, is at least implicitly at work in Malebranche's arguments that finite and particular modes of the mind cannot represent infinite and general realities; see n. 34 above.

But any kind of literal resemblance between divine ideas (ideas in God's mind) and material, extended bodies would be no less problematic than resemblance between ideas which belong to a finite thinking substance and such bodies. Moreover, Malebranche elsewhere explicitly denies that the idea of *x* must resemble *x* in order to represent it.[57] An idea does not have to possess "formally" any of the properties or characteristics possessed by its object. I have already shown that an idea need not be *F* (or even *F*-like) to represent an object that itself is *F* (with the noted exceptions of infinitude and generality).[58]

On the other hand, this does not mean that the representative relationship is only an arbitrary one, a convention set up between *representans* and *representatum*, such as the relationship that exists between a word and its denotation. Foucher accuses Malebranche of following Descartes in holding that the way in which an idea represents an object is just like the nonresembling way in which the word 'tree' represents a tree.[59] Malebranche responds by saying that Foucher has understood neither Descartes's opinion nor his own, and insists further that "l'opinion de Monsieur Descartes est entièrement differente de la mienne" (*Preface*, OC 2:496–97). There is good reason for Malebranche's curt and impatient reply here, and when we understand this we are closer to understanding Male-

---

57. TL I, OC 6:242.

58. Some commentators, however, continue to talk as though Malebranche's ideas *resemble* their objects. McCracken, for example, insists that "the term 'idea' Malebranche restricts to those representations of bodies that *resemble* bodies," and quotes the passage from *Search* III.2.v to support his reading; see *Malebranche and British Philosophy*, pp. 58–59. Church asserts that Malebranche, "like Foucher, takes literally the term 'represent'"—by which I take Church to mean that Malebranche agrees with Foucher that to represent is to resemble (or at least requires resemblance). Church thinks that Malebranche's ideas are "copies" of the objects they represent; see *A Study in the Philosophy of Malebranche*, p. 182.

59. *Critique*, pp. 56–57. While Descartes does claim that some representative relations are simply arbitrary conventions, particularly the way in which words and signs represent (see *La Dioptrique* IV: AT 6:112), it is clear that this is by no means the way in which he considers ideas to represent. Ideas, he insists, are *imagines*, and represent one object rather than another because of their particular content or "objective reality." In fact, Descartes even refers to the idea of an object as a "likeness of that thing [*istius rei similitudinem*]" (see *Meditations* III: AT 7:37; CSM 2:25–26).

branche's conception of 'representation' in its seventeenth-century context.

Malebranchian (and Cartesian) ideas are not just *signs* of objects: they do not merely signify in the nonessential, arbitrary way in which words and many other symbolic systems do (e.g., traffic signs). Rather, there is something about an idea that makes it an idea of one object rather than another; there is some intrinsic feature (or collection of features) possessed by the idea that gives it a particular and determinate objective reference. Because of this intrinsic feature, the idea is associated with a *representatum*. We can call that feature of the idea that gives it its object or *representatum* the idea's *representational content*. The idea of a square, for example, can and does represent a square object and cannot represent a circular object not because of any stipulation, but because its representational content is of a certain character.

Another way of putting this point is to say that an idea, for Malebranche, is an image (une image). To say that an idea is an image is not necessarily to say that it is a copy or a picture or a resemblance of that of which it is an image. It is simply to say that the idea qua representation presents a certain determinate content to the mind, a content that picks out and makes present to the mind some thing that is not itself actually present. It is the content that gives the representation intentionality, or objective reference. In this case it makes it the *idea of* some thing. Now a content *may* be displayed in a pictorial manner (paintings are images; so are the pictures of the imagination), and a representational content *may* involve resemblance with its object. But pictures and imaginative visions and resemblances are not the only possible kinds of images. We recognize that an image can also be constituted out of language; although the individual words are only arbitrarily related as signs to their objects (when they have such reference), a literary portrait of a character or landscape has a content all its own and *is*, as a presentation of that content, a representation of that person or landscape. To represent, to be an image *of* something, is simply to make that thing known without the thing itself being present. Representations, images, all render present and thus make known their objects, whether they are pictures, resemblances, copies, descriptions in language, or ideas present to the mind. In fact, while those ideas which, according to Malebranche, are immediately apprehended by the mind in its union with the divine understanding share with these other kinds of images the essential characteristic of presenting a content to the mind (and thereby re-presenting some object), the way in which they do so is completely sui generis and not reducible to, or explicable in terms of, the way in which other representations present their contents. Ideas "contain" (contiennent) and "present" to the mind "ce qu'on voit en elles," but they do so in a nonpictorial, nonresembling manner.[60] They are a kind of image: spiritual and immaterial, yet capable of representing matter. As Alquié says, "tel est [leur] mystère."[61]

Before continuing, I should note that this broad use of *image* or *imago* to refer to representations generally, pictorial or not, material or immaterial, is in keeping with the seventeenth-century understanding of the term, particularly among Cartesians. Descartes, for example, insists that the defining characteristic of ideas is that they are *tanquam rerum imagines*: "Some of my thoughts are as it were the images of things, and it is only in these cases that the term 'idea' is strictly appropriate" (*Meditations* III: AT 7:37; CSM 2:25). In *La Dioptrique* he claims, in fact, that an image can often represent an object better if it does *not* resemble it ("pour estre plus parfaites en qualité d'images, & representer mieux un objet, elles doivent ne luy pas resembler" [AT 6:113]). And Arnauld, perhaps the harshest and most rigorous critic of Malebranche's doctrine of ideas, repeatedly refers to ideas as *les images*, but distinguishes them from other kinds of representations (pictorial or linguistic): "When I claim that our ideas and our perceptions (for I take them to be the same thing) represent to us the things which we conceive and are images of them [*en sont les images*], it is in a completely different sense from that in which we say that paintings represent their originals and are the images of them, or that spoken or written words are the images of our thoughts" (VFI, 199). To be a representation, then, in this very general sense, is simply to make present that which is absent. Representations are able to do this because of what I have been calling their content. And my claim is that the way in which an idea presents or displays a content, and thereby makes present (or re-presents) to the mind some (absent) object, is basic and inexplicable

60. Malebranche to [?], 14 January 1684 [?]: OC 18:279–80.
61. *Le Cartésianisme de Malebranche*, p. 216.

in terms of the way in which other kinds of representations present their content. This is true for Malebranche, and it is also true for Descartes, Arnauld, and Régis.[62]

So much for at least a somewhat negative and minimal understanding of the way in which ideas, for Malebranche, are representations. Can we make any clearer, however, the peculiar way in which the content of an idea *does* allow that idea to be representative of some object(s), *does* make something known? We can now see that the idea does not represent ("make present") by picturing or resembling an object. The content of an idea is not pictorial. But is representation by idea, then, a completely inexplicable function?

The universal failure of seventeenth-century Cartesians to elaborate a positive and forthright answer to the problem leads one to believe that this is the case. And Malebranche is no exception here. If, as I have suggested, we think of ideas as *les images*, then while this may help us understand in a general way what makes them representations (i.e., they, like all images, present a content and thereby represent some object), it does not help us understand *how* they represent, how their content *does* pick out and make present an object. Ideas qua images are sui generis and, for Malebranche and other Cartesians, constitute an unanalyzable, "self-evident" datum of consciousness. As Arnauld puts it, "the word 'idea' is among those which are so clear that they cannot be explained by any other words, because there are none which are clearer and more simple."[63]

In Malebranche's theory, however, there is an important difference from the standard Cartesian account, a difference that allows us to make some speculative progress toward recognizing certain essential characteristics of the representational content of an idea in his account. The peculiarity of Malebranche's doctrine of ideas (and its salient difference from other Cartesian accounts) is that ideas are in God. According to this neo-Augustinian approach, the divine ideas are the eternal archetypes in accordance with which God creates all finite beings: "God has made animals, plants, even insects, according to the image, or according to the living idea, which he has of them" (*Conversations chrétiennes* III, OC 4:64).

62. Régis, *Système général* II.1.xii (vol. 1, pp. 180ff.). See Watson, *The Breakdown of Cartesian Metaphysics*, pp. 90–91.
63. *La Logique, ou l'art de penser*, p. 65.

What this means is that these ideas (*idées ou images*), which are precisely the ideas which we apprehend, are the "models" or "exemplars" for all created things ("C'est l'idée qui est l'archetype ou exemplaire sur lequel la matière a esté faite" [*Réponse à Régis*, OC 17:287]).[64] Malebranche, in effect, reverses the causal relationship between idea and object as the more orthodox Cartesians see it. Régis, for example, claims that the external object is the "exemplary cause [*cause exemplaire*]" of the idea in the mind representing it.[65] Malebranche replies to him that, on the contrary, the ideas by which we perceive and know external objects are the exemplary causes of those created material beings (*Réponse à Régis*, OC 17-1:307-8).

This suggests that the content of an idea, if it is to serve as a model or archetype in the divine production of things, must specify a set of conditions that its object, if it is created, instantiates. If it is a general idea, it must specify a set of conditions that *any* object of that type instantiates.[66] That is, if God uses these ideas as *modèles*, they must somehow be able to direct God in the production of creatures by providing him with a complete, clear, and precise *description* of an object or a type of object. The idea of a circle describes all those features that an object must possess if it is to be a circle—for example, all radii drawn from the center of the figure to its circumference must be equal; its area must be the product of π and the square on the radius; and so forth—just as the blueprint for a house specifies the features that the house, when constructed, must possess. More generally, the idea of any extended thing specifies a finite extension having such and such a configuration, capable of such and such properties, and standing in such and such relations to other extensions.

In other words, Malebranche's ideas are the pure concepts or definitions of things. They are representative of objects, they make objects known or present, because their content is simply a nonmaterial, nonpictorial presentation of the features of things created from them. The content of an idea, because it *presents* in its own

64. See also Malebranche to [?], 14 January 1684[?], OC 18:280.
65. See *Système général* I.1.iii (vol. 1, pp. 76-77).
66. In an important sense, discussed in chapter 3, *all* ideas for Malebranche are general insofar as they are pure ideas. They become "particularized" only through sensation.

unique way a collection of properties as constituting an object or kind of object, *represents* whatever object or objects instantiate those properties. (If creation follows an idea-exemplar faithfully and correctly, which it does necessarily in the case of divine creation, then the idea that presents the content cannot fail to be representative of those objects that instantiate the specifications set forth therein.)[67]

This way of looking at Malebranche's ideas allows us to make some sense of his claims that the idea of a thing enables one to see both all its actual and possible properties, and all those properties that are excluded from (or incompatible with) it. If the content of an idea specifies a finite set of properties as the definition of a thing or as the conditions for the creation of it, it of course tells us what its *essential* properties are. Now since, in the Cartesian schema, all the possible, nonessential modifications of a substance are simply its essence existing in such and such a manner, all those modifications are defined and understood in terms of that essence. For example, circularity must be understood in terms of extension, and a circular body is simply a particular way of being extended. So the idea or concept that represents an extended body (that is, which specifies the makeup of an extended body) represents it as capable of being modified in certain ways—namely, in all those ways of being modified that can be explicated in terms of extension. And the idea of that body also represents it as incapable of being

67. Among commentators, Radner and Lennon come closest to this kind of reading of Malebranche's ideas, and I am indebted, in part, to their interpretations. Radner insists that "to have access to the idea of pain is to possess a kind of know-how. The idea [of pain] serves as a blueprint for producing pain in a mind. A blueprint need not itself possess the properties of that of which it is the blueprint. To make a thing according to a blueprint is not to duplicate a model but to follow a set of directions. . . . To have the idea of a triangle is to have a generative definition of a triangle. The definition provides the directions for constructing a triangle without itself possessing any 'triangular' features" (*Malebranche*, p. 117). Radner does, however, conclude that Malebranche's ideas are thus *not* images (p. 104). But I do not see why one cannot speak of ideas as images (given the general definition of 'image' I have presented in the text), since the idea, if it is to function in the way Radner suggests, still must (1) present a content to the mind, and (2) *represent* a particular object precisely *because* it presents a particular content to the mind. See also Lennon, "Philosophical Commentary": "Ideas [should] be construed as essences or possibilities. . . . The object of a pure perception of a triangle might be a set of ideal specifications to which any object having the properties of a triangle must conform" (LO 787).

modified in certain other ways—namely, in all those ways that cannot be explicated in terms of extension and its modes. Since color cannot be defined in terms of divisibility, distance, and motion, we see thereby that color is necessarily excluded from our idea of an extended body.[68] In other words, the way in which an idea conveys information regarding compatibility and incompatibility among properties becomes intelligible once we think of ideas as sets of conditions for objects. It is simply a matter of logical relations between essential attributes and nonessential modifications. If the blueprint for a house specifies that the house is to consist of a purely wooden structure of certain dimensions, we then can determine what properties it can have (for example, wooden staircases) and what properties it cannot have (brick walls). It is hard to see how a pictorial image or representation could convey this kind of information in a "clear and distinct manner."

There is another good reason to take Malebranche's representative ideas as concepts of things rather than picturelike images, as specifications of sets of properties that constitute objects rather than some kind of immaterial, visual-like data. Malebranche clearly distinguishes between the sensory apprehension we may have of extension and our access to the pure idea of extension in God. By means of vision and touch, we acquire a *relative* perception of the extension of a physical body.

> Our vision is very limited; but it must not limit its object. The idea it gives us of extension has very narrow limits; but it does not follow from this that extension is so limited. . . . From the fact that God provides us with a given sensible idea of size, as when a fathom ruler is before our eyes, it does not follow that the ruler has only that extension represented to us by the idea. (*Search* I.6.i: OC 1:80–87; LO 26–29)

The sensible "idea" of the size and shape of a body is simply its seen size and shape, its apparent proportions relative to the perceiver's body. Sensible extension does not give us "the truth of things." This "idea" of extension provided by the senses, which plays an important role in Malebranche's discussion of sensation in Book I of the *Search*, is in fact a visual image—it is what we see when we look at a body.

---

68. See *Search* I.10..i: OC 1:122–23; LO 49.

The pure idea of extension, on the other hand, that which represents the true properties of bodies (and not merely their relative properties), must be essentially different qua image from any such sensible datum. It must represent in a nonvisual, nonrelative way. Any kind of pictorial or sensible image will necessarily present only a certain limited aspect of its object. A painting, for example, can capture a thing only from a given perspective, and therefore can never present more than a partial view. A representative idea, however, gives us "complete, perfect, and clear knowledge." It cannot, then, present its content as a sensible image does. Only the full concept of a thing can do the kind of epistemic work that Malebranche's ideas must do.

The kind of distinction Malebranche is working with here between the sensible idea and the pure idea of extension is similar to (but not identical with) that used by Descartes in his wax example of the Second Meditation. On the one hand, there is the extension of the wax as reported by our senses and imagination—the visual or tactile data perceived or the images pictured by the imaginative faculty ([*ceram*] *quam video, quam tango, quam imaginor*). But this idea of the wax is either constantly changing or too limited in its scope, and provides no insight into the "nature" of the wax. On the other hand, there is the clear and distinct idea of the wax "perceived by the mind alone [*sola mente percipere*]" (AT 7:31; CSM 2:20–21). This idea of the wax informs us of the countless ways in which the extension of the wax is and can be modified— information that far surpasses the capabilities of the senses or imagination. This representation constitutes true knowledge of the wax, its essence and properties qua extended body.

Intelligible Extension

Malebranche's discussion of ideas in the *Search*, and my analysis so far, seems prima facie to suggest that ideas are individual, discrete entities, and that there is in the ideal realm (i.e., the divine understanding) a plurality of particular representative ideas—one for every possible object or, at least, every possible *kind* of object. This impression is reinforced by Malebranche's frequent talk of "all our particular ideas of creatures [*toutes les idées particulières que nous avons des créatures*]" (*Search* III.2.vi: OC 1:443), as well as his references in examples to the idea of a triangle, the idea of a square, the idea of the sun, the idea of a house, the idea of a horse, and so forth. On such a view, there would be a one-to-one correspondence between ideas and objects or kinds of objects.

In the Tenth Elucidation, however, Malebranche denies that this is or ever was his position on the nature of ideas.

> It should not be imagined that the intelligible world is related to the sensible material world in such a way that there is an intelligible sun, for example, or an intelligible horse or tree intended to represent to us the sun or a horse or a tree, or that everyone who sees the sun necessarily sees this hypothetical intelligible sun. . . . Thus, when I said that we see different bodies through the knowledge we have of God's perfections that represent them, I did not exactly mean that there are in God certain particular ideas that represent each body individually, and that we see such an idea when we see the body. (*Search*, Elucidation X: OC 3:153–154; LO 627)

Rather, there is in God what Malebranche calls an "infinite intelligible extension," or the idea of infinite extension. This infinite, homogenous, nonmaterial extension contains potentially all individual ideas of bodies. It is capable of being divided and limitied, and its subdivisions configured in various ways to produce the ideas of particular extended things. Taken as a whole, it constitutes the ideal archetype of the material universe, and any bounded segment of it constitutes the intelligible archetype of some possible object or kind. When some finite part of this infinite intelligible extension, for example, takes on the properties of circularity or a horselike configuration, the idea of a circle or a horse is produced.

> It must be realized that God contains in Himself an ideal or intelligible infinite extension; for since he has created it, God knows extension. . . . Thus, since the mind can perceive a part of this intelligible extension that God contains, it surely can perceive in God all figures; for all finite intelligible extension is necessarily an intelligible figure, since figure is nothing but the boundary of extension. (OC 3:151–52; LO 626)

Any part of the intelligible extension can be used to represent any finite extended thing: "Since the parts of intelligible extension are all of the same nature, they may all represent any body whatsoever"

(OC 3:153: LO 627). Thus intelligible extension contains all possible ideas of matter, not actually but potentially, "as a block of marble contains all possible figures."[69]

My account of representative ideas in Malebranche suggests that ideas represent, or make some object present to the mind, because they are the concepts of things. An idea specifies a set of determinate properties as constituting some object. And since bodies are simply finite extended things (matter of a certain size, shape, and motion), the properties specified by any idea of a body will necessarily be properties of extension. Now in spite of the picturesque imagery suggested by my exposition so far of the infinite intelligible extension, the doctrine can be made to fit this interpretation in the following way. The idea of infinite extension in God is simply the ideal, infinite set of specifications for all possible extended figures. That is, this idea conceptually presents extension itself, along with all the possible ways in which it can be modified. It thus tells us what properties any extended thing *must* have (e.g., size), as well as the infinite number of ways in which a thing can be extended or figured. Any particular idea, or the idea of any finite body, is simply some subset of the infinite number of ideal specifications constituting the infinite intelligible extension. Such an idea will include among its own specifications both those general properties that are necessary for any extended figure, plus some finite number of further properties determining it to be one (kind of) extended object (e.g., the circle) rather than another.

Malebranche initially introduces the notion of an infinite intelligible extension in the Elucidations, added to the third edition of the *Search* in 1678, after considering various objections to the original six books of the text. The relevant remarks are occasioned by an objection directed against the view (perceived to be Malebranche's own) that there is a plurality of individual ideas in God: if there were an idea for each object, how could we account for the motions and apparent changes in size we perceive in things? If there were a

69. The best critical studies of Malebranche's theory of the infinite intelligible extension are in Radner, *Malebranche*, chapter 5; Jean Laporte, "L'Etendue intelligible selon Malebranche," in *Etudes d'histoire de la philosophie française au XVIIe siècle*, pp. 153–92; and Robinet, *Système et existence dans l'oeuvre de Malebranche*, pp. 239–55.

particular intelligible sun in God, it would have to move and change
its size in order to account for the apparent motions of the sun, and
for the fact that the sun appears greater when it is near the horizon
than when it is high in the sky. But such *real* motion and change in
God is impossible, the objection continues:

> Nothing in God can be moved, nothing in Him can have figure. If
> there is a sun in the intelligible world, this sun is always equal to
> itself. The visible sun appears greater when it is near the horizon than
> when it is at a great distance from the horizon. Therefore, it is not
> this intelligible sun that we see. The same holds for other creatures.
> Therefore, we do not see God's works in Him. (*Search*, Elucidation
> X: OC 3:151, LO 626)

In his response, Malebranche utilizes finite, bounded parts of the
infinite intelligible extension, accounting for motion by means of
parts taken successively in different positions relative to one
another, and for change by means of parts of different sizes or
standing in different relations. All this can be accommodated by
changes in the specifications constituting the concept of an object.

Most of Malebranche's critics assert that the theory of intelligible
extension represents a distinct change in Malebranche's account of
the nature of ideas. Arnauld was the first to insist that the "manière
de voir les choses en Dieu" in the Tenth Elucidation is different
from the account given in Book III and elsewhere.

> The author of the *Search After Truth* has changed his explanation of
> the way in which [we see all things in God]. First, he believed that we
> see each thing by the particular idea of it in God. But then he
> undergoes a change of sentiment, with his declaration that . . . we see
> all things in God by the application which God makes upon our
> mind with the infinite intelligible extension in a thousand different
> ways. (VFI 247)

Malebranche, in response to Arnauld, claims that the Elucidation account is not at all a *retractation* of the view in the earlier
parts of the work, but merely an *explication* of it, intended especially for those who might have misinterpreted him to be speaking
of a plurality of particular, discrete ideas in God (*Réponse* XV, OC
6:111-12). I do not intend to go into this issue in any detail here.
While almost all recent commentators take Arnauld's side on this

point, I do not believe that there is any good reason to do so.[70] More important, and for the same reasons, I do not think that the introduction of intelligible extension, even if it does represent a retraction of the Book III account, involves any substantive modification in Malebranche's theory of the nature of ideas and their role in perception and knowledge. The finite parts (or subsets) of the single infinite idea of extension in God are indeed ideas of particular extended things. Malebranche insists that "a given part of intelligible extension" which corresponds to a given part of created extension (i.e., a body) is "its idea [*son idée*]" (*Search*, Elucidation X: OC 3:153; LO 627), and continues throughout the Elucidations and elsewhere to refer to "ideas of bodies" just as if they are individual entities.[71] Thus even with the infinite intelligible extension, Malebranche can and does continue to speak of particular ideas of things, as he did before 1678. I see, then, no reason to doubt his claim that the introduction of the intelligible extension is simply an explication of such talk, a way of explaining what, in fact, such ideas are.[72]

70. Scholars who do see a change in Malebranche's view include Radner, *Malebranche*, p. 80; Church, *A Study in the Philosophy of Malebranche*, pp. 139–42; Gueroult, *Malebranche*, vol. 1, chapter 3 and p. 211; and Alquié, *Le Cartésianisme de Malebranche*, pp. 218–26, who insists that Malebranche is just inconsistent on the nature of ideas, even after 1678, when one begins to find a "tension between two tendencies." Some commentators, however, believe that it is possible to see the Tenth Elucidation as indeed an explication of his earlier discussion in Book III and simply consider the apparent differences between the two accounts as the result of the differences in the questions to which each is an answer. See Gouhier, *La Philosophie de Malebranche et son expérience religieuse*, pp. 356ff.; and Lennon, "Philosophical Commentary," LO 786–87. Lennon's point is that the Tenth Elucidation does not contain a change in Malebranche's view, but rather an emphasis on an implication of the account in Book III. There was never any question of individual ideas of *things*, but only of *kinds* of things. And there has been only *one* kind of thing of which we have knowledge by idea, viz., extended things. "Properly speaking, then, there is only one Idea (known to us), intelligible extension" (LO 787).
71. See, for example, the *Réponse à Régis*, OC 17-1:288; and throughout the *Dialogues on Metaphysics*, especially Dialogue I, OC 12:37–38. Both of these are later than the Elucidations.
72. This is not necessarily to say that there are no substantial modifications at all in Malebranche's theory of ideas between the first edition of the *Search* in 1674 and the Tenth Elucidation in 1678. Gueroult, for example, argues that there is an evolution from a theory of finite, created ideas to a theory of eternal, uncreated, and infinite ideas; see *Malebranche*, vol. 1, pp. 62–81. See also Rodis-Lewis, "La Connaissance par idée chez Malebranche."

With regard to a single and isolated act of conception (intellection) or perception, these finite, intelligible parts of the one infinite intelligible extension function in fundamentally the same way as might discrete, mutually independent, individual ideas of particular extended bodies. Essentially, the components of cognition and perception remain the same: an act of the mind and some intelligible (ideal) extended figure, along with whatever sensory elements are present to particularize the ideal content. We can consider that intelligible extended figure either as a bounded sector of the infinite intelligible extension (a subset of the specifications contained in the idea of extension) or simply as the idea of some body.

This is not to say that there are no serious philosophical problems raised by Malebranche's infinite intelligible extension. Arnauld thought it committed him to placing extension "formally" in God and thus making God actually extended.[73] Others saw this same ramification as indicative of an underlying Spinozism in Malebranche's philosophy, whereby God is identical with the extended material universe.[74] These issues are interesting, but go beyond the scope of my concern here.

Malebranche is now in need of two kinds of arguments to complete his theory. First, he must show why one should think that there are such things (êtres) as representative ideas in knowledge and perception in the first place. Second, he must argue for the vision in God; that is, he must show why the ideas which are necessary in knowledge and perception are the ones in the divine understanding.

---

73. See VFI 258. Arnauld presents an extensive critique of an intelligible extension in God, both in VFI and in the *Défense*.
74. See, for example, Dortuous de Mairan's letters to Malebranche, especially OC 19:860f., 877f.

3

The Arguments for Ideas

Conception and Perception

Ideas play a dual role in Malebranche's epistemology. On the one hand, they allow for what Malebranche calls "pure intellection," the conception or rational apprehension of nonsensible natures. On the other hand, ideas are a necessary element (along with sensation) in the perception of objects in the external material world. Malebranche is not always clear in his discussion of ideas whether he is talking about conception or sense perception, and his use of the term *la perception* is ambiguous between the two contexts. It is important, however, to distinguish the one from the other. Let us first look briefly at how ideas function in conceptual thinking.

I argue above that Malebranche's ideas are concepts of things, essences of kinds of objects. It then follows that *all* ideas, for Malebranche, are abstract and general in nature (although, of course, some are more general than others).[1] The pure idea of extension, for example, presents to the mind extension in general. The pure idea of a triangle or of a circle is the universal concept of the triangle or the circle, and contains or specifies only the essential properties for each kind of figure. Even the pure idea of a foot or a hand (or any other body) is only a presentation of an abstract foot or hand, a foot or hand "in general," qua finite extended figure. There are no particulars in the ideal realm. What the pure under-

---

1. Gueroult points out, however, that in the period around the first edition of the *Search* (1674–75), Malebranche appears to be committed to the view that all ideas are particular (although he soon exchanges this for the view that all ideas are universal); see *Malebranche*, vol. 1, pp. 63–67.

standing perceives therein are "universals, common notions . . . [even] material things, extension with its properties . . . a perfect circle, a perfect square, a figure of a thousand sides, and similar things" (*Search* I.4.i: OC 1:66; LO 16). Having identified 'clear perception' with the perception of pure ideas, Malebranche insists that "the mind never sees clearly what is not universal" (*Search* I.1.ii: OC 1:48; LO 5). Restricting the question for the moment to bodies (as opposed to, say, numbers), we find that individual ideas (or finite subsets of the infinite intelligible extension) specify all and *only* those properties of extension that a particular extended object must instantiate, if it is to be of a certain kind.

Conception, or pure intellection, takes place when the mind apprehends an idea by itself, devoid of any sensuous element. I *conceive* a right triangle when I attend to the pure idea of right triangle, without considering existence or any specific sensuous features that would "particularize" the idea, such as color, texture, heat, or taste. The knowledge thus afforded by conception is likewise general and pertains only to *possible* being; in cases such as this, it is knowledge of eternal essences of a geometrical nature and the necessary truths based on them. In an important sense, conception does not tell one anything about what *actually* exists in the material world.[2] (It does, however, tell·one about what there is external to the mind, since the objects of the mind in conception—geometric triangles, circles, squares—are *external* objects for Malebranche: they are not perceptions or modifications of the mind, but ideas that are ontologically independent of it. Thus it can still be said that in conception we have knowledge of "external beings," namely, the ideas themselves.)

Through intellection, then, we have knowledge of universals and mathematical truths. And if the idea grasped is the idea of extension ("intelligible extension"), then we have knowledge of the nature of matter and bodies. Pure intellection is the rational apprehension of eternal, immutable essences and necessary truths—*la science* in the true sense of the term.[3] Thus in spite of Malebranche's

2. This knowledge about possible being provided by conception or pure intellection is not, however, irrelevant to our understanding of the essential nature of material bodies (if they exist). The ideas grasped by the conceiving mind are the archetypes according to which bodies are created.
3. See *Search* VI.2.vi.

frequent use of the term 'perception' to describe the mind's nonsensory apprehension of pure ideas, it is clear that what we have here is not an account of perception per se, but rather a theory of knowledge and understanting.[4] To "perceive" ideas is to have a cognitive grasp of certain concepts and principles. Ideas, and the truths based on them, are, on this neo-Platonic account, the proper objects of human knowledge and serve as the foundation for all certain and necessary cognitions. This is because only ideas (based as they are in the divine understanding) have the immutability, universality, and independence necessary for being *known*. There is no knowledge proper of particulars. Individual existing material things—changeable, singular, "inintelligibles en eux mêmes"—are objects not of knowledge but of sense perception, in which something is added to the pure intellection of the idea. A being can thus be disclosed to us in two ways: "as possible when the idea affecting us is pure, [and] as existing when the perception is sensible" (*Search*, Elucidation VI: OC 3:66; LO 575). This distinction between conception (which Malebranche also calls "illumination [*par lumière*]") and sensible perception, although obscured by a certain degree of ambiguity in Malebranche's use of the terms 'perceive' and 'perception', is central to Malebranche's system, particularly to his project in the *Search* of trying to discover and correct the sources of human error.

What is added to the idea in order to transform pure intellection into perception is sensation, primarily color. The sense perception of an object necessarily involves both a clear idea of some finite extension—which represents the properties of the body qua extended—and some sensuous element. "When we perceive something sensible, two things are found in our perception: *sensation* and pure *idea*" (*Search* III.2.vi: OC 1:445; LO 234). "There is always a *pure idea* and a *confused sensation* in the knowledge we have of the existence of beings" (*Search*, Elucidation X: OC 3:143; LO 621).

Sensation performs two functions in perception. First, it serves as a kind of "natural revelation" of the existence of the object. The sensuous component in perception indicates to us the presence of the perceived body to our own body. Color, heat, pain or pleasure, and other sensible qualities are all nonrational (and nondemonstra-

---

4. Yolton makes this particularly clear; see *Perceptual Acquaintance*, chapter 2.

tive) evidence that the body whose extension is represented by the pure idea is actual (although, as I have shown in chapter 2, these qualities are not in the body itself, but are caused in the mind by God on the occasion of that body's presence to our own). As Malebranche puts it, the sensation "makes us judge that [the object] exists" (*Search*, Elucidation X: OC 3:143; LO 621).[5]

Second, the sensation is required to "particularize" the idea. Without any sensuous component, the extension in the pure idea is general. The sensible quality "colors" the idea, in a manner of speaking, and makes it the idea of this or that physical body. It allows one to distinguish one finite extended figure from another of the same kind (with color apparently doing most of the work here).

> The difference between ideas of visible bodies comes about only by the difference of color. Similarly, the whiteness of the paper allows me to distinguish it from the rug; the color of the rug separates it for me from the table; and that of the table keeps me from confusing it with the air surrounding it and with the floor on which it stands. It is the same with all visible objects. Thus, extension conceived without color is the idea of all bodies . . . the idea of extension is thus general, and always the same. . . . But color particularizes this intelligible extension. (*Réponse* VI, OC 6:61)

In the *Dialogues on Metaphysics*, Theodore, Malebranche's spokesman, clarifies the difference between simply conceiving an object and having a sense perception of it:

> When you conceive a circle, intelligible extension is applied to your mind with indeterminate limits as to size but with all the points equidistant from some given point and all in the same place. You thus conceive a circle in general. . . . When you sense a circle, a determinate part of this extension sensibly affects your soul and modifies it with the sensation of a certain color. For intelligible extension becomes visible and represents some body in particular only through color, since it is only from the diversity of colors that

---

5. Malebranche does not believe, however, that such existential judgment is infallible or absolutely certain. He insists that we can have no "geometric demonstration" of the existence of bodies; see *Search*, Elucidation VI. In this regard he departs from Descartes, who offers in *Meditations* VI a *certum argumentum* for the existence of corporeal bodies.

we judge the difference of objects we see. (*Dialogues* I.10: OC 12:46;
D 39)[6]

Malebranche's favorite example in this regard is our perception of
the sun: "When we have a vivid sensation of light attached or
related to an intelligible circle, distant through a certain intelligible
space, and made sensible by different colors, we see the sun"
(*Réponse* VI, OC 6:55).[7] He elsewhere compares the mechanics of
sense perception to painting: just as the mind "attaches" or projects
the sensation of color onto the pure idea of extension in order to
perceive a body, so the painter applies colors to geometric forms on
a canvas in order to paint real objects.[8]

Unlike the painter's colors, however, Malebranche's sensations
are not *percepta*, or entities perceived by the mind at the same time
it apprehends the idea. They are not, that is, mental *objects*. As
modes of the mind, they are simply *perceptions*, or ways of apprehending. When one perceives the setting sun, the mind does not
apprehend two things—the pure idea of the geometric circle and a
red sensation (or red sensum); rather, it apprehends the sun by the
perception "red." In other words, one apprehends the sun "redly"
(although the color or sensation itself is known or felt by inner
awareness [sentiment interieur]). Malebranche thus appears to
offer an adverbial theory of sensation.

But there is a certain confusion in his account. In several contexts
he suggests that color sensations are ways of apprehending pure
ideas.

> The perception of the soul in someone who sees or feels an arm is
> only the perception, which is called color or pain, of the extension

---

6. See also *Réponse* XIII, OC 6:97ff. Malebranche explains here that without color
there is no sense perception, only pure intellection or conception. See also *Conversations chrétiennes*, OC 4:75–76.

7. See also TL I, OC 6:241.

8. "Parce qu'un arbre est étendu, & que la couleur ne l'est pas . . . il faut que l'esprit
ait l'idée de l'étendu, afin qu'il y attache, pour ainsi dire, le sentiment de couleur: de
même qu'il faut une toile à un Peintre, afin qu'il y applique les couleurs" (*Réponse*
IX, OC 6:78). See also Malebranche's letter to Arnauld, 1 July 1694 (OC 9:998–99).
For a good discussion of this, see Radner, *Malebranche*, pp. 84–90.

which composes the arm; that is to say, the immediate and direct perception of the ideal extension of the arm. (RLA, OC 9:961–62)

In the perception that I have, for example, of a marble column, there is an idea of extension, which is clear, and the confused sensation [*sentiment*] of whiteness which relates to it. . . . It is certain that one only sees extension by the perception and modification of the soul, which is called color. (*Réponse* XIII, OC 6:97–98)[9]

On this schema, to perceive a red body is to apprehend an *idea* of extension redly. The sensible apprehension of the idea is, then, contrasted with the pure perception of the idea (conception) simply in virtue of the nature of the mind's perceptual activity.[10] The idea itself is one and the same in both cases, and it is grasped either by a *perception pure* or a sensation.[11]

I say that there is a "confusion" in Malebranche's account because, if ideas are logical concepts and not visual-like data, as I have argued in chapter 2, how can they be sensibly perceived in this way? Ideas are not colorless pictorial images that are "sensed" by color perceptions. Although he tells us that it is through color and other sensible perceptions that finite parts of intelligible extension are rendered sensible or visible ("une idée claire de l'étendue . . . [est] rendue sensible ou visible par la couleur"), I do not think we should take him literally here. I will return to this in chapter 5.

This exegetical problem notwithstanding, both elements—idea and sensation—are necessary for sense perception. In perceptual acquaintance with material bodies, we both apprehend an idea (in

9. See also *Réponse à Régis*, OC 17-1:282: "Colors are only sensible perceptions which the soul has of extension [*les couleurs ne sont que des perceptions sensibles que l'âme a de l'étendu*]." On the other hand, this talk of color sensations as means of perceiving ideas does not appear at all in the *Search*.

10. It is tempting to claim that Malebranche's *perceptions* are mental acts, and Malebranche often discusses them as if they were. Radner suggests that for Malebranche "sensible qualities are species of mental acts" (*Malebranche*, p. 87). In many contexts, however, Malebranche is careful to insist that they are not actions at all, but "passivities"—particularly when he is emphasizing the causal efficacy of ideas: "Car les perceptions ne sont point des actions mais des passivitez de l'ame produites en elle par l'efficace des idées divines" (RLA, OC 9:921).

11. For a discussion of the differences between *perception pure* and *perception sensible*, see Robinet, *Système et existence dans l'oeuvre de Malebranche*, pp. 275–84.

Malebranche's terms, we "perceive" an idea[12]), which adds the element of understanding and knowledge to the process, and also experience certain sensuous qualities. The pure perception of the idea of the body, without sensation, is conception or intellection. On the other hand, were the mind to have a sensuous *perception* (that is, were it to be modified by a sensation) without at the same time apprehending a pure idea, the process would not qualify as "perception." If there is no idea present to contribute the intelligible and cognitive aspect of perceptual acquaintance, then all that is taking place is mere indiscriminate sensing.[13]

The Arguments for Ideas

There is clearly no need to argue for the presence of sensations in perception—their presence is phenomenologically certain. Sensation is its own evidence. A Cartesian like Malebranche can no more doubt that he is undergoing a sensation (for example, perceiving *redly*) than he can doubt his own existence. The testimony of *sentiment interieur* is incorrigible.

On the other hand, there does seem to be a burden of proof on one who would introduce into knowledge and perception the kind of entity Malebranche calls an 'idea'. Why should we think that in both intellectual knowing (pure thinking) and our perceptual acquaintance with the world, there is, besides the activity of the mind and (in the case of perception) the sensuous element, some ontologically distinct *être représentatif*—an idea which represents certain geometrical features of the extended object? What reasons can be given for so adding to the ontology of knowledge and perception?[14]

12. I am postponing for later discussion the important issue of the difference and relationship between the intellectual "perception" or apprehension of an idea and the perception (in the ordinary sense of the term) of material bodies. In our perceptual acquaintance with a material body, we also "perceive" an idea. Clearly, there is an ambiguity in Malebranche's use of the term 'perception' that needs to be untangled.
13. See *Réponse* XIX, OC 6:137.
14. Arnauld, for one, is quite clear that the burden of proof is on Malebranche to demonstrate the need for such a redundant and ontologically problematic entity; see VFI 221.

Malebranche, in fact, has two kinds of argument which, he believes, demonstrate the necessity of ideas in perception and intellection. Moreover, in some (but not all) contexts, he seems confident that each kind of argument is, by itself, sufficient to prove their existence, although I think his considered position is somewhat more restrained. As should be clear from my discussion, the arguments are intended to cover all our cognitive activities. They are concerned not just with the ordinary (sense) perception of material bodies, but also with thinking and knowing generally. It is important to keep this in mind, since Malebranche has a tendency to slip back and forth between considerations apparently proper to sense perception and conclusions regarding thought and cognition in general. While he may occasionally be guilty of conflating the two cases, I do not think this introduces a fallacy into his arguments. As I show, all the arguments are based on principles he considers to be true of both sense perception and conception, when properly distinguished.

THE ARGUMENTS FROM DISTANCE

An axiom prevalent in seventeenth-century natural philosophy (particularly of the Cartesian variety) is that there can be no action at a distance (*nihil agit in distans*). If a material agent is to bring about an effect in some other material being, it must either be in direct contact with that being, or be in indirect contact with it by means of direct contact with some other material being that is itself in direct contact with it. Nothing can exert its efficacy where it is not.

An epistemological corollary to this axiom is, in effect, that there can be no cognition "at a distance." Just as one body can act only on another body with which it is mechanically united, so the mind can perceive or know only that which is "intimately united with it." As Malebranche insists, "my soul must be united in some manner to whatever it perceives" (TL I, OC 6:212). This corollary serves as a premise in one kind of argument Malebranche gives for ideas. In all instances of the argument (the argument can be expressed in different ways, depending on how 'presence' is understood), Malebranche assumes that *présence* is a necessary condition for (*préalable à*) immediate perception or cognition. What the mind perceives[15] must be present to it. He then shows that since material bodies are not, and cannot be, present to or united with the mind in the necessary manner, they thus cannot be the *immediate* objects of the mind in perception. The intended conclusion is that only ideas, which *can* be so present to the mind, are immediately perceived or known, and thus that they are required to serve as representative proxies in the mind for the material bodies that are at an unbridgeable "distance" from it.

In seventeenth-century physics, the kind of presence or union required is local. The extremity of one body must be spatially contiguous with the extremity of the other body. Malebranche's use of the terms 'presence' and 'union' in his epistemology, however, appears to be ambiguous. Sometimes the argument appears to rely on a premise about local presence; on other occasions the kind of presence required is possible only between entities not ontologically dissimilar; and elsewhere, Malebranche speaks of a *causal* presence.

Malebranche's most famous use of the "presence" requirement to argue for ideas occurs in what has come to be known as the "walking-mind" argument. It first appears in Book I of the *Search*:

> It seems to me beyond question that our souls do not occupy a space as vast as that between us and the fixed stars, even if it be agreed our souls are extended; thus, it is unreasonable to think that our souls are in the heavens when they see stars there. It is not even thinkable that they should be projected a thousand feet from their bodies in order to see houses at a distance. Our soul, then, must see stars and houses where they are not, since the soul does not leave the body where it is located, and yet sees them outside it. Now . . . the stars immediately joined to the soul (which are the only stars it can see) are not in the heavens. (*Search* I.14: OC 1:156; LO 67)

In Book III, where Malebranche turns explicitly to the nature of ideas, the "stars immediately joined to the soul" from the passage just quoted are now *ideas* of stars:

15. At this point it is easier—and more in keeping with Malebranche's own seventeenth-century usage—simply to use, for the most part, the term 'perception' to cover both conceptual thinking and sense perception. I am *perceiving* a thing both when I conceive or think of it and when I have a sense perception of it. In my discussion the context makes clear which in particular is intended.

I think everyone agrees that we do not perceive objects external to us by themselves. We see the sun, the stars, and an infinity of objects external to us; and it is not likely that the soul should leave the body to stroll about the heavens, as it were, in order to behold all these objects. Thus, it does not see them by themselves [*par eux-mêmes*], and our mind's immediate object when it sees the sun, for example, is not the sun, but something that is intimately joined to our soul, and this is what I call an *idea*. (*Search* III.2.i: OC 1:413–14; LO 217)

Later in the same chapter he insists that, "as for things outside the soul, we can only perceive them by means of ideas, given that these things cannot be intimately joined to the soul. . . . [Since] our souls do not leave the body to measure the heavens . . . they can see bodies outside only through the ideas representing them."

It is natural to read these passages as employing a rather literal notion of 'presence', whereby the presence (or union with the soul) required for immediate perception is a spatial or local presence. The soul is located where the body to which it is united is located. Objects in the material world (and in celestial spaces) are at various, measurable distances from this body, hence from this soul. Thus, since these objects are not (locally) present and united to the soul, they cannot be immediately perceived by it.

The two most obvious ways of bridging this distance—the mind leaves the body to "stroll about the heavens" and become present to the object; or the object travels from its own spatial location to enter and unite itself with the mind—are clearly ruled out. The only alternative, Malebranche believes, is that what the mind immediately perceives on such occasions is some entity that is indeed locally present to it: an idea. This reading of the argument as requiring local presence is reinforced by Malebranche's *hypothesis per impossibile*: "even if it be agreed our souls are extended" (i.e., localized in space), the soul still is not where the material object it thinks it perceives is.[16]

16. Yolton suggests that there is a precedent for using the walking-mind argument with a premise requiring "literal" presence (by which I assume he means local presence). Marin Cureau de la Chambre, in *Le Système de l'ame*, insists that since there is no action at a distance, "it is necessary either that the understanding be near the objects, or that the objects be near it." But the mind "is not able to leave the body in order to find" objects, and objects do not move to the mind. Cureau thus argues

Arnauld similarly reads Malebranche as here demanding local presence as a precondition for perception and knowledge, and accuses him of thereby confusing cognition with physics and physiology. More particularly, Arnauld believes Malebranche takes a principle that has at least some prima facie credibility when considered in regard to the sense organs, namely, that an impression can be made on the optical nerve only by an object that is physically present before it, and that the eyes can see only objects that are in their vicinity ("il faloit que l'objet fust devant nos yeux, afin que nous le pussions voir")—and misapplies it to the operations of the mind, which is the faculty truly responsible for all kinds of perception. Malebranche is thus guilty of a tempting but illegitimate (and "infantile") analogy between the corporeal and spiritual realms; that is, between *la vue corporelle* and *la vue spirituelle.*

> It is quite common for the same word being applied to the mind and the body, to be taken by most everyone in the grosser sense [*fort grossierement*], and applied to the mind just as it applies to bodies. Thus, as the word 'presence' signifies a *local presence* with respect to bodies . . . and since local presence is better known to most people, two very false meanings have been attached to this equivocal proposition: 'it is necessary for bodies to be present to the soul in order to be known by it'. First, it is imagined that this *presence* is a prior condition for the knowledge of bodies, and that [presence] is first necessary in order for bodies to be in a state to be known. . . . The second false sense is that they have grossly taken this presence for a *local presence*, as it is applied to bodies. . . . [Malebranche] thus regards local distance as an obstacle, which puts a body out of the

---

for an Epicurean alternative: objects send material representative images to the senses. See Yolton, *Perceptual Acquaintance*, pp. 58–59.

I postpone for now another question, namely, that regarding the kind of theory of perception and cognition to which Malebranche's use of this and the other arguments apparently commits him. He is certainly arguing here, at the very least, for the necessity of ideas in perceiving and knowing. In some sense of the phrase, these ideas are the *immediate objects* of the mind in perception and intellection, because they alone are present to it. But whether ideas are perceived or known *instead* of material bodies (idealism); or whether the immediate perception of the idea is a *means of* perceiving or knowing the material body (indirect or representative realism); or whether some other view is implied—these are all questions I will turn to in chapter 5.

condition of being able to be perceived by our mind. Thus, he believes that it is a *local presence* which is required in order that our mind see its objects. (VFI 216–17)

In fact, Arnauld argues, local presence is completely irrelevant to cognition and perception. We clearly *do* see and know objects distant from the mind: "our soul can know an infinite number of things which are distant from the place where it is situated. . . . I am certain that my soul has seen the sun, the stars and other works of God an infinite number of times" (VFI 214).[17]

In response to Arnauld, Malebranche insists that the walking-mind argument, and its apparent demand for local presence, is not to be taken literally: "Is it not clear that what I said was more a kind of jest [*une espèce de raillerie*] rather than a principle upon which I establish sentiments which undermine this same principle?" (*Réponse*, OC 6:95–96). The point of the argument, he claims, is simply to illustrate that "something different from the sun is necessary to represent it to the soul," that "an idea [is] necessary" for perceiving material things. Malebranche reminds Arnauld that, on his view, we *do* see things distant (éloignez) from the mind; for example, we see things that do not exist.

I see no reason for not taking Malebranche at his word here, when he denies that the kind of presence he intends as necessary for immediate perception (again, 'perception' taken in the broad sense to mean both thinking and perceiving as it is ordinarily understood) is local. Indeed, there are good reasons for thinking that Malebranche has some other notion of 'presence' in mind. Malebranche, being the Cartesian that he is, realizes that there is also a necessary metaphysical (and not merely a contingent spatial) barrier between the mind and material bodies, and that even if the mind were locally present to a material body (that is, even if it were to "travel across the heavens"), it would be of no help in the mind's immediate perception of that body. We need ideas to perceive our own bodies, which of all material things come closest to achieving a kind of "local" presence with the soul.[18] Moreover, the mind is certainly

---

17. I examine Arnauld's arguments in detail in *Arnauld and the Cartesian Philosophy of Ideas*, pp. 90–95.
18. I use quotes here ("local") to indicate that a local presence is, properly speaking, possible only between bodies.

"locally" present to the brain (it is that part of the body to which the soul is "immediately joined"), but the brain is not perceived by it: "Even if the soul is imagined to be in the object and to penetrate it, as it is normally assumed to be in the brain and to penetrate it, the soul could not perceive it, since it cannot even discover the particles composing its brain, where it is said to make its principal residence" (*Search* VI.11: OC 2:100; LO 320).[19] A local presence, for Malebranche, is not what is needed.

In fact, the kind of presence required for immediate perception—in contexts where Malebranche is not employing the walking-mind metaphor—is a species of what might be called an *ontological* presence, and is apparently possible only between entities of the same ontological kind. Two entities can be "present" to each other, in this sense of the term, only if they are not ontologically dissimilar. Ontological presence is, thus, a rather general notion whose application depends on what *kind* of entity is being considered. For a dualist like Malebranche, there are two varieties of ontological presence. Local or spatial presence among bodies is a species of ontological presence— namely, that species which applies among material things. There is another variety of ontological presence, however, which applies in the realm of the mind. Mental things can be (ontologically) present to other mental things (although we do not have a precise name like "local presence" for this species within the genus). For example, a sensation is present to the mind, since the mode of a substance is necessarily ontologically similar to the substance of which it is a mode. Likewise even though, in our present state of being, we do not have immediate knowledge of other minds (but only "knowledge by conjecture"), Malebranche concedes that "there is reason to believe they can be revealed to the soul by themselves and without ideas" (*Search* III.2.i: OC 1:415; LO 218). This is because a kind of "intimate union" between souls is possible. Souls *can* be present to one another in the requisite manner (much as angelic souls are in heaven), and thus there is no metaphysical reason why they cannot have immediate cognition of one another. On the other hand, material bodies *cannot* be so present to the mind. This is because of the radical ontological difference between mind and matter that dualism entails: "Material things . . . certainly cannot be joined to our soul in the way necessary

19. See also *Conversations chrétiennes*, OC 4:30.

for it to perceive them, because with them extended and the soul unextended, there is no relation between them" (*Search* III.2.i: OC 1:417; LO 219). In reply to Arnauld, Malebranche claims that the immediate object of the mind in perception is never an extended, material body, since the soul is not itself extended (TL I, OC 6:231).

Thus, if we reconstruct Malebranche's argument from distance, we get the following: The soul is unextended thinking; bodies are thoughtless extension. Bodies therefore cannot be present to the mind because there is a metaphysical barrier or "distance" between minds and bodies. Bodies therefore cannot be the immediate objects of perception. Even if the mind were to travel the thousand feet separating it from some object in the distance, it still would not be able to unite itself to that material object in the requisite manner. The mind's immediate object in perception, then, is something that is ontologically present to it. According to Malebranche, this object is a representative idea.[20]

Arnauld and Locke are somewhat hard put to understand what kind of presence to the mind Malebranche is working with here. Arnauld insists that if it is not a local presence (which it cannot be), then it must be a cognitive or *objective* presence to the mind. But to be objectively present to the mind, for Arnauld, is to be perceived or known. Presence to the mind, in this sense, is not a prior condition for (*préalable à*) perception and knowledge; rather, it is perception or knowledge itself (VFI 192-93).[21] And if 'presence' is properly understood in this way, then material bodies can surely be present

---

20. Along these lines, Lennon suggests that the object of the "raillery" in the walking-mind argument is the view which Malebranche saw in Cureau, that "what prevents the understanding from being able to unite itself [*se . . . unir*] to corporeal objects is that it cannot leave [*sortir*] the body where it is contained to join [*joindre*] them. . . . But when the soul is separated, it no longer has any obstacles preventing it from uniting itself to objects, for it is free to move toward them" (*Système de l'ame*, p. 38; Lennon's translation). According to Lennon, "the thrust of the walking-mind argument is . . . something like the following: 'The mind does not physically approach the material objects, as if that would explain its knowledge of them anyway!'" ("Angelus Domini: Malebranche's Argument for Ideas," p. 6).

21. Arnauld's point here has the historical evidence on its side. For thinkers such as Duns Scotus, Ockham, Suarez, and Descartes, to be present to the mind is simply to have what they call *esse objectivum*, to exist in the mind as something known or thought (as opposed to actual existence in the world, *esse subjectivum* or *esse formalis*). See Nadler, *Arnauld and the Cartesian Philosophy of Ideas*, pp. 147-65.

to the mind. Since Malebranche considers presence to be a condition for perception, it is clearly not objective presence he has in
mind. What, then, is it?

Locke is even more baffled. He can conceive what union or
presence between two bodies involves, but has trouble understanding what meaning this notion can have in the mental sphere. What
is it for something to be "present" to the mind, in a sense of
'presence' that disqualifies bodies?

> What it is to be intimately united to the soul; what it is for two souls
> or spirits to be intimately united; for intimate union being an idea
> taken from bodies when the parts of one get within the surface of the
> other, and touch their inward parts; what is the idea of intimate
> union, I must have, between two beings that have neither of them
> any extension or surface? And if it be not so explained, as to give me
> a clear idea of that union, it will make me understand very little more
> of the nature of the ideas in the mind. . . . He says that "certainly
> material things cannot unite themselves to our souls." Our bodies are
> united to our souls, yes; but, says he, not after "a manner which is
> necessary that the soul may perceive them." Explain this manner of
> union, and show wherein the difference consists betwixt the union
> necessary and not necessary to perception, and then I shall confess
> this difficulty removed.[22]

Locke's point is well taken. While ontological presence is clearly
conceived in the realm of bodies, where it means *local* presence (or
spatial contiguity), it is not clear what Malebranche means by
'present to the mind', if he does not mean what Arnauld means, that
is, present as known or perceived. What *is* that other species of
ontological presence?

One possible way of explaining ontological presence in the mental realm could make sense of Malebranche's premise. Unfortu-
nately, this way is not open to Malebranche. It might be suggested
that the Cartesian ontology Malebranche accepts furnishes a
scheme within which we can talk meaningfully of something being
present to the mind (hence, capable of being immediately perceived
by it), and do so in a way such that only things which are ontologi-

---

22. "Examination," p. 213. To be fair, it must be admitted that Locke has a similar
problem in defining what he means when he says in the *Essay* and elsewhere that
ideas are "in the mind"; see Aaron, *John Locke*, pp. 100–101.

cally similar to the mind can be so present. 'Present to the mind', in this ontological sense, might simply mean being a modification of a thinking substance, or belonging to the mind as one of its properties. Sensations and other perceptions, for example, belong to the mind as its modes and are immediately known by it. And it is clear that anything which so belongs to the mind must necessarily be ontologically similar to the mind, since a modification of a substance is simply that substance existing in such and such a way. Perhaps, then, when Malebranche claims that something must be present to the mind for the mind to be able to perceive it immediately, he means it must be a mode of the mind.[23]

But if Malebranche is arguing for *ideas* as the objects present to and hence immediately perceived by the mind, he clearly cannot intend 'presence' to be understood in terms of the relationship between a substance and its modifications. For Malebranche, ideas are not (and cannot be) modifications of the mind at all. They are ontologically distinct from and independent of any finite thinking substance. In fact, Malebranche insists that ideas, while they are "in" God, are not modifications of the divine mind either.[24] This would appear to imply that, strictly speaking, ideas are not "mental" at all, if by 'mental' is meant either being a mind or belonging to a thinking substance (finite or infinite). But if ideas are not mental, if they are neither minds nor modifications of minds, then in what sense are they of the right ontological type for "intimate union" with the mind? If the presence required for immediate perception is possible only between entities of the same ontological kind (that is, if it is an *ontological* presence), then Malebranche's ideas would seem to be as "distant" from the mind as material bodies.[25]

Malebranche, I believe, realizes that his notion of 'presence' or 'union' can stand some clarification; as he admits to Régis, the word

23. Watson offers a more extreme suggestion. He claims that "the *only* possible explication of direct acquaintance in the Cartesian system is that which makes it the same as the relation between a substance and its modifications" (emphasis added). In fact, according to Watson, the relation of direct acquaintance "is nothing more than the relation of a substance to its own modifications." On this reading, the cognitive relation between mind and object is reducible to the ontological one between mind and mode; see *The Breakdown of Cartesian Metaphysics*, pp. 112–13.
24. See *Search*, Elucidation X: OC 3:149; LO 625.
25. This is a point made by Foucher; see RCP, p. 107.

'union' is "un des plus équivoques qu'il y ait" (*Réponse à Régis*, OC 17-1:294). We thus find in later editions of the *Search* (in what is probably an attempt at clarification), one further "argument from distance" for ideas, in which the kind of "presence" required for immediate perception is of a *causal* nature. To be present to the mind is to be in a causal relationship with the mind; thus only that which can act on the mind, which can "touch" or modify it by causing a perception in it, is visible or intelligible by itself. For example Malebranche, when he reiterates his premise for Arnuald, phrases it as follows: "My soul must be united in some manner with whatever it perceives, it must be touched or affected by it" (TL I, OC 6:212). To say that material bodies cannot be "present" to the mind, and hence are not directly and immediately perceived or known, is to say that they cannot themselves act upon the mind.

> Although something must be in order to be perceived, everything that is, is not thereby perceptible in itself; for in order to be so, it must be able to act immediately upon the soul, it must be able of itself to enlighten, affect, or modify minds. Otherwise, our soul, which is purely passive so far as being able to perceive, will never perceive it. (*Search* IV. 11: OC 2:99–100; LO 320)[26]

Bodies are inefficacious, incapable of causing perceptions in the soul, on two counts. First, since a material body is nothing other than extension, it is essentially and necessarily causally inefficacious. A body is by nature devoid of any active power and hence is incapable by itself of causing a modification in any other thing, whether material or immaterial. It cannot bring about motion in another body or thoughts in a soul. Extension is purely passive, and has only the faculty of "receiving various figures and movements."[27] This is evident from the clear and distinct idea of extension, which tells us that an active causal power is, in fact, incompatible with the nature of body.

---

26. See also *Search* III.2.vii: "We know things by themselves and without ideas when they are intelligible by themselves, i.e., when they can act on the mind and thereby reveal themselves to it" (OC 1:448; LO 236); and RLA: "[L'ame] n'apperçoit que ce qui la touche, que ce qui l'affecte" (OC 9:921).
27. *Dialogues* VII.1–2: OC 12: 148–51; D 145–49. See also *Search*, Elucidation XV. This point about the causal inefficacy of bodies is central to Malebranche's occasionalism.

Second, for Malebranche it is axiomatic that "nothing can act immediately upon the mind unless it is superior to it" (*Search* III.2.vi: OC 1:442; LO 232). And the soul, as a simple substance, is more perfect than bodies, which are complex and composed of parts. Hence, even if bodies were in some way active, they could not act on the soul and thus cannot be immediately present to it.

On the other hand, Malebranche argues, "it is certain that ideas are efficacious, since they act upon the mind and enlighten it" (*Search* III.2.vi: OC 1:442; LO 232). In fact, he defines an idea as "that which affects and modifies the mind [*ce qui touche & modifie l'esprit*] with the perception it has of an object" (*Search* III.2.i: OC 1:414; LO 217).[28] More precisely, God alone (the only being superior to a finite thinking substance) is capable of acting on minds. And the ideas "which are located in the efficacious substance of the Divinity" affect and enlighten us through God's power. Thus ideas (via God) are what are immediately present to the mind.

We thus see that while a necessary condition for immediate perception is "presence to the mind," the kind of presence required apparently varies from a local presence (although, as I note, I do not think that Malebranche ever intends this seriously) to an ontological presence (presence as possible only between entities of the same ontological kind) to a causal presence (whereby an object is present to the mind when it enters into a causal relationship with it). In all cases, material bodies lack the capacity to be present to the mind and hence are not immediately perceived and known.

Now it might appear from my presentation of these arguments

---

28. As Robinet has shown, the notion of *idée efficace* in its "precise meaning" does not appear in Malebranche's oeuvre until 1695, in the Preface to the *Dialogues*, and not in the *Search* until the fifth (1700) edition. But it does clearly appear in the *Réponse à Régis* in 1693 (OC 17-1:282-83, 288). Robinet suggests, however, that this does not represent a usage of the term "en son sens précis"; see Robinet, *Système et existence dans l'oeuvre de Malebranche*, pp. 259-72. This novelty in Malebranche's theory of ideas clearly results from questions raised by Régis (and Arnauld) regarding Malebranche's understanding of the "union" between the human mind and God (Régis's text is cited by Malebranche at OC 17-1:293-94). For other discussions of this notion, see Alquié, *Le Cartésianisme de Malebranche*, pp. 208-12; Gueroult, *Malebranche*, vol. 1, pp. 153-202; and Farfara, *The Notion of the "Idée Efficace" in the Philosophy of Malebranche*.

that Malebranche also believes that they, singly or together, establish the further claim that representative ideas, as he understands them, are necessary for perception and cognition; that Malebranchian ideas can be, and are, present to the mind in the requisite manner; that ideas alone are immediately perceived, and that they thus make up for the absence (or "distance") from the mind of the material body.

But in fact, all these arguments from distance prove is that bodies by themselves are not perceivable or knowable; or as Malebranche puts it, that bodies "en eux-mêmes" are "invisibles et inintelligibles." Each argument, by employing a notion of 'presence to the mind' that effectively excludes bodies, shows only that material objects cannot be present to the mind in the manner required for immediate perception. But the arguments do not by themselves tell us what *is* so present to the mind. In particular, they do not prove that representative ideas of the Malebranchian variety are present to the mind in perception and knowledge.[29] To do this, they would have to show as well that such ideas are *exclusively* capable of being present to the mind in the necessary way, that only they can fit the bill (so to speak) as opposed to, say, ideas such as Arnauld understands them. Moreover, I believe that Malebranche indeed recognizes the limitations of his arguments here. In response to Arnauld, he states that in the arguments from distance in Book III, Part 2, of the *Search*,

> I was only claiming that something different from the sun was required to represent the sun to the soul. Whether this be a *modification of the soul*, according to the opinion of Mr. Arnauld; or an *express species*, according to certain philosophers; or a *being created* with the soul, according to others; or, finally, a *part of*

29. Gueroult makes this point well. He claims that the arguments from distance (which he groups together with other arguments under the summarizing title "Les corps sont inconnaissables par eux-mêmes") prove only "that bodies . . . are invisible and unintelligible . . . that the material world is absolutely unknown and unknowable directly in itself." Further arguments are needed to show that what we directly perceive are Malebranche's representative ideas; see *Malebranche*, vol. 1, pp. 88–90. See also Robinet, *Système et existence dans l'oeuvre de Malebranche*, p. 217: "The collection of arguments relative to the demonstration of the invisibility of bodies by themselves do not allow one to conclude the necessary existence of ideas."

> *intelligible extension rendered sensible by color or light,* as I claim:
> this is what I have not yet examined. (*Réponse*, OC 6:96)[30]

The arguments from distance, then, demonstrate only that some kind of representative entity (être représentatif) present to the mind is needed to stand in for the material body. To complete the case for his theory of ideas, and to exclude other kinds of representative entities, Malebranche also needs to argue that what does the representing here is something distinct from the human mind. In other words, Malebranche's arguments that representative ideas are not modifications of the soul (examined in chapter 2) supplement the arguments from distance and allow him to draw the conclusion that in perception and knowledge the mind's immediate object is a Malebranchian idea.

THE ARGUMENT FROM INTENTIONALITY

Malebranche has a stronger—and what I think he takes to be a more persuasive and important kind of—argument for ideas. It is an argument for intentional objects that appears both in medieval philosophical thought on cognition and in later phenomenological analyses of consciousness. In some important respects the argument also anticipates the "argument from illusion" offered for the existence of sense data in perception.

---

30. In this response, written in 1684, Malebranche cannot be referring to the passage from *Search* III.2 insofar as it includes the reference to "ce qui touche et modifie l'esprit" (that is, insofar as it employs the notion of *causal* presence), since this phrase was not added until 1712 (6th ed.). It might be suggested, then, that Malebranche adds the reference to causal presence as a result of this interchange with Arnauld and in order to complete the argument for Malebranchian ideas, and that thus Malebranche's response to Arnauld about the limited scope of the arguments from distance is not intended to apply to the argument as it involves a causal presence. But then why does he not make the addition in the fourth edition published in Amsterdam in 1688? Moreover, as I note above, the references to causal presence seem to be made rather in response to Régis's queries. Thus I think that Malebranche's answer to Arnauld regarding the import of the passage from the *Search* can be taken to be applicable to the argument from causal presence as well; that is, that argument, too, is offered only to show that *something* is needed to be present to the soul and immediately perceived, since material bodies cannot be. Along these lines, Gueroult notes that the causal argument by itself could equally be used to demonstrate the Berkeleian view that God acts directly on the soul by means of sensations without the use of representative ideas distinct from these sensations; see *Malebranche*, vol. 1, p. 91.

The issue of intentionality plays an important role in the Arnauld–
Malebranche debate, although scholars have tended to ignore it in
favor of the more celebrated issue of direct realism vs. indirect or
representative realism.[31] Both Arnauld and Malebranche regard
intentionality (or "object-directedness") as an essential feature of
much of mental life. They agree, that is, that every *perception*,[32]
every act of the mind is object-directed. Every thought is the
thought *of* something; every perception is the perception *of* something. Intentionality constitutes an inseparable and evident feature
of the mind's operations.[33] Arnauld puts it in a way that would
allow Malebranche to agree:

> One cannot think without thinking of something; to think of nothing
> is not to think at all; that is, there is no thought which does not have
> its object. (*Défense*, 383)

> Just as it is clear that I am thinking, it is also clear that I am thinking
> of something; that is, that I know and that I perceive something; for
> this is essential to thought. (VFI 184)

What Arnauld and Malebranche disagree about, however, is how
to characterize and account for this feature of thought. They both
recognize that it cannot be accounted for by claiming that every act
of consciousness is, in fact, immediately confronted with and directed toward an actually existing material object. Such a claim is
clearly false. We often think of or imagine objects that are fictitious,
and we often see things that do not in fact exist (for example, in
hallucinations and dreams). In such cases the mental act has intentionality even though there is no corresponding material object.
Hence the absence of such an object must be irrelevant to the act's
object-directedness.[34]

Arnauld accounts for the intentionality of mental acts by insisting that every act of the mind, every *perception*, is a representation

31. See Nadler, "Intentionality in the Arnauld–Malebranche Debate."
32. *Perception* here, however, does not include sensations for Malebranche, since he
does not recognize them as intentional phenomena.
33. For Arnauld, *all* mental phenomena are intentional, and intentionality serves as
the mark of the mental. Malebranche, on the other hand, insists that while perceptions or mental acts are intentional, sensations and other passions are not. See
Nadler, *Arnauld and the Cartesian Philosophy of Ideas*, pp. 175–78.
34. See Arnauld, VFI 221; Malebranche, RLA, OC 8:915.

of some object or another. Each perception or thought has a representational content—what Arnauld, after Descartes, calls its "objective reality." This content, intrinsic to the mental act, is what
gives the act its object-directedness, that is, directedness to the
object presented by (or represented in) that content. All perceptions
thus have intentionality, whether or not there exists outside the
mind something corresponding to the act's content.[35]

Malebranche likewise insists that every thought has its object: "to
perceive is to perceive something, since to perceive nothing, to
perceive no thing, is not to perceive at all [*voir le néant, voir rien,
c'est ne point voir*]" (TL I, OC 6:202). Malebranche, however,
understands this intentionality thesis to mean that every perception
or thought is immediately directed at some entity really (ontologically) present to it. Every act of the mind essentially and necessarily
has a direct and immediate object which it apprehends. And it is the
real presence of this object (and its apprehension by the act) which
confers intentionality upon the act.

Put another way, Arnauld insists that intentionality is a nonrelational property of the mental act, a function of its (intrinsic) content. Malebranche, on the other hand, takes intentionality to be a
relation between the perception (mental act) or the perceiving agent
(mind) and a really present entity of some ontological sort or
another.[36]

Malebranche employs the thesis of intentionality, understood in
this way, to argue for his claim that in perception and cognition the
mind directly and immediately apprehends an external representative idea. His argument is, in effect, that whenever we have an
intentional conscious state, there must be some immediately intended object to account for that state's intentionality; material
bodies cannot be the immediately intended objects of such states;

---

35. See VFI, chapter 5. For a detailed discussion of Arnauld's theory of intentionality, see Nadler, *Arnauld and the Cartesian Philosophy of Ideas*, chapter 6.
36. This view of intentionality as a species of relation is found in certain medieval
theories; see, for example, Ockham, *Commentary on the Sentences* (*Ordinatio*),
Book I, D. 2, Q. viii, in *Opera Theologica*, vol. 2, pp. 271–74. It also reappears in
later philosophical thought on perception and cognition; see, for example, Brentano,
Psychology from an Empirical Standpoint, pp. 77–92; and Meinong, "The Theory
of Objects." For a philosophical discussion and critique of the relational account of
intentionality, see Prior, "Intentional Attitudes and Relations."

therefore it is some nonmaterial, representative entity which is the intended object. In its simplest form, the argument runs as follows:

AI-1 (1) Every thought has its object ("Il n'y a point de pensée qui n'ait son objet . . .").

(2) That is, every thought or perception is the direct and immediate thought or perception *of* something (" . . . si par l'objet de la pensée l'on entend son objet immédiat et direct").

(3) On many occasions our thoughts or perceptions have no corresponding material objects (e.g., when we think of possible but nonexisting beings ["une montagne d'or"] and mathematical entities).

(4) Even in these cases there must be an object immediately and directly perceived ("Il n'est pas vrai qu'on ne pense à rien car . . . penser à rien, c'est ne point penser du tout").

(5) Since there is no material object there to fill this role in these special cases, there must be some nonmaterial object present to the mind serving as its direct and immediate object, and representing to it these possible and abstract objects.[37]

Premises (1) and (2) represent the intentionality thesis, as Malebranche understands it, and allow him to conclude to (4) and (5). As it stands, however, the argument does not do the kind of work that Malebranche wants it to do. He seems to believe that it establishes the *general* claim that in *every* case of perception or thought we apprehend an idea. In fact, it shows only that ideas are the mind's direct and immediate objects in the special cases mentioned, that is, when there is no material object to fill this role. The argument explains how we still perceive something, still have a perception or thought, when there is nothing in the material world to correspond to our perception. But it is consistent with this explanation that in the veridical cases the immediately intended object is a material one.

37. The argument from intentionality in this form appears in RLA, OC 9:910.

Malebranche, however, offers a second version of the argument from intentionality, one based on the general possibility of hallucination and on the logical possibility of error in all our perceptual judgments. This second version can be reconstructed from the texts in two ways.

AI-2a   (1) Every thought or perception is *of* something ("voir le néant, voir rien c'est ne point voir").

(2) That is, every thought or perception is the direct and immediate thought or perception of some really present entity.

(3) If material bodies were the direct and immediate objects of thought or perception, we would never see or think of things that do not exist.

(4) But we do often see or think of things that do not exist (in hallucinations and dreams).

(5) Therefore material bodies are not the direct and immediate objects of thought and perception. Rather, this role is filled by ideas, themselves really present to the mind, that represent bodies.[38]

Premises (1) and (2) again represent the intentionality thesis. Behind premise (3) seems to lie a principle that all direct and immediate objects of perception or thought must be of the same ontological kind. It is inconceivable, that is, that veridical perceptions have as their direct objects one kind of entity (viz., material bodies), while hallucinatory perceptions have as their direct objects another kind of entity. All perceptual acts must be directed toward the same *kind* of object. In other words, the intentionality of perception must be accounted for *in the same way* for *all* perceptions.[39] Now on the assumption that the intended (direct) objects of

38. See TL I, OC 6:202.
39. One plausible justification for this principle could be the phenomenologically qualitative similarity between a veridical perceptual experience and a hallucinatory one, that is, the similarity that allows us to mistake the latter for the former and thus be taken in by our hallucinations and dreams. Since the two kinds of perceptual experience are so qualitatively similar, they must have as their direct objects the same kind of entity.

perception are material bodies, every perception would then be the direct perception of an actually existing material body. It follows that we could never have hallucinatory perceptions (where the body perceived does not exist), for in such a situation there would be *no* directly intended object, which is to perceive nothing, hence not to perceive at all. On this assumption, then, all perceptions would be veridical, which is clearly not the case. We thus must seek some other kind of entity to serve as the directly intended object of perception (again, in *all* cases of perception): representative ideas. The argument from intentionality, in this second version, does appear to have the kind of generality which Malebranche needs, and which the first version lacks.

Malebranche explicitly presents this second version of the argument to Arnauld in a way that can be reformulated as follows[40]:

AI–2b   (1) Every thought or perception is *of* something.

(2) That is, every thought or perception is the direct and immediate thought or perception of some really present entity.

(3) For every existential perceptual judgment we make, it is logically possible that that judgment is false ("la vûë sensible des objets renferme necessairement un jugement qui peut être faux").

(4) If material bodies were the direct and immediate objects of our perceptions ("si on voyait les corps en eux-mêmes"), there would be no possibility for such false existential perceptual judgments.

(5) We thus do not perceive material bodies themselves; they are not the direct objects of our perceptions.

(6) The direct objects of our perceptions are ideas, which represent such bodies to the mind.

The kind of error Malebranche has in mind in premise (3) consists primarily in a false judgment regarding the existence of the material body perceived: we erroneously judge that body *x*, of

---

40. TL I, OC 6:202.

which we are now having a perception, actually exists.[41] Malebranche is insisting that if material bodies were the direct and immediate objects of perception, such false judgments would not even be logically possible: since we would always and necessarily be in perceptual acquaintance with a material body (viz., the one perceived), on every occasion the judgment that the body perceived exists would necessarily be true. For every perception of x (where x is a material body), there would really be some actually existing x corresponding to the perception and serving as its direct and immediate object. If the direct objects of perception were ideas representing bodies, however, we could explain such errors as cases of mistaking the real presence of the directly intended object (an idea, presenting an extension to the mind) for the presence of some actually existing material body. For Malebranche, apparently, this is what occurs in a hallucination and the false existential judgment resulting from it: we perceive an idea having certain quantitative properties and colored by certain sensations, and we are thereby led to believe that we are perceiving some material body possessing just those properties.[42] The logical possibility of error in every perceptual experience is thus preserved by introducing representative entities to account for the intentionality of perception.

Malebranche offers a third version of the argument from intentionality,[43] and likewise formulates it in such a way that it does appear to argue for the broader claim that perceptions in general (and not just hallucinatory ones) are immediately directed toward ideas.

41. Malebranche's argument can also be reconstructed for the case of qualitative error, whereby we falsely attribute some perceived quality to a material body. In fact, he may actually have this in mind when he says that in such false judgments "one refers [*on rapporte*] to objects that which necessarily relates only to the ideas [*ce qui n'a de rapport necessaire qu'aux idées*] which represent them, and to the sensations by which one judges of their existence" (*Réponse*, OC 6:202).

42. See *Search* III.2.i: OC 1:414–15; LO 217–18.

43. Malebranche does not seem to recognize that there are any significant differences in the ways in which he formulates the argument. When going over the third version of the argument, he tells Arnauld (to whom all three versions are offered) that "je réponds donc encore une fois . . ." (RLA, OC 9:915).

AI-3   (1) Every perception has a necessary, essential, and direct relation to its immediate object ("les perceptions ont un rapport direct nécessaire essentiel à son objet immédiat").[44]

(2) It is clear from experience that perceptions do not have any necessary and essential relations to material bodies ("je nie que nos perceptions aïent essentiellement rapport aux objets de dehors").

(3) Thus material bodies are not the immediate objects of our perceptions.

(4) Therefore that to which any perception is essentially and necessarily related and which is immediately perceived is not a material body but an idea which represents some body or other object.[45]

Premise (1) represents the intentionality thesis: every perception or thought is necessarily *of* something. Given Malebranche's understanding of the thesis, this means that every perception or thought stands in a necessary relation to some really present object, an object without which the perception would not occur ("voir rien, c'est ne point voir"). To say that it is a *rapport nécessaire* is simply to say that if the perception occurs, then an object is there (and conversely, if an object were not there, then the perception would not occur). It is *not* to say, however, that if the object is there, then some perception of it likewise takes place; for Malebranche, the existence of the objects of knowledge and perception is independent of any perception of them. Nor is it to say that there is a necessary relation between the perceptual act and any one particular object, since the perception can move on to another object, or could just as well have had a different object to begin with. Rather, the necessary relation Malebranche has in mind here is between perception and a *kind* of object, or between perceptual acts and objects of a certain kind.[46]

---

44. In exposition of this premise Malebranche once again repeats, in a modified form, his standard encapsulation of the intentionality thesis: "Appercevoir le néant, c'est ne rien appercevoir, c'est ne point penser du tout" (RLA, OC 9:916).
45. RLA, OC 9:915–16.
46. We might put the question this way: Is there a kind of object such that whenever a perception occurs there is necessarily an object of that kind present?

Now as premise (2) reminds us, we know that there is no necessary relation between a perception and some external material body. First, it is clear that there are many cases in which we have perceptions of things that do not exist (here Malebranche uses the vivid experience of dreams: "Nous avons souvent des perceptions [des] objets, quoiqu'ils n'existent point: nos perceptions n'y ont donc point essentiellement rapport"). Perceptions do occur without corresponding material objects.

Second, even when we have a normal veridical perceptual experience, where there *is* some external material body corresponding to the perception, there is still no *necessary* relation between the perception and that body. One can always conceive of a situation in which one still perceives that body, that is, in which the perceptual experience is phenomenologically identical to that of the veridical case, yet there is *no* such material body. Just because one has a perception of x (where x is a material body, e.g., a pink elephant), it does not follow necessarily that x really exists.[47] There is never any necessary connection between the perception of x (a mental event) and the existence of x (a physical event), even when both are in fact simultaneously present.

It follows, then, that material objects are not the kind of things to which our perceptions are necessarily and essentially related, hence not the kind of things which serve as the immediate objects of perception. But there must always be *some* object really present to which that perception *is* necessarily and essentially related. There must be some object, that is, which is the direct and immediate object of the perception and without which the perception would not occur (by premise [1], the intentionality thesis); otherwise we would be perceiving nothing, which is not to perceive at all. This role is filled by representative ideas ("C'est donc à nos idées . . . que nos perceptions ont un rapport essentiel" [RLA, OC 9:916]). Thus every perception will be the perception *of* something (or every perception will be necessarily related to some present immediate object)—an idea—whether or not some corresponding material body exists.

---

47. 'To perceive' is not, of course, used here as the "success term" it is often taken to be, whereby if I *perceive* something, it follows that that thing exists, that it is there to be perceived. I think Malebranche does not intend it to be taken as a success term.

All these formulations of the argument from intentionality rely on Malebranche's relational understanding of the intentionality thesis: to say that every thought or perception is the thought or perception *of* something means, according to Malebranche, that there is always some external entity ontologically present to the mind that the act of perception directly apprehends or intends. Since material bodies clearly do not fill this role (and the reason for this varies with each version of the argument), some kind of immaterial representative entity must be the immediately intended object: ideas. The whole point of the argument is to account for the intentionality of perception and thought (and this must be accounted for in the same way for all perceptions and all thoughts) in a way that allows for the possibility of hallucination or false judgment (AI–1 through AI–2b) and preserves the necessary and essential relation between mental act and immediately intended object (AI–3).[48]

Malebranche's use of the argument from intentionality raises a number of questions. First, does it commit him to the counterintuitive (and, on the face of it, patently false) claim that whatever we perceive actually exists? His version of the intentionality thesis apparently implies this. Malebranche puts this objection, first raised by Arnauld, into the mouth of Aristes in the *Dialogues*. Malebranche's response is, in one sense of the claim, yes, but in another sense of the claim, no. It certainly does *not* commit him to the claim that whenever we have a perception of a material body, that material body really exists. In fact, his argument clearly relies on denying just this sort of claim. And I take it that the force of the question (and the counterintuitiveness of the claim) depends on interpreting it in this way. Malebranche, on the other hand, willingly admits that he *is* committed to the claim that whenever we have a perceptual experience or whenever we think of something,

---

48. The argument from intentionality and the *voir rien* . . . principle are only casually mentioned in the *Search* (e.g., IV.11: OC 2:99; LO 320), and then not until the fifth (1700) edition. See Robinet, *Système et existence dans l'oeuvre de Malebranche*, pp. 217–18, where he argues that the *voir rien* principle plays no role in the *Search*. Malebranche apparently uses the intentionality thesis to argue for ideas as the direct and immediate objects of the mind for the first time in his polemic with Arnauld. It also appears in the *Dialogues* (I.4).

there is at least *some* (immaterial) external entity really present that we apprehend: an idea.[49]

This brings out once again the fundamental equivocation in Malebranche's use of the word 'perceive'. When we *perceive* material bodies that do not exist, we still *perceive* ideas. But surely to say that we perceive an idea is to have in mind a different sense of 'perceive' and 'perception' than when we ordinarily speak of perceiving bodies. Clearly, a distinction needs to be made between the two senses of 'perceive' at work here. Malebranche does make such a distinction, which I will examine in chapter 5 when discussing the role of ideas in perception.[50]

An equally pressing question is suggested by an objection Arnauld makes in regard to the argument from (local) presence. Arnauld accuses Malebranche of taking a principle that apparently has some prima facie credibility with respect to visual sight (viz., an object must be present to the eyes to be seen) and illegitimately applying it to the way the mind perceives (something must be present to the mind to be perceived or known). In other words, according to Arnauld, Malebranche takes a premise about optical vision (which is one sense of 'perceiving') and uses it to draw a conclusion about thought ('perceiving' with the mind), thus committing the fallacy of equivocation. Now is not Malebranche, with his peculiar interpretation of the intentionality thesis, performing a similar (and, to Arnauld, similarly fallacious) move here? That is, while we might be willing to grant that, if there is nothing there in front of us to see, then we cannot see anything and thus are not in fact *seeing* at all ("voir rien, c'est ne point voir"), and that vision can

49. See *Dialogues* I.4: OC 12:36; D 29.
50. Lennon insists that, because of this equivocation regarding 'perceive' (or 'awareness'), Malebranche is not entitled to use ideas to account for the intentionality of perception, as he does in the argument. Lennon argues that when the question of intentionality is raised, it is naturally a question about how what is "ordinarily" called perception is object-directed. Hence the principle of intentionality cannot be satisfied by any kind of nonordinary, philosophically special direct awareness of ideas. "The principle of intentionality is not satisfied by construing an idea as the object of nonveridical awareness; for what we are ordinarily said to be aware of in such cases is what would be represented by that idea if the awareness were veridical, i.e., if there were (ordinary sense of 'to be') something for it to represent." See "Philosophical Commentary," LO 796.

apprehend only objects that are really present, it does not follow that we can *think* only of things that are really present before us. Perhaps 'seeing' is a success verb, and its proper use in a true proposition implies the existence of something seen. But this does not seem to be true of 'thinking'. Is Malebranche guilty of a conflation here?

To be sure, Malebranche occasionally uses the following two principles interchangeably: "to see nothing is not to see [*ne rien voir, c'est ne point voir*]" and "to think of nothing is not to think [*penser à rien, c'est ne point penser*]." In fact, he sometimes seems to switch carelessly from one principle to the other, even within the same sentence.[51] But more often than not he is quite conscious of the fact that there is indeed a difference between seeing (sensing) and thinking (conceiving), and is careful to distinguish the claim that nothingness is not *visible* from the claim that nothingness is not *intelligible*.[52] In fact, both these claims are entailed by a more general and fundamental principle—one, moreover, that lies at the heart of the different versions of the argument from intentionality: nothingness is not *perceivable*. To *perceive* nothing is not to *perceive* at all ("appercevoir le néant, c'est ne rien appercevoir").[53] For Malebranche, acts of seeing and acts of thinking are species of *perception*.[54] Thus what is true about and essential to perception in general will also be true of seeing and thinking. And the relevant point about perception in general is that *les perceptions* are intentional phenomena. Thus thinking or conceiving necessarily has its direct and immediate object (one perceives a pure idea), as does seeing or sense perception. With this broad notion of 'perception', then, Malebranche is not guilty of a conflation of seeing and thinking and of using seeing as a model for thinking. Rather, he is simply moving from the essentially intentional character of percep-

51. See, for example, RLA, OC 9:910.
52. See *Search* IV.11: OC 2:99; LO 320.
53. See RLA, OC 9:915–16.
54. See *Search* I.1.i: OC 1:42; LO 2; and I.2.i: OC 1:49–50; LO 7. This seems to be a standard seventeenth-century way of cataloguing the mind's functions. See Descartes, *Les Passions de l'âme*, I.19: "Our perceptions are also of two kinds: some have the soul as their cause, others the body. Those having the body as their cause are the perceptions of our volitions and of all the imaginings or other thoughts which depend on them" (AT 11:343). See also Arnauld, VFI 198.

tion in general to the essentially intentional character of these two kinds of perception. From the latter, given his understanding of the intentionality thesis, he can argue to the real presence of ideas, the immediately intended objects of these acts. There are interesting precedents before Malebranche for this kind of argument, whereby one moves from the intentionality of thinking and perception to the "existence" of certain nonmaterial intended objects. While it may seem paradoxical to draw parallels between the views of an archnominalist like William Ockham and Malebranche's theory of ideas—which is equally a theory of universals, and a realist one at that—nonetheless the Franciscan's early views on universals contain an argument quite similar to that used by the Oratorian.

Ockham insists that there is a mode of existence distinct from real or actual existence, a mode he calls "objective existence [*esse obiectivum*]." This is the kind of existence possessed by universals, abstract objects (such as propositions, relations, and mathematical entities), possible but uncreated beings, and beings that combine existentially incompatible properties (e.g., chimeras, goatstags). All these things have objective being, or a *cognitive* being, in some mind, but do not have actual existence (or what Ockham calls *esse subiectivum*).[55] Ockham's argument for positing this ideal mode of existence, like Malebranche's argument from intentionality for ideas, is grounded on the following two premises: (1) Whenever we think, we always think *of* something; to think of nothing is not to think at all; and (2) We often do think of things that do not really exist, that do not have *esse subiectivum* (e.g., universals, goatstags). And like Malebranche, Ockham takes (1), the intentionality thesis, to mean that whenever we think of something, there must be an object of thought that has *some* ontological status; it must exist in some mode or another distinct from the act of the mind which apprehends it: "Just as it is impossible that there should be vision and nothing seen, or that there should be desire and nothing desired, so it is also impossible that there should be a cognition and nothing cognized by that cognition. If something is known by that cognition, it is either something in the soul or something outside the

---

55. *Commentary on the Sentences* (referred to hereafter as *Ordinatio*), Book I, D. 2, Q. viii, in *Opera Theologica*, vol. 2, pp. 271–74.

soul."[56] When we think of things that really exist, the object of the cognition has *esse subiectivum*. When we think of things that do not really exist, however, the object of the mental act must still have some nonordinary kind of existence, some mode of being distinct from *esse subiectivum*. Otherwise we would be thinking of nothing, which is impossible. Thus such things have a being in the mind; not an *esse subiectivum* in the mind, however (such as its acts or operations, real properties of the mind, have), but an *esse obiectivum*—a being as the object of thought.[57]

THE ARGUMENT FROM PROPERTIES

Malebranche's argument from intentionality is, to all appearances, similar to the argument from illusion commonly offered in defense of sense data theories. In the case of completely hallucinatory perceptions, where nothing at all exists in the material world to correspond to the illusory perceptual experience, there still must be some (nonmaterial) entity apprehended by the mind to explain why one sees this object (a pink elephant, an oasis in a desert mirage) rather than some other. This immediately apprehended entity is called a sensum, or sense datum, and performs an explanatory role similar to (but not identical with) that played by Malebranche's ideas. (Malebranchian ideas, as nonsensible concepts, are different from sense data both in nature and in the way they are apprehended by the mind.)

The argument from illusion for sense data is also made from less extreme perceptual situations than those Malebranche appeals to,

56. *Commentary to Perihermenias*, chapter 1; the text can be found in Böhner, "The Realistic Conceptualism of William Ockham," p. 323: "Sicut impossibile est esse visionem et nihil videri, vel esse dilectionem et nihil diligi, ita impossibile est esse cognitionem et nihil cognosci illa cognitione. Si aliquid cognoscitur ista cognitione, aut aliquid in anima aut aliquid extra animam." Ockham is here presenting an argument for the objective existence theory, although he himself has apparently moved toward his later view; see n. 57 below.

57. *Ordinatio* I.2.viii, *Opera Theologica*, vol. 2, pp. 268, 271–73. In his later works Ockham abandons the objective existence theory, apparently as a result of criticisms made by Walter Chatton, a fellow Franciscan. See Adams, "Ockham's Nominalism and Unreal Entities" and "Universals in the Early Fourteenth Century"; and Böhner, "The Realistic Conceptualism of William Ockham," pp. 315–19.

An argument of this sort is also commonly attributed to Meinong in his discussion of ideal or subsisting entities as the intended objects of certain acts of consciousness; see Findlay, *Meinong's Theory of Objects and Values*, pp. 17–22, 35.

such as ordinary cases of qualitative (instead of existential) illusion. For example, a penny appears elliptical when viewed at an oblique angle, although the penny itself is round, not elliptical. The argument is that there must be some object, distinct from the penny, which really *is* elliptical, which we apprehend, and whose apprehension explains why our perceptual experience is of an elliptical rather than a round object. More generally, whenever I have a perceptual experience of a material object x that is present before me as having a certain sensible quality q, and it is certain that x does not itself really possess q but rather some other, incompatible quality p, then there must nevertheless be some nonphysical y, not identical to x, which I apprehend and which really does have q, and which explains why an x-like object having q now appears to me.[58] As C. D. Broad puts it, "it is very hard to understand how we could seem to ourselves to *see* the property [q] exhibited in a concrete instance if, in fact, *nothing* was present to our minds that possessed that property."[59] Broad calls this y a "sensum" and generalizes the argument to cover the perception of *all* qualities, illusory and veridical.

This kind of argument for immediately apprehended nonmaterial entities, which Chisholm calls the "sense-datum inference,"[60] like the more extreme argument from hallucination, does not explicitly use the intentionality thesis. Rather, it uses a principle that is also at the heart of a further argument for ideas used by Malebranche—the principle, namely, that "nothingness has no properties." The argument for sense data presented clearly relies on an instance of this principle: there cannot be ellipticality without there also being some real entity that has this property.

In the first of the *Dialogues*, Malebranche has Theodore reason in the following way: "Now the circle I perceive has properties

---

58. The more extreme version of the argument can be similarly generalized as follows: Whenever I have a perceptual experience of a material object x as having a certain sensible quality q, and x does not exist, there must nonetheless be some nonmaterial object y that really does have q and explains why an x-like object having q now appears to me.

59. "The Theory of Sensa," p. 91.

60. According to Chisholm, the inference moves (fallaciously) from a statement about appearing ("There exists something which appears diamond-shaped") to a statement about the existence of something which *is* diamond-shaped; see "The Theory of Appearing," p. 173.

which no other shape has. Hence the circle exists at the time I think of it, since nothing has no properties [*le néant n'a point de pro-priétez*] and one nothing cannot differ from some other nothing" (I.4: OC 12:35; D 29). If one expands this brief statement into a full argument for ideas, such as Malebranche apparently intends it to be, one might come up with the following line of reasoning:

(1) When I think of a geometric circle, my mind directly and immediately apprehends a number of properties, properties that are clearly and distinctly apprehended as being uniquely and indubitably possessed by this particular kind of figure.

(2) These properties do not belong to any material body, such that by perceiving that body I perceive precisely these mathematical properties, for there is no material body corresponding to the geometric circle.

(3) These properties, however, must belong to *some* object, to some entity present to the mind. If they belonged to nothing, there would be no such properties perceived ("le néant n'a point de propriétez").

(4) Thus they belong to some intelligible circle that really exists, and which I directly and immediately perceive.

In other words, if there are properties present before the mind and perceived by it, but no corresponding material object, there must nevertheless be something real making those properties so present. In this case the "something" is the idea of a circle. The argument could then be extended to cover cases of qualitative illusion—where there is a material body present, but one which clearly does not have the perceived property—and then generalized to the perception of all properties or qualities of objects whatsoever, material and abstract. In this way Malebranche could be viewed as employing the so-called "sense-datum inference" to prove that ideas are the immediate objects of perception.

But as tempting as this reading of Malebranche's reasoning is, it is evident from the texts that he does not really use the argument from properties in this way. Whenever he employs the principle "nothingness has no properties," he does so *not* in the context of proving that we directly perceive ideas instead of material objects, but rather in the context of demonstrating that ideas, whose existence is already granted, are what he calls "real beings." That is, Malebranche wants to guard against the common error of supposing that ideas are "nothing real."

> Given that men are naturally led, as it were, to believe that only corporeal objects exist, they judge the reality and existence of things other than as they should. For as soon as they perceive an object, they would have it as quite certain that it exists, although it often happens that there is nothing external. In addition, they would have the object be exactly as they see it, which never happens. But as for the idea that necessarily exists, and that cannot be other than as it is seen, they ordinarily judge unreflectingly that it is nothing.[61]

Malebranche then goes on to show, with the argument from properties, why such a judgment must be wrong.

> As if ideas did not have a great number of properties, as if the idea of a square, for example, were not different from that of a circle or a number, and did not represent completely different things, which can never be the case for nothingness, since nothingness has no properties. It is therefore indubitable that ideas have a very real existence [*une existence très-réelle*]. (*Search* III.2.i: OC 1:414–15; LO 217–18)

Note that Malebranche here assumes that there *are* such things as ideas, as "everyone would grant." What is at issue, however, is their degree of reality. Are ideas "mere and insignificant beings [*des êtres minces et bien méprisables*]," with an inferior degree of reality? This is the view ordinarily held by more orthodox Cartesians such as Arnauld and Régis, for whom an idea, qua perception or mental act, is a *pur accident*, a mere modification of the mind.[62] Or are ideas "real beings"? Malebranche's argument would have us believe that ideas must be real beings, since they clearly present properties

---

61. See also *Dialogues* I.5: "As men take their ideas of things to be nothing, they give far more reality to the created world than it has. They are not in doubt about the existence of objects, and they attribute to them many qualities which they do not have. Yet they do not even think about the reality of their ideas" (OC 12:36; D 29).
62. See also Descartes, for whom an idea is simply a modification of a thinking substance, hence lower down on the ontological scale than the substance itself; *Meditations* III: AT 7:40; CSM 2:28. Moreover, Descartes insists that the mode of existence possessed by ideas is, compared to real existence, "much less perfect [*imperfectior*]," although it is not quite nothing; see "Replies to First Objections," AT 7:183; CSM 2:75.

to the mind, properties that allow us to distinguish one idea from another. And properties can belong only to something real ("le néant n'a point de propriétez; le néant n'a aucune propriété").[63]

It is not quite clear, however, precisely what Malebranche is arguing for here. More particularly, it is not clear in what sense the term 'real being' is to be understood when it is used to characterize an idea. Malebranche must be careful lest his argument prove too much. Descartes, for example, uses the principle "nothingness possesses no attributes or qualities [*nihili nulles esse affectiones sive qualitates*]" to prove that whenever we find some attributes or qualities, there is also necessarily some substance (*substantia*) in which they inhere.[64] Surely Malebranche does not want to argue that ideas are substances, and he says as much.[65] He admits that, compared to substances, ideas are "bien petits & bien méprisables" (*Search* III.2.iii: OC 1:423; LO 223). But, he insists in the same paragraph, "they are still beings . . . [an idea] is still a spiritual thing [*être*]." But in what sense of 'thing'? It is not a spiritual "thing" in the same sense in which a mind is a spiritual thing; an idea is not a spiritual substance.

Once again, as with the argument from distance, it seems we are brought back to a fundamental problem in Malebranche's theory of ideas. What *is* the ontological status or nature of ideas? They are neither substances nor modifications of any substance. Yet in the Cartesian schema these are the only alternatives: something is either a substance or a modification of a substance. And Malebranche, however modified his Cartesianism, is at least explicit in accepting this ontological dualism.[66] Where, then, do ideas fit in? In what sense are they "real" or "beings"?[67] As far as I can tell, Malebranche

---

63. See also *Search* III.2.iii: "Since ideas have real properties, no one can doubt that they are real beings [*des êtres-réelles*]" (OC 1:423; LO 222). As Robinet notes, the point of this argument is to show that ideas, whose existence is already certain on other grounds, are *quelque chose*, have an existence that is *très réelle*; see *Système et existence dans l'oeuvre de Malebranche*, p. 218.
64. *Principles of Philosophy* I.11: AT 8-1:8; CSM 1:196.
65. See *Search* III.2.iii: "If it be said that an idea is not a substance, I would agree" (OC 1:424; LO 223).
66. See *Search* III.2.viii: OC 1:461; LO 244; and VI.2.ix: OC 2:425; LO 573. See Descartes, *Principles of Philosophy* I.51. For a discussion of the substance/modification duality in Malebranche's Cartesianism, see Radner, *Malebranche*, pp. 1–5.
67. Foucher is similarly puzzled about the ontological status of Malebranche's ideas; see RCP, pp. 103–8.

does not provide an answer to this question—and in the context of his Cartesianism, I do not see how he can.

The various arguments examined in this chapter are all employed by Malebranche to demonstrate that representative ideas—the entities examined in chapter 2—are required for perceiving material bodies—indeed, that they are needed for perceiving and thinking generally: whenever we think or perceive, an idea is present and is what is directly and immediately apprehended by the mind. Ideas are meant to account for the intentionality of mental acts (perceptions) and, by the same stroke, to provide a solution to the philosophical problems of illusion and hallucination. Moreover, they explain how it is that we actually do perceive material bodies, given what, at least to Malebranche, appear prima facie to be serious obstacles to such perceptual acquaintance (no perception at a distance, etc.). Ideas, then, serve as representative proxies, standing in the mind for the material bodies that it cannot perceive *en euxmêmes*. They are the mind's direct and immediate objects in knowledge and perception. It still remains to be seen, however, precisely what cognitive role ideas play in knowledge and perception; how "perceiving" an idea forms an integral part of the perception of a material body; and what Malebranche's claim about ideas being the direct and immediate objects of the mind amounts to. I will address these issues in chapter 5, after examining in the next chapter Malebranche's arguments for the vision in God, whereby he purports to show that the ideas needed in cognition and perception are in the divine understanding.

4

The Vision in God

Up to this point I have been considering Malebranche's theory of ideas mainly in its Cartesian context. Ideas are immaterial representative beings (êtres représentatifs) that both provide for clear and distinct knowledge of essences and truths, and in some way mediate our perceptual acquaintance with and knowledge of material bodies. These general Cartesian elements are accompanied by a number of significant departures from Descartes's theory of ideas, most notably in Malebranche's contention that ideas are ontologically distinct from the human mind. This gives rise to two questions: If ideas are not modifications of a finite thinking substance, then "where" are they? And how is it that they then come to be present to the mind?

Malebranche tells us that it was his recollection of what St. Augustine had to say on these matters which "allowed me to escape happily from the difficulty in which I found myself" (TL I, OC 6:199). Ideas, he claims, are in God or, more particularly, in the divine understanding. In knowledge or pure intellection, as well as in perception, the human mind apprehends an idea. And it can do so only because God wills that this idea, which like all ideas exists eternally in God's intellect, be revealed to that finite mind. Thus our ideas (the ideas we apprehend in cognition and perception) are God's ideas. And Malebranche means this in the strictest possible sense. He is not saying merely that the ideas we apprehend are caused in us by God and are qualitatively similar to but distinct from God's own ideas, as Berkeley is often taken to be claiming.[1]

---

1. Berkeley, on what is probably the more widely accepted reading of his theory, claims that the ideas in my mind are numerically distinct both from the ideas in another finite spirit and from the ideas in God. See for example *Three Dialogues*,

Rather, Malebranche means that the ideas we perceive are numerically identical with God's ideas. This is true not just of our ideas of abstract and mathematical entities and eternal essences, but also of our ideas of material bodies. In fact, if it is true of the former, it is necessarily true of the latter, since those abstract mathematical ideas just *are* our ideas of bodies: the idea of a body is nothing other than the idea of a finite extension, a purely geometric quantity. Malebranche suggests that with respect to the role of ideas in our knowledge and perception of material bodies, his doctrine of the vision in God is really more a development or logical extension of Augustine's doctrine than a mere uncritical adoption of it. And it is a development made possible, he insists, only by Descartes's "discovery" that sensations are not real properties of bodies but merely mental modes.

Malebranche's vision in God, then, is a synthesis of Cartesianism and Augustinianism on the matter of ideas.[2] And this is true in two respects. First, Malebranche's doctrine combines the (Cartesian) clear and distinct representative character of ideas (at least those with a geometric content) with their (Augustinian) ontological dependence on God. Second, the vision in God is a response to two distinct problems, one of which Malebranche inherits from Descartes, the other from Augustine. The Cartesian problem concerns

---

Third Dialogue, where Hylas claims that the "same idea which is in my mind cannot be in yours" (*Works*, vol. 2, p. 247), and where Philonous grants that there are two kinds of ideas, or a "twofold state of things—the one ectypal or natural, the other archtypal and eternal. The former was created in time; the latter existed from everlasting in the mind of God" (p. 254). At one point, Berkeley says, in a reference to Malebranche, "I do not understand how our ideas, which are things altogether passive and inert, can be the essence, or any part (or like any part) of the essence or substance of God, who is an impassive, indivisible, purely active being" (Second Dialogue, pp. 213–14). For comparisons of Berkeley and Malebranche on ideas, see Luce, *Berkeley and Malebranche*; McCracken, *Malebranche and British Philosophy*, chapter 6; and Bracken, "Berkeley and Malebranche on Ideas."

2. This is certainly how Malebranche himself sees it; see TL I, OC 6:201. See also Alquié, *Le Cartésianisme de Malebranche*, pp. 185–90. But Connell argues that "the traditional interpretation, which sees in the vision in God a synthesis of Cartesian and Augustinian thought, can no longer be accepted as adequate" (*The Vision in God*, p. 357), and offers alternative Scholastic sources for Malebranche's doctrine.

how an immaterial thinking substance can know and perceive external material bodies. Representative ideas are generally required if we are to have any kind of cognitive access to the material world, and Malebranche believes that their value as representations can be guaranteed, and thus this epistemological problem can be resolved, only if the ideas that mediate between us and the world are God's ideas. The Augustinian problem concerns our knowledge of eternal essences and truths. The vision in God explains how such knowledge is possible. In fact, for Malebranche, it is the only possible explanation of how particular, finite, and mutable spirits can know immutable, universal Truth.[3]

In this chapter I examine the various arguments, both positive and negative, that Malebranche offers for the claim that the ideas we apprehend in knowledge and perception are in God. I am primarily concerned with the philosophical motivations that lie behind Malebranche's doctrine. Except for a brief discussion of Malebranche and Augustine, I do not go into questions of influence and tradition, nor do I consider the development of and changes in the doctrine between the first edition of the *Search* and later writings.[4] Moreover, I do not examine in an exhaustive fashion all of Malebranche's arguments and reasons for the vision in God. Rather, I focus generally only on what I take to be Malebranche's main arguments, as well as those secondary ones which are of a particularly philosophical interest.[5]

3. Commentators generally recognize that the Cartesian problem informs the discussion of the vision in God in the *Search* proper, while the Augustinian problem does not really appear until the Elucidations; see Connell, *The Vision in God*, especially chapter 7; and Robinet, *Système et existence dans l'oeuvre de Malebranche*, Book II, section 1.

4. The question of influence and tradition has been well examined in the literature. See, for example, Connell, *The Vision in God*; and Gaonach, *La Théorie des idées dans la philosophie de Malebranche*. For the question of development, see Connell; Robinet, *Système et existence dans l'oeuvre de Malebranche*; and Gueroult, *Malebranche*, vol. 1.

5. For exhaustive (but not necessarily detailed and analytical) presentations of the arguments, see Gueroult, *Malebranche*, vol. 1, pp. 101–18; McCracken, *Malebranche and British Philosophy*, pp. 61–70; and Radner, *Malebranche*, pp. 20–22, 47–59.

Malebranche and Augustine

Malebranche frequently acknowledges St. Augustine as his authority on the question of ideas. As he says in his response to Arnauld's initial attack on his theory, "I avow that it is principally [St. Augustine's] authority which has given me the desire to put forth the new philosophy of ideas" (*Réponse*, OC 6:80).[6] To bolster his case for his theory of ideas, particularly in the face of criticism from Arnauld (who in fact insists that Malebranche gets Augustine wrong) and others, Malebranche frequently cites from Augustine passages such as the following:

> Ideas are Original Forms or fixed and changeless [*stabiles atque incommutabiles*] patterns of things which have not been fashioned from the Forms themselves and consequently, being eternal and always the same, are contained in the Divine Mind [*continentur in divina intelligentia*]. And while these themselves neither come to be nor cease to exist, it is maintained that, in accordance with them, everything capable of having a beginning and an end is fashioned, as well as whatever actually comes into, or goes out of, existence. They insist that a soul cannot contemplate these Forms unless it is rational and then, only by that part of it which accounts for its excellence, namely, by the mind itself and reason. . . . Once this is established and granted, who can dare to declare that God has made everything in an irrational manner. If one cannot say or believe such a thing, then it follows that all things have been fashioned according to an intelligible principle. . . . But where are we to suppose these intelligible principles to exist, if not in the very mind of the creator? He was not fixing His gaze upon anything located outside Himself to serve as

6. "Car j'avouë que c'est principalement son autorité, qui m'a donné l'envie de pousser la nouvelle Philosophie des idées." The best and most thorough examination of the Augustinianism of Malebranche's vision in God is in Gouhier, *La Philosophie de Malebranche*, pp. 279–311. Connell has argued, however, that in fact "the teaching of St. Augustine had little if any influence upon Malebranche's original conception of the vision in God" (*The Vision in God*, p. 236). Malebranche, he insists, conceived the vision in God independently of Augustine, although he found in the latter's writings "authoritative confirmation that supplied the courage he required in order to proceed with his view" (ibid.). Connell suggests that Scholastic sources probably played a more influential role in the genesis of the doctrine than did Augustine. Gaonach presents an interesting discussion of what he sees as possible origins of Malebranche's doctrine in Plotinus and St. Thomas; see *La Théorie des idées dans la philosophie de Malebranche*, pp. 113–24.

a model when He made the things he created. . . . But if the intelligible principles of things created, and of those to be created, are contained in the divine mind and if only the eternal and changeless can exist there . . . then not only are these realities Ideas but they are themselves true. . . . Among the things made by God, the rational soul stands superior to all and, as long as it is undefiled, is close to God. To the degree that it is united to Him by charity, by so much does it contemplate these intelligible principles through the vision of which it is made supremely happy, being bathed and illuminated by Him with a spiritual light.[7]

Malebranche finds in Augustine, in passages like this, a number of theses regarding ideas and human knowledge—theses which, he claims, lend authoritative support to his own doctrine.[8]

First, ideas are eternal and immutable objects of knowledge, ontologically distinct from (yet present to) the knowing mind. The claim that ideas are eternal, immutable, independently existing entities (in Augustine's words, *sunt ideae aeternae & semper eodem modo sese habentes*) is, as Malebranche sees it, the philosophically orthodox way, since Plato, of characterizing them. Augustine, then, is here simply following philosophical tradition in his use of the

---

7. *De diversis questionibus*, LXXXIII, qu. 46; translation by R. P. Russell, in *Introduction to the Philosophy of Saint Augustine: Selected Readings and Commentaries*, pp. 203–5. This passage is cited and glossed by Malebranche in *Dialogues*, Preface, OC 12:10–11, and he translates it into French in RLA, OC 9:914–15. For a complete collation of all the passages from Augustine cited or quoted by Malebranche, see Gouhier, *La Philosophie de Malebranche*, Appendix, pp. 411–20.

8. The question of the correctness of Malebranche's interpretation of Augustine is a rather difficult and contentious one. Gilson insists that Malebranche's reading seriously distorts Augustine's thought; see *The Christian Philosophy of St. Augustine*, pp. 94–96. For a contrary view, see Hessen, *Augustins Metaphysik der Erkenntnis*, pp. 210ff., and "Malebranches Verhältnis zu Augustin." Gouhier shows that Malebranche's primary source for Augustine's texts is Ambrosius Victor's *Philosophia Christiana* (1667), and he claims that Malebranche took his Augustine straight from Victor, only occasionally going to the full original texts themselves. This suggests that Malebranche's interpretation of Augustine is greatly influenced by that of Victor. As Gouhier notes, "L'augustinisme que Malebranche a connu, c'est celui de la *Philosophia Christiana*"; see *La Philosophie de Malebranche*, pp. 279–84. My presentation is intended only to point out some important elements Malebranche finds in Augustine, and not to pass judgment on the accuracy of Malebranche's reading.

term *Idea.* Now when ideas, so understood, are taken in conjunction with an assumption about knowledge that Malebranche also finds in (and shares with) both Plato and Augustine, it follows that ideas are the proper objects of human knowledge. That assumption is that knowledge, properly speaking, can only be of eternal, immutable things, and not of particular entities subject to change and becoming. Knowledge is of Truth, and Truth is by its nature "immuable et éternelle."

> It would not be difficult to prove, as St. Augustine has done, that there would not be any certain sciences, any demonstrated truths, any clear difference between the just and unjust, in a word, any necessary truths or laws known by all minds, if that which is contemplated by all intelligences . . . was not, by its nature, absolutely immutable, eternal, and necessary. (TL I, OC 6:199)

The reality of human knowledge (*scientia*, la science) is preserved only if the objects of the finite knowing mind are eternal, immutable essences (*Ideae, Formae*, Idées) that are independent of the mutable acts or perceptions of that mind ("modifications changeantes & particulières de l'esprit humain").[9]

Second, ideas are the archetypes or exemplars for God in creation, and thus exist in the divine intellect. (In Malebranche's own words, in his gloss on the preceding passage from Augustine, "idées sont les exemplaires, ou les archetypes des creatures" [*Dialogues*, Preface OC 12:11].) This explains the rationality of God's creative activity and, in Malebranche's eyes, is just the proper Christian modification of Plato's theory.[10] If God creates the world, and does so in accordance with certain rational and intelligible principles (*rationes*), as he must, and if an omnipotent God cannot be guided (or constrained) by anything outside his own being, then the principles (ideas or forms) that guide God must be found *in ipsa mente Creatoris*, to use Augustine's phrase. Again, here is Malebranche's commentary on the above passage: "It is an impiety to suppose that in creating the world, [God] looked outside himself [*hors de lui-*

---

9. See also *Réponse à la 1ère lettre de M. Arnauld*, OC 9:1000: "Ce Saint Docteur ait distingué souvent les *idées* de la souveraine Raison qui nous éclaire, d'avec nos ténébreuses modalitez."
10. See *Dialogues*, Preface, OC 12:12.

même] to a model on which he formed it" (*Dialogues*, Preface, OC 12:12). Moreover, if ideas are truly eternal and immutable, they can exist only in an eternal and immutable being. These kinds of considerations play a role in Malebranche's arguments for the vision in God.

Third, Malebranche sees in Augustine a theory of divine illumination that forms the core of his account of human knowledge. "St. Augustine believed that the eternal wisdom is the light of all intelligences [*La Sagesse éternelle est la lumière des intelligences*], and that it is only by the manifestation of his substance . . . that God illuminates us internally" (*Dialogues*, Preface, OC 12:18).[11] Finite spirits have knowledge of mathematical essences and truths, speculative and moral principles, and eternal laws only because they see them in God. And we can see them in God only because "God presides over all finite spirits, and immediately enlightens them."[12] There is one common universal Reason in which we perceive and know all truths.

Malebranche's reading of Augustine on ideas is, among other places, summed up in a letter for Arnauld.

> It must be that, as St. Augustine has said in five hundred places, ideas are eternal, immutable, necessary, and common to all minds, in order for there to be certain truth and falsehood, justice and injustice, eternal truths and laws; and that our minds are enlightened [*éclairez*] by these same ideas in consequence of their union with the universal Reason which contains them all in its substance, which alone is the life and light of all intelligences. . . . All speculative and practical sciences are founded only upon the immutability of the eternal ideas which generally enlighten all minds in consequence of their attention. (RLA, OC 9:933).

Malebranche admits that his doctrine of the vision in God departs from the theory of ideas and divine illumination that he finds in Augustine. "These are the arguments of St. Augustine—ours are somewhat different, and we have no wish to make improper use of the authority of so great a man in order to support our view"

---

11. See also *Réponse*, OC 6:64: "It seems to me that I ought to say to Monsieur Arnauld these words of S. Augustine . . . *Dic quia tu tibi lumen non es*"; and *Search* III.2.vi.
12. Malebranche is here quoting from Augustine; see TL I, OC 6:199.

(*Search* III.2.vi: OC 1:444; LO 234). Malebranche sees two obvious differences between his own views and those of Augustine. First, Malebranche's claim is that the primary objects of the mind are *ideas* in God, while Augustine's explicit claim is that we see *truths* in God. But, Malebranche insists, truths are nothing but relations among ideas, and as such are nothing real. Ideas *are* real, and thus we see truths only because we first grasp the ideas themselves, and then relations between them. Therefore this difference, he believes, is really a nominal one, and Augustine's considered position is most likely the same as (or reducible to) his own.

> Thus, we do not claim, as does Saint Augustine, that we see God in seeing truths, but in seeing the *ideas* of these truths—for the ideas are real, whereas the equality between the ideas, which is the truth, is nothing real [*n'est rien de réel*]. . . . Thus, our view is that we see God when we see eternal truths, not because these truths are God, but because the ideas on which these truths depend are in God—it might even be said that this ws St. Augustine's meaning. (*Search* III.2.vi: OC 1:444; LO 234; translation modified)

Second and more significant, Malebranche is aware that Augustine never claimed, as he himself does, that "changeable and corruptible things are known in God," that is, that we see in God not just eternal and immutable truths, but also corporeal bodies. Augustine's explicit view, as Malebranche reads him, is that we see in God only eternal laws and truths, mainly mathematical objects and principles and moral rules. "He never asserted that we see in God corruptible things or things subject to change, such as all the bodies which surround us . . . sensible objects which have come into being and may cease to exist, and which by their nature are subject to change" (TL I, OC 6:199). Malebranche's view, on the other hand, is that we *do*, in fact, perceive and know bodies in God. But this does not mean that the immediate objects of knowledge in God are themselves changeable, corruptible things. What we see in God are the *ideas* of bodies, "their essences, which are immutable, necessary, and eternal." Thus to Augustine's doctrine of illumination, which is basically a theory concerning our knowledge of eternal truths alone, Malebranche's vision in God adds a second dimension: it is also a theory concerning our knowledge of the nature (but not the existence) of corporeal bodies, of the material world surrounding us. What makes this knowledge possible is the Augustinian thesis that the ideas in God are the archetypes which God employed in creating the world.

Malebranche argues that Augustine did not develop his theory of illumination so far as to include the knowledge and perception of bodies for two reasons. First, he believed that we see bodies by themselves (en eux-mêmes) and not by means of ideas. Second, he was not yet aware of the fact, demonstrated by Descartes, that color, heat, pain, and other sensory qualities are not really in material objects but are mental events occasioned by those objects. Now if color, for example, really were, like size and shape, a property of the material object itself, "une qualité répandue sur la surface des corps"—and the color of a body is not something "immutable, intelligible, and common to all minds"—then to say that we see bodies in themselves in God would mean that something changeable and relative (a colored body itself) is in God. And Augustine would clearly (and, in Malebranche's eyes, rightly) reject such a conclusion.[13] "Surely, if we see bodies in themselves, it is not in God that we see them" (*Dialogues*, Preface, OC 12:20).

Malebranche believes he was able to expand the scope of the vision in God to include bodies by the grace of *deux vérités*, one of which he learned from Descartes, the other consisting in his own doctrine of ideas. From Descartes he has learned that bodies are not really colored, that "colors are not spread upon the surface of objects, and are only modifications or perceptions of the soul." And his own investigation into knowledge and perception has convinced him that we do not perceive bodies in themselves; rather, we immediately apprehend *ideas* of bodies.[14] Thus we can safely say that we know bodies through the vision in God without implying that changeable, corruptible entities are in God: we apprehend the *ideas* of bodies in God, and these ideas, as representative of bodies, do not include those changeable sensible features occasioned by bodies in the mind. In fact, Malebranche insists that once these two principles are granted, his own doctrine is simply a logical exten-

13. See *Réponse*, OC 6:68; *Dialogues*, Preface, OC 12:20; TL I, OC 6:200–201.
14. *Dialogues*, Preface, OC 12:18–20.

sion of Augustine's, a drawing out of what is implicit in Augustine's own remarks on our knowledge of eternal truths.[15] If bodies are not colored, warm, sweet, and so forth, then the idea of body is simply the idea of extension, and the idea of a particular body is simply the idea of a particular, finite extension. Augustine clearly asserts that we perceive intelligible extension—"the object of the science of the Geometers"—in God. He also asserts that we thereby see particular geometrical figures in God. But after the Cartesian reduction of body, this is tantamount to saying that we perceive the ideas of bodies in God. "Thus, according to the doctrine of this holy Doctor, it is in God that we see bodies" (*Dialogues*, Preface, OC 12:19–20).[16] With respect to his relationship to Augustine on the nature of ideas, Malebranche ultimately concludes that "il n'y a nulle différence dans le fond entre son sentiment & le mien" (*Réponse*, OC 6:68).

One wonders whether Malebranche is attributing to Augustine epistemological motivations and concerns that in fact could belong only to a seventeenth-century Cartesian. Malebranche is suggesting that the reason Augustine did not include bodies in the vision in God is because he had not yet discovered either the primary/secondary quality distinction or the representative function of ideas. Malebranche is then apparently assuming that Augustine would indeed have liked to use his theory of illumination to explain how it is that we know and perceive bodies, but saw no way in which this could be done without profaning God. But it seems more likely that the problem for which Malebranche initially employs the vision in God (in the first edition of the *Search*)—namely, the problem of how we know and perceive material bodies—was not a problem at all for Augustine. Malebranche's reading of Augustine, then, is perhaps tailored for his own convenience, even at the risk of

---

15. See TL I, OC 6:201: "I believed that . . . without fundamentally distancing myself from the principles of S. Augustine, or rather, I believed, in following them, I could assert that one sees, or that one knows in God even material and corruptible objects." See also *Dialogues*, Preface, OC 12:18: "It is proper for me to prove here that, following the doctrine of [Augustine], it must necessarily be said that *we also see bodies in God*."

16. See also TL I, OC 6:201.

distorting the Bishop of Hippo's thought. Yet Augustine is obviously an important inspiration for and influence on Malebranche's theory of ideas. No matter what other thinkers or traditions may have played a role in the genesis of Malebranche's vision in God, and no matter how much Malebranche may have diluted Augustine with elements of Cartesianism, there is no question that Malebranche himself sees his own doctrine as fundamentally and essentially Augustinian.

The Argument from Elimination

Malebranche claims that his recollection of Augustine's theory of divine illumination rescued him from what initially appeared to be a dead end. The impasse he found himself in, he says, resulted from his having considered the various ways in which we might come to know and perceive bodies—a consideration which, he insists, was exhaustive and covered "toutes les manières dont nous pouvons voir les objets"—and from his finding "manifest contradictions" in all of them (TL I, OC 6:198–99). These contradictions are sufficient for rejecting each of the theories as a viable account of our perceptual and cognitive acquaintance with the world. Once they are eliminated, only one further theory—the vision in God—remains, a theory presumably free of the problems plaguing the others. This first argument for the doctrine, then, is a negative one, an argument by elimination whereby all competing alternatives are shown to be untenable.[17]

THE THEORY OF SPECIES

The first theory Malebranche considers, and rejects, involves material bodies emitting resembling species, which are transmitted into the mind. The emitted or impressed species are material analogues (this presumably allows them to *resemble* corporeal bodies). They travel through space to the sense organs, where they are "impressed" upon the external senses. The impressed species are then taken up and made intelligible (or "spiritualized") by the agent or

17. Malebranche clearly believes the enumeration of competing theories to be exhaustive; he calls it a "division exacte . . . de toutes les manières" (TL I, OC 6:198).

active intellect ("l'intellect agent ou agissant"). This intellectualiza- tion or dematerialization process results in expressed species that can be received by the passive intellect ("l'intellect patient").
Expressed species thus are the means by which the passive intellect knows and perceives the material object ("c'est par elles que l'intel- lect patient connoît toutes les choses matérielles") (*Search* III.2.ii: OC 1:418; LO 220).

Malebranche claims that this is the theory held by the Peripatet- ics.[18] In fact, it conflates at least two distinct and different accounts: the Peripatetic and the Epicurean. According to the traditional Peripatetic or Aristotelian–Scholastic theory, what happens in per- ception and knowledge is that the knowing mind takes on the form, but not the matter, of the object known. The material object (a substance composed of matter and form) operates upon the sense organ and causes upon it a sensible impression, which impression is called a *species* or *phantasma*. This impressed species is an image or likeness of the object, and is conveyed to the inner "common sense" by the external senses. It is then taken up by the active intellect (*intellectus agens*) which, by a process of abstraction, causes the sensible species to become "intelligible" and capable of being re- ceived by the passive or possible intellect (intellectus patiens). The species, thus intellectualized or spiritualized, constitutes the form of the sensible object, yet separated from that object's matter. When the form is abstracted from the sensible species and passed into the possible intellect, the mind thereby becomes informed by the form itself of the material object. This informing of the mind is the act of cognition, while the identity of form between mind and object makes the cognitive act to be *of* that particular object.[19]

Clearly, there are significant parallels between this neo-Aristote- lian account and the theory Malebranche is describing in *Search*

---

18. He does not explicitly call it a "Peripatetic" theory until the third (1677) edition.
19. This account is abstracted from St. Thomas, *Summa theologiae*, Ia, Question 84, articles 6–7 and Q. 85, art. 1, and is supplemented by several later Scholastic sources: Eustacius a Sancto Paulo, *Summa philosophica quadripartita*, Part III; the Conimbrian commentaries on Aristotle's *De anima* (*Commentarii in tres libros de Anima Aristotelis*, henceforth referred to as *Comm. de Anima*), Book III, chapter 6; and Franciscus Toletus, *Commentaria una cum questionibus in tres libros Aristotelis de Anima* (henceforth referred to as *Comm. cum quest.*), Book II, chapter 12, questions 33–34.

III.2.ii. St. Thomas, for example, insists that the *phantasmata* or impressed species are likenesses (*similitudines*) or images (*imagines*) of the sensible objects which cause them.[20] Later Scholastics also stressed the representative character of the species.[21] But it is essential to Malebranche's characterization of what he calls the "Peripatetic" theory—a characterization crucial to his critique of it—that the species emitted or "transmitted" (envoyés) by corporeal objects are themselves corporeal, being tiny material images or models. (Malebranche calls them *petits corps*, to contrast them with the thoroughly spiritualized expressed species.) But both Thomas and later Peripatetics explicitly deny that impressed species or *phantasmata* are material. Thomas, for example, rejects outright the view that material resemblances issue forth from objects. To be sure, the impressed species results from the material object "operating" upon the senses; but such an impression is not by way of a discharge of tiny corporeal images, a transmission of Democritean *eidola*.[22] The *form* of the object, but none of its matter, is received by the sense organ. The nonmaterial nature of the (impressed) species is even clearer in late-sixteenth- and early-seventeenth-century Scholastic sources. Toletus, for example, argues at length for the immateriality and nonspatiality of species. Species, or that by which (*qua media*) an object is perceived, have what he calls an "intentional existence [*esse intentionale*]"—both in the intervening medium and in the sense organ—but not a real or material exist-

20. See *Summa theologiae*, Q. 84, art. 7, resp. 2. The Conimbrian commentators call the impressed species a *similitudo objecti*; see *Comm. de Anima* II.6.ii.2. Toletus calls the species both a *rei simulachrum quoddam* and an *imago obiectum repraesentans*; see *Comm. cum quest.* II.12, qu. 33–34.
21. See Eustacius, *Summa philosophica quadripartita* III, pp. 332–33 (Gilson, *Index scolastico-cartésien*, p. 98).
22. Thomas is admittedly vague on the nature of the phantasms. He says that "the operations of the sensitive part are caused by the impression of the sensible on the sense; not indeed by a discharge, as Democritus said, but by some kind of operation [*sed per quamdam operationem*]" (*Summa theologiae*, Ia, Q. 84, a. 6). Yet he does not say explicitly what the nature of this operation is. Gilson believes that Thomas's impressed species are ontologically between the material and the immaterial: "Les phantasmata ne sont ni matériels ni intelligibles . . . le phantasma se trouve ainsi placé entre la matière et l'esprit" (*Etudes sur le rôle de la pensée médiévale dans la formation du système cartésien*, pp. 22–23).

ence.[23] They certainly do *not* occupy any space (whereas part of
Malebranche's *reductio* argument against the "Peripatetic" view
relies on the spatiality of the species).

Thus, according to the orthodox Peripatetic account, the form of
the individual material object is conveyed into the understanding
(or passive intellect) by means of the impressed species, which is
itself caused by the object working on the sense organ, but not by
the discharge of tiny material images. This is not to imply that
Malebranche's understanding of the Peripatetic view is without any
foundation whatsoever. Consider, for example, Eustacius's description of *species* as *ab objecto immissa et in sensu recepta*, and the
fact that they are *propogata* through a material medium and received by the corporeal sense organs.[24] This vague language would
ordinarily lead one to imagine something being sent off by a material object. And what, to Malebranche's Cartesian mind, could a
material body send off except something material?[25] Moreover, the
Peripatetic account does indeed require the species to be spiritualized and rendered acceptable to the passive intellect. And if they
need to be spiritualized, this could be only because they are initially
nonspiritual, that is, material—or so Malebranche may have been
thinking.

Latter-day Epicureans, on the other hand, believe that bodies
transmit to the sense organs certain extremely fine material films or
images that resemble the bodies and thus make sense perception
and knowledge possible. Gassendi, for example, describes these
images as "remarkably subtle corporeal textures" and as "tenuous
membranes" that pass from the body to the senses.[26] He notes that

23. "Species habent esse intentionale in medio, & in organo. . . . Primo, quia sunt
immaterialiores, quam ipsum obiectum reale, unde prodeunt . . . [Aristotle ait]
sensus recipere formam sine materia" (*Comm. cum quest.* II.12, Q. 34, *Opera omnia
philosophica*, pp. 110–11). According to the Conimbrians, species are *forma absque
materia* (*Comm. de Anima* II.6.ii.2).
24. *Summa philosophica quadripartita* III, p. 330 (Gilson, *Index scolastico-
cartésien*, p. 98).
25. For suggestions regarding the possible influence of Malebranche's Cartesianism
(and mechanism) on his understanding of the Peripatetic theory, see Radner, *Malebranche*, p. 21; and Connell, *The Vision in God*, pp. 170–72.
26. *Syntagma philosophicum*, "Physica", Section I, Book 6, chapter xiii, *Opera
omnia*, vol. 1, p. 443.

bodies send off these *eidola* in two ways, either by spontaneous emission or by continuous "direption" (tearing off). Walter Charleton, a self-described Epicurean-Gassendist, insists that "Sight . . . discerns the exterior Forms of Objects, by the reception . . . of certain *Substantial* or *Corporeal Emanations* . . . as it were Direpted from their superficial parts." He calls these emanations "a kind of most thin film," "tenuous concretions, or subtle contextures, holding an exquisite analogy to solid bodies." In fact, they are structured collections of atoms, taken from the outermost surface of the body (again, either spontaneously emitted or stripped away by the action of light), and carried by the particles of light to the sense organ. After this corporeal image is received by the external membranes of the eyes, it is transmitted to the retina and then received by the optic nerves, where it serves to represent the external object. The "inner faculty" then "perceives" or judges of the object on the basis of this image on the optic nerve.[27]

In Malebranche's critique of the theory he presents in *Search* III.2.ii, which he labels "Peripatetic," he focuses only on the claim that bodies send forth material resemblances of themselves. That is, in his critique Malebranche really only addresses an Epicurean theory of corporeal simulacra, which constitutes just a part of the complex hybrid account he is considering under the Peripatetic label. His objections to this theory are as follows:

1. The material species must be "little bodies" and as such are solid and impenetrable. Given the great multitude of such bodies that must be flying around, however subtle and thin they may be, it is clear that they must constantly run into one another and impede one another's progress. Thus they can never travel uninterruptedly across the spaces between bodies and the senses. Moreover, we can see a great number of objects from a single vantage point. But this implies that all the various species coming from these bodies must be capable of being reduced to a point, which, given their impenetrability, is impossible. Similarly, we can see a great number of objects from any vantage point whatsoever, which implies that

27. Charleton, *Physiologia Epicuro-Gassendo-Charltoniana*, Part I, Book 3, chapter ii, pp. 136ff. Charleton explicitly contrasts Epicurean *eidola* with Peripatetic species, which are immaterial.

there is no point in the universe where all the species do not meet—"ce qui est contre toute apparence de vérité."

2. The appearances of an object change, depending for example on whether one moves closer to or farther away from it. This would seem to imply that the object emits species of different sizes, increasing or diminishing their size as the occasion demands. Yet on the other hand, it would appear that an object can emit species only in a regular and unchanging manner, and that the species are immutable. In this regard the theory is inconsistent.

3. The species clearly do not—nor need they—resemble the object that produces them. When we look at a perfect cube, the species that reach the eyes have unequal sides and angles, for such is how the cube appears to the senses. And yet we still perceive a cube with equal sides and angles.

4. It is inconceivable ("on ne peut pas concevoir") that a body that constantly emits species in all directions—species taken from the outermost layer of the body—should not sensibly diminish in its bulk as layer after layer is stripped away.[28] Moreover, how can corporeal species travel through space from a body to the sense organ with the inconceivable speed that would be required in order to explain how a body can be seen *immediately* upon its discovery, even though it be "several million leagues away"?

It should be clear from this summary that Malebranche's critique in the *Search*, while it may raise certain ontological problems for the Epicurean theory of simulacra, does not address any epistemological issues. He does not consider here that part of the alleged "Peripatetic" account according to which the species, in conjunction with the active and passive intellects, play a cognitive role in our knowledge of bodies.[29]

Moreover, it is curious that Malebranche categorizes the theory he is criticizing as a theory according to which "the *ideas* we have of bodies and of all other objects we do not perceive by themselves

---

28. Charleton answers this kind of objection merely by insisting on "the almost Incomprehensible TENUITY of these substantial Emanations"; *Physiologia Epicuro-Gassendo-Charltoniana*, I.3.ii, pp. 141–43.

29. He partially addresses these aspects of the theory elsewhere; see the *Méditations chrétiennes*, Meditation I. See also Gueroult, *Malebranche*, vol. 1, pp. 103–4.

come from these bodies or objects" (*Search* III.2.i: OC 1:417; LO 219; emphasis added). The material species that bodies emit are not *ideas*.[30] The species themselves never pass into the mind. Rather, the sensory reception of the species is part of the material conditions necessary for the mind to have ideas (or in this case, *intelligible* species) that make bodies known.[31] For this reason, the first theory Malebranche considers really belongs, insofar as it can count as a theory of ideas at all, with the second theory he considers, under the class "Empiricist Theories of Ideas." In both these theories, "ideas" arise in the mind only on the occasion of some kind of causal interaction between the sense organs and corporeal bodies (with the difference that on the first theory, the idea as intelligible species is directly derived by abstraction from the material or impressed species). Malebranche's critique of the "Peripatetic" theory is thus directed only at one particular (Epicurean) account of the material causal processes that are deemed necessary for the mind to have ideas of bodies. It is not until his remarks on the second theory that he addresses the more general and important issue of how the soul can produce ideas on the occasion of some sensory stimulation.

Malebranche's rejection of the "Peripatetic" theory represents, I believe, a general rejection of abstractionism. The ideas we have of bodies, and of corporeal natures, are not derived by abstraction from experience or sensory data. To be sure, the theory represents only one possible abstractionist account. But Malebranche's Cartesian persuasions clearly compel him to reject out of hand any theory which asserts that our idea of extension (and our ideas of extended bodies) are drawn from the senses. As Descartes insists in the wax example of the Second Meditation, extension is grasped by

---

30. The question of whether the species emitted by bodies are corporeal or not should not be confused with the issue of whether or not ideas themselves are corporeal. Gassendi does, in fact, believe that there are corporeal ideas in the mind (i.e., in the brain), but this is logically independent of his position on the materiality of the images transmitted from the body to the sense organs. See Michael and Michael, "Corporeal Ideas in Seventeenth-Century Psychology," especially pp. 40–44.

31. On the other hand, it may be that Malebranche believes that the material species are in fact like ideas in at least one very important respect, namely, they are resembling or representative images.

the pure understanding, by a "purely mental scrutiny [*solius mentis inspectis*]" (AT 7:31; CSM 2:21). The difference is that for Descartes the idea of extension is innate in the human mind, whereas for Malebranche it is in God.[32]

THE PRODUCTION THEORY

The second theory Malebranche considers is that "our souls have the power of producing [*produire*] the ideas of the things they wish to think about, and that our souls are moved to produce them by the impressions that objects make on the body" (*Search* III.2.iii). Motions communicated from an external body to the sense organ through an intervening medium are then transmitted by the nerves to the brain. The soul, on the occasion of the brain motions, produces an idea of the object. Like the first theory, the second theory asserts that ideas arise in the mind on the occasion of some kind of causal interaction between the external object and the sense organ, such that an impression left on the organ gives the mind material for its cognitive activity, with the differences that (1) in the first theory but not in the second, the corporeal impression conveyed by the object is a resembling image of the object; and (2) in the second theory, a soul actively producing its own ideas is substituted for the active intellect deriving the intelligible species directly from the impressed species.[33]

The question as to who is the object of Malebranche's critique in *Search* III.2.iii can be divided into two parts: First, who (if anyone) actually held the theory Malebranche presents? And second, whom did Malebranche have in mind as a proponent of this theory? A clear answer to the general question has eluded Malebranche scholars for quite some time. Gouhier and Gueroult initially believed that Malebranche's critique is directed, like the critique of the first theory, against *la théorie scolastique*,[34] but they have since aban-

32. Bracken suggests that "once empiricist, i.e. abstractionist, accounts of concept acquisition are rejected . . . innateness or 'seeing all things in God' become the only philosophically intelligible answers"; see "The Malebranche–Arnauld Debate: Philosophical or Ideological?"
33. Connell labels the first two theories the "passive" and "active forms of the empiricist hypothesis"; see *The Vision in God*, pp. 167–83.
34. See Gouhier, *La Philosophie de Malebranche*, pp. 225–26; and Gueroult, *Malebranche*, vol. 1, pp. 104–5.

doned this view.[35] Beatrice Rome preserves that hypothesis in a modified form. Referring to "theologians before and after Thomas," she contends that the second theory represents "an adulterated form of the philosophies of both Plato and Aristotle."[36] Rodis-Lewis suggests that it is Henricus Regius (Henri le Roy), Descartes's erstwhile disciple in Holland, whom Malebranche particularly has in mind with the second theory.[37] To be sure, Regius holds an extreme empiricist view, whereby ideas result in the mind on the occasion of certain corporeal movements (he even suggests that ideas are "impressed" on the mind by objects),[38] and he denies that there are any innate ideas. But as Connell points out, for Regius the mind is *passive* in its reception of ideas. Its power to form ideas is limited to the capacity to put together ideas already received from the senses.[39] The theory under consideration, however, claims that the mind is *active* in the original production of ideas from material impressions. Connell himself believes that the theory critiqued in chapter 3 is that of Cureau de la Chambre, although, as I will show, the evidence for this is rather inconclusive.[40] One recent commentator simply throws up her hands: "no individual or group comes readily to mind."[41]

There is, however, an anser to the first part of the question in certain Cartesian writings of the period. I have in mind, in particular, the so-called *Port-Royal Logic*. The first edition of the *Logic* was published in 1662, twelve years before the first edition of Malebranche's *Search*. In chapter 1 of Book I the authors, Antoine Arnauld and Pierre Nicole, attack proponents of the brand of empiricism which holds that ideas are conveyed into the mind through the senses. In particular they specify Gassendi and others who hold the opinion that *nihil est in intellectu quod non prius fuerit in sensu* (they suggest also that their critique is directed at

35. See OC 1:524, n. 344.
36. *The Philosophy of Malebranche*, p. 82.
37. See her textual remarks in OC 1:524, n. 344ff.
38. *Philosophia naturalis*, Book V, chapter 7: "Probatur menti ab objectis ideas esse impressas, quibus rerum recordantur" (p. 399).
39. *Philosophia naturalis*, Book V, chapter 1, pp. 353–54. See Connell, *The Vision in God*, pp. 178–79.
40. Connell, "Cureau de la Chambre, source de Malebranche."
41. Radner, *Malebranche*, p. 22.

Scholastic theories). This opinion, they assert, is "absurd." In what way, they ask, could such ideas as "being" or "thought" enter through the senses? Nor does it seem possible for ideas of this nature to be formed from other, more primary sensible images, whether by composition, diminution, or amplification. The only reasonable hypothesis, they conclude, is that "the mind has the faculty of forming these ideas for itself [*la faculté de les former de soi-même*], although it often happens that it is aroused [*excitée*] to do this by something which strikes the senses."[42] This opinion is then generalized to cover all the mind's ideas:

> It is false, therefore, that all of our ideas come through our senses. On the contrary, it may be affirmed, that no idea which we have in our minds has its origin [*tire son origine*] in the senses, except by occasion, in that the movements which are made in the brain, which is all our senses can do, give occasion to the soul to form [*de se former*] different ideas which it would not have formed without them.[43]

They explicitly compare the soul's creative ability to produce ideas on the occasion of bodily changes to a painter's capacity to paint a picture ("faire un tableau") on the occasion of a proffered commission. The schema here, artistic analogy and all, is identical to the theory Malebranche has in mind in *Search* III.2.iii. In fact, in his critique Malebranche takes over the painter analogy and turns it against the theory.

These remarks in the *Logic*—a work permeated by Cartesian methodological and metaphysical principles[44]—echo certain of Descartes's own statements on the origin of ideas, particularly those in his response to Regius's claim that the mind has no need of innate ideas. Descartes, in the *Comments on a Certain Broadsheet*, insists that, in a sense, all our ideas are innate: they arise out of the mind's own faculty of thinking; nothing literally passes from the external world into the mind. He denies that "things transmit ideas to our mind through the sense organs." Rather, "they transmit something

42. Arnauld and Nicole, *La Logique, ou l'art de penser*, p. 71.
43. Ibid., pp. 71–72.
44. For a study of Arnauld's commitment to Cartesianism, see Nadler, *Arnauld and the Cartesian Philosophy of Ideas*, chapter 2. Nicole's case is a bit more problematic; see Nadler, "Cartesianism and Port-Royal."

which, at exactly that moment, gives the mind occasion to form
[*efformandas*] these ideas by means of the faculty innate to it" (AT
8-2:358–59; CSM 1:304). What bodies do communicate are simply
corporeal motions. These motions serve as the remote or accidental
cause, which gives the primary cause—the mind itself—occasion to
produce its effect at one moment rather than another.[45]

Thus we have an answer to the first part of the question. I suggest
that the theory Malebranche is rejecting in chapter 3 is a Cartesian
one. It is found in the *Port-Royal Logic*, in the precise chapter
where Arnauld and Nicole present their views on the nature and
origin of ideas, and also in certain published remarks of Descartes
himself.[46]

This is not, of course, to claim that such a theory is the exclusive
property of Cartesians. Cureau de la Chambre, for example, presents in his *Systeme de l'ame* (1664) an account of knowledge that
resembles in important respects the view described in *Search*
III.2.iii. According to Cureau, the understanding produces ideas or

45. This theory is also explicitly offered by La Forge. Noting that material substances can communicate only motions to the body, these motions, which do not
reach the spiritual soul, nonetheless give occasion to the *faculté que nous avons de
penser* and "determine it to the production of these ideas of which it is the principal
and efficient cause" (*Traité de l'esprit de l'homme*, chapter 10, in *Oeuvres philosophiques*, p. 176).

Rodis-Lewis, citing precisely the same passages, identifies the account in the
Logic and in Descartes's *Comments on a Certain Broadsheet* with the fourth theory
Malebranche considers in the enumeration (see OC 1:527–28, n. 359; also Lennon,
"Philosophical Commentary," LO 784). But the fourth theory is not a theory about
the origin of ideas, as the first three theories are. It is about only the ontological
status of ideas. Malebranche makes no mention, either in his description of the
fourth theory or in his critique of it, of a faculty in the soul for producing ideas on
the occasion of bodily motions; yet it is precisely this faculty that constitutes the core
of the account found in the *Logic* and in Descartes's remarks (and in the second
theory).

46. The *Comments on a Certain Broadsheet* [*Notae in Programma quoddam*] were
published by Elzevir in 1648. It contains probably Descartes's most considered view
on ideas, since the *Comments* were written expressly to clarify his view in the face of
a misunderstanding of it. The account in the *Comments*, however, is not consistently
and clearly present in all Descartes's works. In the earlier *Meditations*, for example,
he presents, with regard to "adventitious" ideas, a more strictly causal picture; see
especially the Sixth Meditation. The question of Descartes's views on the origin and
nature of ideas is a notoriously ambiguous and difficult one; see Kenny, "Descartes
on Ideas."

immaterial *images* of objects when objects communicate material images through the sense organs to the imagination.[47] Moreover Cureau, like Malebranche in his characterization of the second theory (and like Arnauld and Nicole in the *Logic*), compares the understanding's ability to produce ideas representative of objects to the work of a painter creating images.[48] Connell, on the basis of this general resemblance, concludes that the theory under attack in *Search* III.2.iii is that of Cureau.[49] But Connell himself admits that when it comes to details, the fit between the second theory and Cureau's account is rather imperfect. In the theory Malebranche describes in chapter 3, the impressions communicated to the brain from the object are emphatically "not images resembling the objects causing them" (OC 1:422; LO 222). For Cureau, on the other hand, objects transmit representative material images (phantasmes) to the imagination, which are then employed by the understanding as models for the ideas it produces.[50] In this apparently important regard, there is more agreement between the second theory and the Cartesian account. In the *Logic*, what is communicated from objects to the brain to occasion ideas are motions, not representative images.[51]

Connell also admits that the evidence for his claim that Malebranche has Cureau explicitly in view in *Search* III.2.iii—certain "implicit" (and, he admits, "superficial") textual similarities, along with the fact that Malebranche knew Cureau's work—is inconclusive. This of course brings us to the second part of the question: Is there any good evidence that Malebranche, in his own mind, identifies this second theory as a "Cartesian" one? It might be objected

47. *Systeme de l'ame*, I.1.vi, p. 11.
48. Ibid., I.1.viii, p. 18.
49. "Cureau de la Chambre, source de Malebranche," pp. 167–68.
50. "Parce que tous les objets n'ont pas le mouvement nécessaire pour s'approcher et s'unir aux puissances de l'âme, la nature a pourvu à cela par les images qui sortent de ces objets-là qui les représentent, lesquelles passant dans les organes des sens s'unissent à l'imagination" (*Systeme de l'ame* I.1.ii, p. 7). Connell recognizes the discrepancy here between Cureau's theory and the one Malebranche describes; see "Cureau de la Chambre, source de Malebranche," pp. 167–68.
51. See also the previously cited passages from Descartes's *Comments on a Certain Broadsheet*, wherein no reference is made to images, but only to corporeal motions. Yet elsewhere Descartes does refer to the motions terminating in the brain as "images" of the objects causing them; see *La Dioptrique*, Discourse 6.

that there are good reasons for thinking that he does not. Malebranche explicitly identifies the fourth theory in the enumeration as that proposed by Arnauld[52] (it is also the theory held by Régis), and it is generally agreed that Descartes and other Cartesians are the target when Malebranche considers the third theory ("Ideas are innate or created with us").[53] This makes it seem unlikely that the second theory is a Cartesian candidate as well.

To be sure, there is no doubt that the third and fourth theories represent, for Malebranche, elements of the Cartesian doctrine of ideas (the fourth theory presents its ontological component).[54] But there is also at least one very good piece of evidence for thinking that the second theory is likewise, in Malebranche's eyes, a Cartesian one. In the "Elucidations" added to the *Search*, Malebranche considers the following objection to the vision in God: Our soul thinks or has ideas not because of its union with God, but because such is its nature. In creating the soul, the objection runs, God gave to it the faculty of thinking, the capacity to produce in itself its own ideas, although it exercises this capacity only when occasioned to do so by the senses. Malebranche begins his response to this objection—an objection which relies on precisely the same theory of ideas he considers in *Search* III.2.iii—by attributing it to certain "Cartesian gentlemen [*Messieurs les Cartésiens*]." And his response to *this* Cartesian objection is generally the same as his response to the theory in chapter 3, namely, that the soul simply does not have the causal efficacy the theory attributes to it.[55]

I believe, then, that in *Search* III.2.iii the theory under attack is a Cartesian one (presented by Arnauld and Nicole in the *Port-Royal*

---

52. He does so somewhat obliquely in a note added to the *Search* in the fifth (1700) edition (see OC 1:433–34), and more explicitly in the *Réponse* (OC 6:53–54) in 1684. This is because it would have been possible for him to make this connection only after having read VFI (1683).

53. See Rodis-Lewis, OC 1:526–27, notes 356–57; and Gueroult, *Malebranche*, vol. 1, pp. 106–7.

54. Lennon, in fact, briefly (and without elaboration) suggests that all four alternative theories "coalesce into an account that in various ways was being proposed in the late seventeenth century as the Cartesian theory" ("Philosophical Commentary," LO 785). It is clear, however, that Malebranche himself does not view them this way, as the "Peripatetic" label on the first theory testifies.

55. *Search*, Elucidation X: OC 3:144; LO 622.

Logic and by Descartes in his *Comments*), and that Malebranche intends it to be understood in this way.

Whereas in his critique of the first theory, Malebranche basically ignores what is purported to go on in the mind and concentrates only on the emission by bodies of material species, in his critique of the second theory he focuses only on what is alleged to be the soul's ability to produce its own ideas. He ignores the claim that it is the external, physical processes that occasion the soul's creative ability. Thus if the second theory does represent an empiricism about the causal origination of ideas (as I suggested earlier, both the first and second theories are "empiricist" in the sense that in both cases sensory stimulation is a necessary condition for the presence of ideas), Malebranche's critique of that theory hardly constitutes a critique of empiricism per se.[56] For Malebranche's purposes, the empiricist elements in the second theory are only accidental. His real target is the claim that the human mind produces its own ideas.

Malebranche objects to the production theory on three counts. First, he argues that it grants to the soul a power of creation that the soul clearly cannot possess. Ideas are "real beings," spiritual entities that are "more noble" than bodies. Thus, were finite minds able to produce ideas, they would be able to create beings greater than those God himself has created. But even if it be granted that ideas are not more noble than bodies, indeed, even if it be granted that they are not substances at all, they are still spiritual beings (êtres spirituels) and as such have a degree of reality. And in order to bring something real into being, the power of "true creation" is required, that is, the power to produce something ex nihilo.

---

56. Malebranche does not really include in the enumeration of theories for the argument from elimination of full-bodied empiricist theory of ideas, in which external bodies cause motions in the brain (via the sense organs and nerves), which motions themselves in turn cause ideas in the mind. (On the other hand, in his arguments for occasionalism he does demonstrate that bodies cannot cause effects in the soul.) Such an empiricism is the theory proposed by Locke in his remarks on Malebranche (and is likewise the theory that informs the *Essay*). Locke agrees with Malebranche that bodies do not emit resembling material species. But he insists that the motion of the particles of matter striking the eye do cause ideas or perceptions in the mind, although he grants that how this happens is "inconceivable to us"; see "Examination," pp. 214–17. Thus, just as I argue that Malebranche's critique of the second theory does not constitute a critique of empiricism, so Locke argues that the same is true of Malebranche's critique of the first theory.

Defenders of the theory might respond that in fact it is not true creation that is required, for the soul produces its ideas from the material impressions communicated to the brain. Malebranche replies that to create ideas from corporeal images is no less an act of creation than creation ex nihilo. "It is no more difficult to produce something from nothing than to produce it by positing another thing from which it cannot be made and which can contribute nothing to its production" (*Search* III.2.iii: OC 1:423–24; LO 223). In other words, one thing can be produced from another thing only if they are of the same nature (Malebranche gives the example of producing bread from stone, material beings whose transmogrification can be accomplished presumably by a change in internal particle structure because they are but "extension differently configured"). But spiritual ideas cannot be formed from material impressions, for they are of incommensurable natures ("[ils] n'ont point de proportion"). Thus on the production theory the soul's production of ideas, even if "from" material images, is tantamount to creation ex nihilo.[57] And human souls simply do not have the power of true creation.

Second, this alleged power of creation by itself would be useless, Malebranche argues, because we would still be unable to form the ideas we need. Ideas cannot be produced blindly, even on the occasion of material impressions. In order to form the idea of an object, we would have to know beforehand the object whose idea we are to produce. Similarly, a painter cannot produce a picture of an animal unless he first has some idea or knowledge of the animal to be painted. But in the case of ideas, this implies that in order to create the idea of *x*, one must already have an idea of *x*. "A man could not form the idea of an object unless he knew it beforehand, i.e. unless he already had the idea of it, which idea does not depend on his will" (OC 1:424–25; LO 223). And if he already has an idea of the object, it is useless (inutile) for him to form another idea of it.

It is not clear that Malebranche's objection is to the point. Would the mind really need an idea to produce an idea? I take it that on the theory Malebranche is considering, the nature of the material im-

---

57. "If, then, the mind produces its own ideas from the material impressions the brain receives from objects, it continuously does the same thing, or something as difficult, or even more difficult, as if it created them" (OC 1:424; LO 223).

pression plays some role in the soul's production of the idea, and that the soul does not create just any idea on the basis of any impression. Rather, the material impression must provide information or serve as a cue or guide that directs the soul in the production of the idea. And the impression can perform this role even if—as the theory Malebranche is considering asserts—it is not an image resembling the object that causes it. The mind, as the "faculty of thinking," is simply that which is capable of "reading" and translating corporeal (brain) motions into ideas.

In the *Conversations chrétiennes* Malebranche in fact considers the possibility that the soul forms its ideas on the basis of certain "models," and argues that the idea would then be superfluous, since the model itself could do the cognitive work the idea is allegedly required to do.

> From what will you form the idea of a square—will you form it from nothing or from the bodies which surround you? If from nothing, you can thus create it. But on what model? And where does this model come from? If you have a model that you did not make, then what good will your idea that you claim to create serve you? The model will suffice. For in this case, it will truly be your model, and not your idea, which will enlighten you and which you will consult. (OC 10:13)

But again, Malebranche's point does not quite strike home. Material impressions, even if they serve as informative but nonimagistic models for the production of ideas, are just brain motions and hence are themselves not cognitive at all.

Malebranche could, however, make the following reply: It is inconceivable that the soul could, on the basis of the corporeal impressions alone, determine what idea to produce and how to produce it. There is no necessary connection between any corporeal motions and any spiritual event (such as an idea or sensation) such that from those motions alone one can know what idea or sensation should follow.[58] Whatever connections do exist are established by God's free decrees. Thus in order for the soul to be able to "read"

---

58. See *Search* V.1: OC 2:129; LO 338–39. In fact, Malebranche makes this precise point in the context of criticizing the third theory (innate ideas), with the added claim (also relevant here) that the mind does not perceive the motions in the brain anyway; see III.2.iv: OC 1:431; LO 227.

the impression and translate it into the appropriate idea, the soul would have to have access to the divine lexicon, which is clearly not the case.

Malebranche's third objection to the production theory is of an occasionalist nature. The theory, he claims, is guilty of a common error, namely, the supposition that if one event A is constantly conjoined with and followed by another event B, then A is the cause of B.

> Men never fail to judge that a thing is the cause of a given effect when the two are conjoined, given that the true cause of the effect is unknown to them. This is why everyone concludes that a moving ball which strikes another is the true and principal cause of the motion it communicates to the other, and that the soul's will is the true and principal cause of the movement in the arms . . . because it always happens that a ball moves when struck by another, that our arms move almost every time we want them to, and that we do not sensibly perceive what else could be the cause of these movements. (OC 1:426; LO 224)

Very often we have ideas present to the mind as soon as we want them, and in these cases an act of will always precedes the appearance of an idea. Thus we conclude that the soul's volitions must be the true causes of the ideas. But, Malebranche insists, this constant conjunction gives us the right to assert only that acts of will are *necessary* conditions for these ideas, *not* that acts of will are *sufficient* conditions, that is, that the will itself has the power to bring them about. Hence constant conjunction does not support the claim that the will is "the true and principal cause" of ideas. In fact the soul, as a finite creature, has no power, force, or efficacy to bring about any effect on its own, either in the body or in itself (*Search*, Elucidation XV: OC 3:204; LO 658). What we should conclude is that the volitions are simply the occasions for the only being that has any real causal efficacy—God—to make the ideas present.

> We know through inner sensation that we will to think about something, that we make an effort to do so, and that at the moment of our desire and effort, the idea of that thing is presented to our mind. But we do not know through inner sensation that our will or effort

produces our idea. We do not see through reason that this could happen. It is through prejudice that we believe that our attention or desires are the cause of our ideas; this is due to the fact that a hundred times a day we prove that our ideas follow or accompany them. Since God and His operations contain nothing sensible, and since we sense nothing other than our desires preceding the presence of ideas, we think there can be no cause of these ideas other than our desires. But let us take care. We do not see in us any power to produce them; neither reason nor the inner sensation we have of ourselves tells us anything about this. (*Search*, Elucidation XV: OC 3:229; LO 671)

Thus the will might be the "occasional cause" for the presence of ideas, but it cannot be the real cause.

THE THEORY OF INNATE IDEAS

Malebranche next turns to the theory of innate ideas. As Malebranche describes the theory in *Search* III.2.iv, its claim is that "all ideas are innate or created with us." While on the production theory all ideas are "innate" in the trivial sense that all ideas arise from the faculty of thinking alone, and none are literally conveyed into the mind from the external world, the innateness doctrine now under consideration holds that the soul does not itself produce ideas but rather that God creates and places preformed ideas in the soul. The mind is thus considered to be a "storehouse [*magazin*]" from which the will can bring into consciousness the appropriate ideas on any given occasion.

This innateness claim is intended to hold for *all* ideas, although it is not quite clear here what the scope of 'idea' is in Malebranche's characterization of the theory. On the one hand, it might broadly include both the clear and distinct concepts that Malebranche himself recognizes as ideas, as well as sensory perceptions (which Descartes and others call "ideas"). On this broad view, the theory is that both sensations (heat, color, etc.) and clear and distinct ideas are innate and created with us at birth.

On the other hand, there are good reasons for construing 'idea' more narrowly than this.[59] In chapter 4 Malebranche, for the pur-

59. See Jolley, "Leibniz and Malebranche on Innate Ideas," pp. 80–81.

poses of his critique of the innate ideas theory, considers only ideas of triangles and other "simple figures," suggesting that the theory is intended to cover *only* clear and distinct concepts. This is in keeping with his own strict notion of 'idea', and it is important to remember that the whole point of Malebranche's exercise in *Search* III.2.ii–vi is to discover where ideas—as he himself conceives them—come from. Moreover, were the theory to be taken in the broad sense, it would be both rather implausible and one that no one actually held. To be sure, Descartes says that, in a sense, all our ideas—both sensory and clear and distinct—are innate. But this is only in the trivial sense mentioned above, whereby all ideas derive immediately and proximately from the faculty of thinking alone.

> [T]he very ideas of the motions themselves and of the figures are innate to us. The ideas of pain, colors, sounds and the like must be all the more innate if, on the occasion of certain corporeal motions, our mind is to be capable of representing them to itself, for there is no similarity between these ideas and the corporeal motions. (*Comments on a Certain Broadsheet*, AT 8-2:359; CSM 1:304)

Still, even on the narrow reading—whereby all clear and distinct ideas of primary qualities are innate because God preforms them and places them in us when he creates us—one wonders whether Malebranche is in his critique of innate ideas setting up a straw man, as Locke is often accused of doing.[60] Locke's famous attack on innate ideas is directed at a doctrine so extreme that it is surprising anyone ever held it. According to Locke, some contend that "there are in the Understanding certain *innate Principles*; some primary Notions [*eidola*], Characters, as it were stamped upon the Mind of Man, which the Soul receives in its very first Being; and brings into the World with it"; they further contend that these notions and principles are "universally agreed upon by all Man-

---

60. See, for example, Peter Gay, *John Locke on Education*, p. 7: "The precise target of [Locke's] long polemic remains a matter of discussion." But Yolton has shown that the theory Locke attacks is held in various forms throughout the seventeenth century in England; see *John Locke and the Way of Ideas*, chapter 2. Locke actually ascribes one version of the theory to Lord Herbert of Cherbury, in his *De Veritate*, and many elements of Herbert's theory do in fact conform to Locke's characterization, for example, the criterion of "Universal Consent."

kind."[61] The innate ideas that Locke rejects are both preformed at creation and actually in consciousness.[62]

Now Malebranche is not attacking, as Locke is, a theory that holds innate ideas to be conscious thoughts. But he is attacking the theory that ideas are preformed in our mind when God creates us. Moreover, unlike the view Locke attacks, the view Malebranche opposes is that *all* ideas, not just some, are innate. Did anyone hold such an extreme view? Lord Herbert of Cherbury's innate "Common Notions," one ostensible object of Locke's attack,[63] are not ideas of bodies, of figures or extension (i.e., ideas of the Malebranchian variety), but rather are certain rules or principles according to which we judge truths.

Most scholars agree that Descartes is the object of Malebranche's critique in III.2.iv.[64] But does Descartes in fact hold such a view of innateness? That there are certain ideas innate in us, preformed and actual albeit subconscious, is suggested by some of his remarks. The idea of God, for example, is "implanted [*indita*] in the same way in the minds of all" (First Replies, AT 7:105; CSM 2:76), and is apparently complete and actual, although it may have become obscured by other (most likely sensory) material. It is an idea that I can "bring forth from the treasure house [*thesauro*, trésor] of my mind" (*Meditations* V, AT 7:67, 9-1:53; CSM 2:46). And our ideas of certain essences—of body, mind, number, geometrical objects— are innate, such that when I first turn my attention to them (and Descartes describes this as "discovering [*detego*]" them, thus suggesting that they are completely there to begin with), "it seems like noticing for the first time things which were long present within me although I had never turned my mental gaze on them before"

---

61. *Essay* I.2.i–ii.
62. Leibniz, as a partisan of innate ideas, rejects both these alleged features of the theory; see *New Essays on Human Understanding*, Book I.
63. John Yolton has pointed out to me that the reference to Herbert in the *Essay* I.3 is in fact a late addition in its composition, and that anyway the doctrine Locke attacks is found in many contemporary writers in England.
64. See Gueroult, *Malebranche*, vol. 1, p. 106; Gouhier, *La Philosophie de Malebranche*, p. 227; and Alquié, *Le Cartésianisme de Malebranche*, pp. 194–97. Connell, on the other hand, suggests that it is directed at Suarez and not Descartes; see *The Vision in God*, pp. 191–92.

(*Meditations* V, AT 7:63–64; CSM 2:44). Descartes also says that "I find within me countless ideas of things [*invenio apud me innumeras ideas*]," ideas that are "not my invention."

But there are two problems with attributing the extreme account of innate ideas of *Search* III.2.iv to Descartes. First, Descartes is quite clear that *not all* our ideas (even restricting the term 'idea' to our clear and distinct ideas of figure, motion, etc.) are innate in the strict[65] sense of "innate." He draws an explicit contrast between strictly innate ideas and adventitious ideas that are "foreign to me and coming from outside" (although they do not literally enter into the mind "from outside," but are generated by the faculty of thinking on the occasion of certain externally caused corporeal motions).[66] And it appears that among our adventitious ideas are our ideas of external bodies—precisely those ideas that the innateness theory Malebranche is considering is supposed to account for.[67]

Second, it is far from clear that Descartes's innate ideas are fully actualized, preformed concepts that need only to be brought into consciousness. In fact, in one context Descartes expressly denies this, and says that innate ideas are more like potentialities inherent in the faculty of thought.

> I have never written or taken the view that the mind requires innate ideas which are something distinct from its own faculty of thinking. I did, however, observe that there were certain thoughts within me which neither came to me from external objects nor were determined by my will, but which came solely from the power of thinking within me; so I applied the term 'innate' to the ideas or notions which are the forms of these thoughts in order to distinguish them from others, which I called "adventitious" or "made up." This is the same sense as that in which we say that generosity is "innate" in certain families, or that certain diseases such as gout or stones are innate in others: it is

65. In the trivial sense of 'innate" already discussed, Descartes grants that all our ideas, even sensations, are innate.
66. See *Meditations* III, AT 7:37–38; CSM 2:26 (the phrase "foreign to me" was added in the French version).
67. See *Meditations* VI: AT 7:79–80; CSM 2:55, where he argues that many of his ideas are "produced [*emitti*]" by the corporeal things they clearly and distinctly represent.

not so much that the babies of such families suffer from these diseases in their mother's womb, but simply that they are born with a certain "faculty" or tendency to contract them. (*Comments on a Certain Broadsheet*, AT 8-2:357-58; CSM 1:303-4)

The idea of God "derives its being" from our faculty of thinking, "in which [it] is innate." But to say that this idea is innate is to say only that it "always exists within us potentially [*potentia*], for to exist in some faculty is not to exist actually, but merely potentially" (AT 8-2:360-61; CSM 1:305). As Alquié notes, "Descartes considers innate ideas as certain *virtualités*, or potentialities of thought; not as preformed cognitive entities sitting in a *magazin* waiting to be retrieved."[68]

Malebranche does not explicitly specify his opponent in chapter 4, but he probably does have Descartes in mind. But the theory he critiques and eliminates is not one that Descartes himself held.[69]

Malebranche's most ready criticism of this theory derives from his own conception of what an idea is.[70] As we have seen, Malebranche insists that representative ideas are not and cannot be modifications of the human mind. But if ideas cannot be in the mind in the first place, then a fortiori they cannot be innate in the mind.

Second, the doctrine involves too much complexity to be reconcilable with the ways of God, who always acts in the simplest way possible. We can, Malebranche notes, conceive or think of an infinite number of things and kinds of things, as for example an infinite number of variations upon a particular kind of geometrical

---

68. *Le Cartésianisme de Malebranche*, p. 195. See also Rodis-Lewis, OC 1:526, n. 356.

69. Alquié agrees that while Descartes may be the explicit object of Malebranche's attack, the preformation theory Malebranche critiques is not really Descartes's. This is not to say that Malebranche conveniently substitutes for Descartes's theory a caricature that is easier to attack. Rather, Alquié argues, if Descartes's innateness theory is to make any sense in Malebranche's eyes, innate ideas must be construed in it as actual and preformed: "Any voluntary evocation of an idea already supposes its presence . . . and no presence can be merely virtual"; see *Le Cartésianisme de Malebranche*, p. 195.

70. For a good discussion of Malebranche's critique of innate ideas, see Jolley, "Leibniz and Malebranche on Innate Ideas."

figure. This implies that we have access to an infinite number of ideas. On the innateness theory, the mind itself would contain all these ideas. "[The mind], then, has an infinite number of ideas—what am I saying?—it has as many infinite numbers of ideas as there are different figures; consequently, since there is an infinite number of different figures, the mind must have an infinity of infinite numbers of ideas just to know the figures" (*Search* III.3.iv: OC 1:430; LO 227). In fact God would, on the innateness theory, have to create an indefinite number of sets of infinite ideas, one for every human mind that ever existed. And this, to Malebranche's mind, is a highly implausible hypothesis. "For as God always acts in the simplest ways, it does not seem reasonable to explain how we know objects by assuming the creation of an infinity of beings, since the difficulty can be resolved in an easier and more straightforward fashion," namely, by appealing to the vision in God.

Moreover, even if the mind did contain this storehouse of ideas, it would be of no cognitive use, because there would be no way for the mind to determine and choose which ideas to bring forth on a given occasion. This objection is similar to that made against the production theory.

> For since the image the sun imprints in the brain does not resemble the idea we have of it . . . , and as the soul does not perceive the motion the sun produces in the brain and in the fundus of the eyes, it is inconceivable that it should be able to determine precisely which among the infinite number of its ideas it would have to represent to itself in order to imagine or see the sun and to see it as having a given size. (OC 1:431; LO 227)

In III.2.iv Malebranche briefly considers another theory, one that, like the innateness doctrine, claims that God is the cause of ideas in the mind. In this case, however, the ideas are not created in us all at once in the beginning. Rather, God produces a new idea each time we think of or perceive a new object. More particularly, on the occasion either of a volition in the soul or of the appropriate motions in the brain (communicated from the object through the sense organs), God causes an idea representing the object to appear in the mind. In a sense, Malebranche's rejection of this hypothesis is curious, since it would seem to be a fine occasionalist way of explaining the origin of ideas in the mind.[71] In fact, such an explanation is suggested by some remarks of Géraud de Cordemoy, an early occasionalist.[72]

Malebranche argues against this theory on the grounds that it lacks explanatory power. We can, he notes, at all times will to think about all things. At any given moment one can will to think of any one of an infinite number of things. But this would not be possible unless an infinite number of ideas were already present to the mind (even if perceived only confusedly). For how could we will to think about an object of which we have no idea? The will needs the idea of an object in order to direct the mind to think of that object. On the theory under consideration, however, these ideas are not present to the mind until after the volition (and after God has produced them). Thus it does not explain how it is that we can at any time will to think of anything.

Malebranche's general rejection of innate ideas is particularly elucidating, because it is clear that he intends his doctrine of the vision in God to serve precisely the same purposes that the partisans of innateness intend their doctrine to serve. Innate ideas are em-

71. There are still occasionalist elements in knowledge and perception for Malebranche. First, he claims that our attention is "the occasional and natural cause of the presence of ideas to our mind in consequence of general laws of its union with universal Reason" (*Dialogues* XII.9: OC 12:289; D 291). Following these laws, God reveals the appropriate idea to the mind on the occasion of our attention. Malebranche regards this as a simpler occasionalist explanation—and one more worthy of God's mode of action—than the one which has God creating new ideas. Second, the sensations in perception are caused in the mind by God on the occasion of the appropriate motions in the sense organs and the brain, in consequence of the general laws governing mind–body union. For a discussion of how, with respect to knowledge and perception, the two doctrines of occasionalism and the vision in God divide the field, see Jolley, *The Light of the Soul*, chapter 6.
72. Cordemoy notes that "Dieu, à qui nous devons nos pensées, & les mouvements de nôtre langue, veut bien exciter les uns, dès que nous voulons faire entendre les autres" (*Discours physique de la parole*, in *Oeuvres philosophiques*, p. 246). Later he makes a direct link between occasionalism and the origin of ideas: "il est aussi impossible à nos âmes d'avoir de nouvelles perceptions sans Dieu, qu'il est impossible au corps d'avoir de nouveaux mouvements sans luy" (p. 255). Dom Robert Desgabets, writing in 1675 (one year after the first edition of the *Search*), sees a basis for this account of ideas in Cordemoy's occasionalism, and insists that, in spite of Malebranche's miserly consideration of it, "c'est cette manière qui me paraît indubitable" (*Critique de la critique de la Recherche de la vérité*, p. 210).

ployed by Leibniz, Herbert, Descartes, and others to explain how
we can have knowledge of certain immutable and necessary truths.
For Descartes our knowledge of essences, of "true and immutable
natures," and of the principles based upon them cannot be derived
from experience, which can provide only contingent, mutable
truths. Such knowledge must come from certain innate ideas or
"seeds of truth" implanted within us. This alone can account for the
certainty, universality, and necessity of the truths one can discover
by such ideas.[73]

Similarly, Malebranche's vision in God is, in one of its aspects,
an account of how we can have knowledge of certain mathematical,
logical, and moral truths—truths that are eternal, universal, and
necessary, and thus which cannot be derived from sense experience.
Truths, for Malebranche, are relations within and between ideas.
And if the ideas themselves are eternal, then so are the necessary
truths based on them. "The intelligible ideas or perfections that are
in God and that represent to us what is external to God are
absolutely immutable and necessary. Now, truths are but relations
of equality or inequality between these intelligible beings . . .
Truths, therefore, as well as ideas, are necessary and immutable"
(*Search*, Elucidation X: OC 3:136; LO 617–18). Like innate ideas,
Malebranche's ideas (via God) are already there from the start,
indelible, a priori, independent of sense experience, waiting to be
discovered by an attentive mind. Malebranche even, at times, employs the language of innateness: "We must actually have in us the
ideas of all things" (*Search* III.2.iv: OC 1:432; LO 227). Alquié,
taking his cue from Voltaire, seems to be correct when he claims
that the vision in God is, at least as presented in the *Search*, an
"innéisme transposé et extériorisé."[74]

73. See *Meditations* V. See also Leibniz, *New Essays on Human Understanding*,
Preface, pp. 49–50, and Book I.
74. *Le Cartésianisme de Malebranche*, p. 195. See Voltaire, *Lettres philosophiques*,
Letter 13: "M. Malebranche, of the Oratory, in his sublime hallucinations, not only
allowed the existence of innate ideas but was certain that all we perceive is in God
and that God, so to speak, is our soul." For a comparison of the vision in God and
innateness, see also Moreau, "Le Réalisme de Malebranche et la fonction de l'idée,"
pp. 118–20. On the other hand, Nicholas Jolley is certainly right when he cautions
me against drawing strong analogies between the vision in God and the doctrine of
innate ideas, lest I thereby underestimate the significance of Malebranche's view that
ideas are not mental entities.

THE MODIFICATION THEORY

Malebranche considers last what he takes to be the final alternative to the vision in God. "The fourth view is that the mind needs only itself in order to see objects, and that by considering itself and its own perfections, it can discover all external things" (*Search* III.2.v: OC 1:433; LO 228). Ideas, on this account, are nothing but modifications or "perfections"[75] of the soul, mental events of one kind or another. As ideas, they also possess a representational character.

It is not clear, however, that this modification theory is an explanation of the *origin* of ideas (as the first three theories are). Rather, it seems to amount only to a claim about the ontological status of ideas, whatever their causal origin may be. This fourth theory is certainly compatible with the innateness doctrine. Innate ideas, created with the mind, would (or at least could) be modifications of the mind. It is also compatible with the production theory: ideas produced by the mind would also be mental modifications. The fourth theory merely states that ideas exist in the mind as its modifications; it is not a theory about how ideas get into the mind.[76] And yet, because the modification theory does make this particular ontological claim, it represents the exact antithesis of the

75. Malebranche's use of the term 'perfection' in his description of the theory should not be misconstrued. A "perfection" of a substance, in the seventeenth century, is simply a property or attribute modifying it. Descartes uses the term this way; see *Discourse on Method*, AT 6:34; CSM 1:128, and *Principles* I.18. For an interesting discussion of Locke's use of the term and the "ladder of perfections," see Ayers, "Mechanism, Superaddition, and the Proof of God's Existence in Locke's *Essay*."
76. See Radner, *Malebranche*, p. 50. Gueroult claims that this fourth theory is, with the third theory, an innatist doctrine (*Malebranche*, vol. 1, p. 102; see also Rodis-Lewis, OC 1:528, n. 359). Connell labels it the "active hypothesis of innate ideas" (to distinguish it from the "passive" version, according to which the mind receives ideas from God), because Malebranche describes it as the view that the soul is able to "modify itself in such a fashion as to perceive all that the human mind is capable of knowing. In a word, they would have the soul be like an intelligible world, which contains in itself all that the material and sensible world contains" (see *The Vision in God*, p. 194–96). But what is essential to the fourth theory, so far as Malebranche is concerned, is only its ontological claim—ideas are modifications of the soul—and not any claim about innateness. In fact, the phrase "modifying itself," used with respect to the soul, means only that on this theory ideas arise from the soul's own faculty of thinking, at least in their material being or "formal reality." Perhaps this implies that they are "innate," but surely only in the trivial sense in which we saw ideas to be innate according to the production theory.

theory Malebranche himself wants to defend, namely, that ideas are not "modalitez de l'ame" but are in God. Thus Malebranche's immediate critique of the theory in III.2.v is really only an opening salvo in a long debate (with Arnauld and others) concerning whether or not modifications of the soul can be representative of nonmental realities—that is, whether or not ideas are modifications of the soul.[77]

The modification theory is the orthodox Cartesian account. Malebranche explicitly attributes it to Arnauld,[78] although it is also the position held by Régis and La Forge, as well as by Descartes himself. In VFI, Arnauld attacks Malebranche's view of ideas as mind-independent objects of perception. He argues that ideas, on the contrary, are the mind's perceptions, mental acts directed at objects. "I take the idea of an object and the perception of an object to be the same thing" (VFI 198). Ideas, as such, have two aspects: ontologically, they are modes of the soul, mental events; but they also possess intentionality, or object-directedness, by means of their "objective reality" or representational content.

> I have said that I take perception and idea to be the same thing. Nevertheless, it must be remarked that this thing, although single, stands in two relations: one to the soul which it modifies, the other to the thing perceived, in so far as it exists objectively in the soul. The word *perception* more directly indicates the first relation; the word *idea*, the latter. (VFI 198).

Because our perceptions are representative of, and thus directed toward, objects, because each has its own particular content, we are able to know and perceive objects by means of, or "through," these mental acts.[79]

---

77. See, for example, *Réponse* V–VII, OC 6:50–69.

78. See n. 52.

79. Malebranche, as is clear from his description of the fourth theory, takes claims such as this to mean that on this theory we directly perceive the ideas (mental modifications) themselves, and only indirectly perceive objects. But Arnauld is quite explicit (if confusing) in his direct realism. He insists that, while there is a sense in which we *do* perceive ideas/perceptions immediately, this does not dilute our direct cognitive access to material objects; see VFI, chapter 6. For an analysis of Arnauld's theory of ideas, see Nadler, *Arnauld and the Cartesian Philosophy of Ideas*, especially chapters 5 and 6.

The view that the ideas by means of which we know and perceive objects in the world are mental events, modes of the soul having a representative character, is Descartes's own position. Ideas, he claims in the Third Meditation, are "simply modes of thinking [*modos cogitandi*]," and as such do not differ one from another in terms of their formal reality or ontological status: "they all appear to come from within me in the same fashion" (AT 7:40; CSM 2:27). Where they differ is in terms of their objective reality/representational content, whereby one idea represents one object, another idea a different object, and so on. Elsewhere Descartes says that the word 'idea' taken "materially" as an operation of the intellect (*operatio intellectus*) refers solely to a modification of the mind, which "cannot be said to be more perfect than me" (*Meditations*, Preface, AT 7:8; CSM 2:7). There is some debate as to whether Descartes's ideas are perceivings or mental acts (as Arnauld insists), or mental objects that are themselves perceived by the mind.[80] The modification theory considered by Malebranche is apparently neutral with respect to this question.[81]

Malebranche's main contention against the Cartesian view consists in precisely the arguments he offers that representative ideas

80. In *Arnauld and the Cartesian Philosophy of Ideas*, I argue that Descartes's ideas should be construed as perceptions or mental acts (pp. 126–30). See also Yolton, *Perceptual Acquaintance*, chapter 1. For the idea-object reading (a standard and widespread one), see Smith, *Studies in the Cartesian Philosophy*, p. 14 and passim, and Williams, *Descartes*, pp. 240ff., among many others. For a discussion of the confusion in Descartes's use of the term 'idea', see Kenny, "Descartes on Ideas," pp. 241–42.

81. See also La Forge, *Traité de l'esprit de l'homme*, chapter 10:

> When we consider ideas in themselves, we can define them as forms, modes, or manners of the mind's thoughts, by the immediate perception of which we perceive the thing they represent to us. . . . I call them 'modes' or 'manners' because none of them can be conceived without a substance which thinks. . . . Thus, they do not differ from the substance of the mind, nor even among themselves, otherwise than as different modes of the substance to which they belong; these forms are not different from our particular thoughts. (*Oeuvres philosophiques*, p. 173)

Régis, in his *Système général* (Part I, chapter 1 of the *Logique*), identifies *idées* with *perceptions*, which are modes of the soul (dans l'ame). He claims that "by the terms 'idea' and 'perception', I do not understand anything besides the modes of thinking which I know by themselves; but which represent to me things which are external to myself" (*Métaphysique* I.2, *Système général*, vol. 1, pp. 72–73). Malebranche acknowledges that this fourth theory is Régis's in his *Réponse à Régis*, OC 17-1:291.

cannot be modifications of a finite thinking substance. I examined those arguments in detail in chapter 2. In *Search* III.2.v Malebranche concentrates on the finite character of the human mind in two respects. The mind can know all beings ("tous les êtres"), including infinite beings, even though it cannot comprehend them. It follows, then, that (1) the mind has access to the ideas of all beings, that is, an infinite number of ideas, and (2) the mind has access to infinite ideas, that is, to ideas of infinites. As for (1), a finite mind cannot have an infinite number of modifications at the same time (although it is presumably theoretically capable of undergoing an infinite number of successive modifications). Yet as Malebranche asserts in his argument against the innateness doctrine, at any given moment we *do* have simultaneously present to the mind an infinite number of ideas. Thus these ideas cannot be modifications of the human mind. With respect to (2), I examined in chapter 2 Malebranche's arguments that a finite substance cannot have any infinite modifications. Thus the idea of the infinite cannot belong to a finite mid.[82]

Moreover, Malebranche asserts, the idea of extension is clearly not a mode of the mind. We perceive intelligible extension by itself, without thinking of anything else. It is grasped by the mind as an independent being capable of being modified in various ways. It is not, above all, perceived as being a mode of the mind. Thus intelligible extension is not a mode of the mind at all, since modifications of a substance cannot be conceived without at the same time conceiving the substance to which they belong. "We perceive this extension without thinking about our mind; we cannot even conceive that this extension could be a modification of our mind" (*Search*, Elucidation X: OC 3:148; LO 624).[83]

Behind all Malebranche's philosophical arguments against the doctrine that ideas belong to the human mind, however, there lies a more fundamental theological (and even personal) conviction

82. For a concise discussion of Malebranche's arguments here, see Radner, *Malebranche*, pp. 50–52.
83. Once again, Malebranche here denies Descartes's distinction between the formal reality of ideas and their objective reality. For Descartes, the idea that, by means of its representational content, presents extension as a substance need not itself, in its formal reality, be a substance; it can be (and is) a mode of the mind (see *Meditations* III).

against any such theory. Malebranche, I believe, is just not willing to countenance the possibility that the human mind can know and perceive external material objects, or even to have knowledge in general, "by regarding *itself*" or by means of its own inner resources. "Say not that you are a light unto yourself," Malebranche is fond of quoting from St. Augustine. The mind simply does not have the kind of independence from God that the modification theorists, in their vanity, claim it has. They underestimate both our ontological and our epistemological dependence upon God.

In fact, this same conviction probably underlies Malebranche's objections to the other three theories as well.[84] Any theory, for example, that gives to the mind a creative power (as the production theory does) certainly elevates and deifies the mind. Only God has the power to create. And while on the innateness theory God is the cause of the "warehouse" of ideas the soul finds in itself, the theory still attributes to the mind and its knowledge an ongoing independence from God—an error similar, perhaps, to that made by those who say the world, once created, subsists by itself, without the need of God continuously sustaining it by a kind of constant (re-)creation.[85] For Malebranche, only the vision in God captures the full relationship we as knowers have with God.

ELIMINATION AND ENUMERATION

The argument from elimination is now complete:

> In the preceding chapters, we have examined four different ways in which the soul might see external objects, all of which seem to us very unlikely. There remains only the fifth [the vision in God], which alone seems to conform to reason and to be most appropriate for exhibiting the dependence that minds have on God in all their thoughts (*Search* III.2.vi: OC 1:437; LO 230)

The alternative theories have all either been refuted or shown to be less than satisfactory. Ideas are not conveyed into the mind from external bodies; the mind does not produce its own ideas; God does

---

84. As Gouhier puts it, "the false hypotheses, in Malebranche's eyes, are not only poorly linked syllogisms; they express intellectual vices, which must be vanquished if one sincerely loves truth" (*La Philosophie de Malebranche*, p. 224).

85. This divine sustenance doctrine is central to Malebranche's occasionalism; see *Dialogues* VII.

not create the soul with its own store of ready-made ideas, nor does God create each idea every time the soul needs one. In fact, ideas are not even in the human mind at all. They are in God. And we perceive ideas only because we have cognitive access to the ideas in God through a kind of ongoing revelation. Thus as Malebranche puts it, we see all things in God.

> God must have within Himself the ideas of all the beings He has created (since otherwise He could not have created them), and thus He sees all these beings by considering the perfections He contains to which they are related. We should know, furthermore, that through His presence God is in close union with our minds, such the He might be said to be the place of minds as space is, in a sense, the place of bodies. Given these two things, the mind surely can see what in God represents created beings, since what in God represents created beings is very spiritual, intelligible, and present to the mind. Thus, the mind can see God's works in Him, provided that God wills to reveal to it what in Him represents them. (*Search* III.2.vi: OC 1:437; LO 230)

The representative ideas that are present to human minds in knowledge and perception are the Ideas which serve God as archetypes in creating the material world.

Malebranche's argument by elimination naturally raises the following question: In order for the argument to be conclusive, it must be the case that the enumeration of alternative theories is complete and exhaustive, representing all possible ways ideas might become present to the mind. Only then would the elimination of the first four theories be sufficient to establish the fifth theory (the vision in God). Locke, for one, is skeptical that Malebranche's enumeration is exhaustive. He suggests that there may be many other possible ways of apprehending ideas besides the five hypotheses examined, ways beyond our limited comprehension but not beyond God's power. Thus, Locke insists, Malebranche provides only an *argumentum ad ignorantiam*, not an argument from elimination.[86]

Now we have seen that there is clearly some historical basis for the division Malebranche makes among the competing theories.

86. "Examination," p. 212.

Each is related to a school or figure(s); indeed, each is derivable from works it is certain Malebranche knew. Thus the enumeration can be seen as a historical catalogue of the ways ideas have been said to be given to the mind. But the real (and philosophically interesting) question is: Is there a *logical* basis for the enumeration, such that it is plausible to think that *all* possible theories of ideas are included? Malebranche suggests that there is when he introduces the enumeration.

> We assert the absolute necessity, then, of the following: either (a) the ideas we have of bodies and of all other objects we do not perceive by themselves come from these bodies or objects; or (b) our soul has the power of producing these ideas; or (c) God has produced them in us while creating the soul or produces them every time we think about a given object; or (d) the soul has in itself all the perfections it sees in bodies; or else (e) the soul is joined to a completely perfect being that contains all intelligible perfections, or all the ideas of created beings. We can know objects in only one of these ways. (*Search* III.2.i: OC 1:417; LO 219)

He later tells Arnauld that chapters 2–6 represent "une division exacte de toutes les manieres dont nous pouvons voir les objets" (TL I, OC 6:198).[87] But Malebranche never explicitly tells us what principles generate the division. And without this clue, or a demonstration that the division is exhaustive, his argument must remain essentially inconclusive.

It is worth mentioning here two possible ways, offered by recent commentators, in which some kind of logical basis for the division could be provided. First, it has been suggested that two principles are at work: (1) ideas must either originate from experience or be innate—the two horns of empiricism and rationalism are exhaustive and exclusive; and (2) the soul must in each case be either passive or active in the reception or generation of ideas. Thus the first two alternatives represent the passive and active forms of the empiricist hypothesis, and the third and fourth theories represent

---

87. See also *Réponse à Régis*, OC 17-1:291: "J'ai fait un denombrement de toutes les manières possibles de voir les corps." Gouhier believes that the division represents a "logical deduction of all possible combinations"; see *La Philosophie de Malebranche*, pp. 223–24.

the passive and active forms of the innatist (or rationalist) doctrine.[88]

This makes for a tidy picture, but not an entirely accurate one. For example, while it may be true that on the first theory the impressed species are passively received, the active intellect (which in fact does most of the cognitive work) is still required to complete the process. And in Malebranche's characterization of the second theory, the empiricist element is hardly a distinguishing feature. Rather, he focuses on the creative power the theory imparts to the soul, making the theory appear to an active (albeit trivial) version of the innatist doctrine.

A more plausible suggestion is made by McCracken. Ideas, according to the organizing argument he provides, exist only in minds. And they must be either in our minds or in some other mind to which ours can be united. If they are in our minds, they must have been produced there by bodies (the first theory), by our own minds (the second theory), or by God (the third theory), since bodies, finite minds, and God are the only substances of which we have any knowledge.[89] This proposal has the advantage that it accurately captures in a simple form the nature of the division, and that it does so in a Cartesian framework. Still, we do not know whether or not Malebranche has in mind precisely this ground of the division.

Positive Arguments for the Vision in God

Malebranche offers, in addition to the argument from elimination, a number of positive considerations (several of which each amount to something less than an argument proper) for his claim that the ideas we apprehend are in God.[90]

---

88. See Connell, *The Vision in God*, pp. 162–64. For a similar view, see Gueroult (*Malebranche*, vol. 1, p. 102), who separates the theories into empiricisms and innatisms, as does Rodis-Lewis (OC 1:528, n. 359). Connell also suggests that the logical division derives from Suarez (*The Vision in God*, chapter 4 and pp. 163–64).
89. *Malebranche and British Philosophy*, pp. 61–62.
90. These are examined in detail by Gueroult, *Malebranche*, vol. 1, pp. 107–18; and Radner, *Malebranche*, pp. 52–59.

Simplicity. "God never does in a very complicated fashion what can be done in a very simple and straightforward way." Since God clearly has ideas of all he creates, it is simpler, more economical, and more direct for him to have us know bodies in the world by revealing his own ideas to our minds rather than by producing as many sets of infinite ideas as there are created minds. This solution has God accomplishing "greater things" by fewer and more straightforward means, which is more in keeping with his wisdom and power than more complex means (*Search* III.2.vi: OC 1:438; LO 230-31).[91]

Creaturely dependence. Unlike any of the four alternative theories, only the vision in God demonstrates and fosters a proper sense of our ontological and epistemological dependence on our creator. "This view places created minds in a position of complete dependence on God—the most complete there can be . . . and it is good that men should distinctly know that they are capable of nothing without God" (*Search* III.2.vi: OC 1:439-40; LO 231). We as knowers are not self-sufficient, no more than we as beings are self-sufficient substances. In a sense, the vision in God is the epistemological correlate of occasionalism. The theory anchors our cognitive activities as strongly in God's understanding as the causal doctrine anchors our bodies' motions in God's will.

Efficacy. Ideas are clearly efficacious, capable of causally affecting the mind: "they act upon the mind and enlighten it . . . they make it happy or unhappy through the pleasant or unpleasant perceptions by which they affect it." Nothing can act upon the mind except that which is superior to it. And the only being superior to a finite mind is an infinite mind: God. Only God can bring about changes in the modifications of human minds. Thus those ideas that so affect us must be "located in the efficacious substance of the Divinity" (*Search* III.2.vi: OC 1:442; LO 232).

Perception. Malebranche claims that "the strongest argument of all" is based on the mind's way of perceiving anything. It is certain, he states, that whenever we want to think about some particular thing, we first glance over all beings and then direct our attention to

---

91. Arnauld argues against Malebranche on the basis of this same premise. He claims that Malebranche has God accomplishing by complex and indirect means what can be done in a simpler fashion; see VFI 222-25.

and consider the object we wish to think about. This, it seems, is for Malebranche an evident phenomenological fact, although it also apparently follows from a premise he employs in his argument against the production theory, namely, that we can desire to think of a particular object only if we already have, at least in a confused and general fashion, a perception of it. I can willfully direct my attention only onto an object that is already present to my mind in some manner. Since at any given moment we can desire and will to think of any of an infinite number of beings, "it is certain that all beings are present to our mind." But only God can contain an infinity of beings. Thus all beings can be present to our mind, and the perception of any one of them is therefore possible, only because God is present to it and reveals these beings to us (*Search* III.2.vi: OC 1:440–41; LO 232).

There seems to be at least two ways of reading this argument. On one reading, Malebranche is arguing that the presence of God to our minds explains the simultaneous presence of an infinite number of ideas to our minds, ideas of which we have a "confused and general perception." We can then narrow our attention to focus on specific ideas with a clear and distinct perception (to apprehend an idea is to perceive the thing represented in the idea, which is why Malebranche, in the argument, speaks about how we perceive or think about "things").

A somewhat different, more ontological reading—and one that I believe would be preferred by Malebranche—is that God's presence to our minds explains not the simultaneous presence of an infinite number of particular ideas, but rather the presence of "all beings contained in one." God is "He who includes all things in the simplicity of His being." Malebranche says that the idea of God is the idea of infinite being, of being in general. This idea or perception of the infinite,[92] which is possible only by means of union with God, is necessarily prior to and explains the perception of finite beings. "In order for us to conceive of a finite being, something must necessarily be eliminated from this general notion of being, which consequently must come first. Thus the mind perceives noth-

---

92. Strictly speaking, for Malebranche we do not have an *idea* of God, of infinite being. Rather, our direct knowledge/perception of God is evidence that God himself is present to our minds; see *Search* III.2.vii, section 2.

ing except in the idea it has of the infinite." We thus have a general and confused perception of all beings in our perception of being, and particular ideas (ideas of finite beings) are always drawn (by an act of attention) on the ground of being in general, that is, God. "All these particular ideas are in fact but participations in the general idea of the infinite" (*Search* III.2.vi: OC 1:440–42; LO 232).[93]

Truth. In the "Elucidations" added to the *Search*, the nature of Malebranche's argumentation for the vision in God takes a more Augustinian turn.[94] For Augustine, what we see in God are eternal and immutable truths. Truth is by its nature eternal, changeless, and uncreated. Moreover, truth is higher than and common to many minds. Hence it can be nowhere but in the divine reason, in God himself (in Augustine's words, truth *is* God).[95] Malebranche similarly examines the character of truth and concludes that the ideas it is based on can only be those in God's understanding.

First, Malebranche claims, truth is universal. I have knowledge of certain mathematical and moral truths, and I am certain that others see the same truths I do. Moreover, I do not perceive these truths in the minds of other people, just as they do not perceive them in my mind. Hence there must be some universal Reason wherein the ideas on which these truths are based are found, a Reason that enlightens all finite intelligences. "For if the reason I consult were not the same that answers the Chinese, it is clear that I could not be as certain as I am that the Chinese see the same truths as I do" (*Search*, Elucidation X: OC 3:129; LO 613).

Second, truth is immutable. It is not determined or changed by my will or by the will of any other creature. In fact, it is even

93. See also *Search*, Elucidation X: OC 3:133–34; LO 616: "It seems clear to me that if we did not have within us the idea of the infinite, and if we did not see everything through the natural union of our soul with infinite and universal Reason, we would not be free to think about all things." Three different interpretations of the "perception" argument are given by McCracken, *Malebranche and British Philosophy*, pp. 66–67; Radner, *Malebranche*, pp. 53–55; and Connell, *The Vision in God*, pp. 215–26. Radner and Connell clearly reject the first interpretation, while McCracken accepts it.

94. Connell insists, in fact, that "the proof for the vision in God from the eternal truths represents a profoundly significant development of Malebranche's thought," leading to an altered conception of the doctrine; see *The Vision in God*, p. 316.

95. See St. Augustine, *On Free Will*, Book 2. See Robinet, *Système et existence dans l'oeuvre de Malebranche*, pp. 237–39.

independent of the will of the creator.[96] But truths are nothing but relations among ideas, and what makes them eternal and necessary is simply the immutability of the ideas themselves. And eternal and immutable ideas must be found in an eternal and immutable understanding.

> I am certain that the ideas of things are immutable, and that eternal laws and truths are necessary—it is impossible that they should not be as they are. Now, I see nothing in me of a necessary or immutable nature. . . . There might be minds unlike me, yet I am certain that there can be no mind that sees truths and laws different from those I see. . . . It must be concluded, then, that the reason consulted by all minds is an immutable and necessary Reason. (*Search*, Elucidation X: OC 3:130; LO 613–14)

Theodore, in the *Dialogues*, explains to Aristes that "if our ideas are eternal, immutable, necessary, you plainly see they can only exist in a nature which is immutable" (OC 12:45; D 39).

Finally, truth is infinite. That is, there is an inexhaustible store of truths deriving from the infinite number of ideas. In mathematics, for example, the human mind clearly conceives that there are an infinite number of intelligible triangles and other figures, from which can be derived an equally infinite number of truths. "In a word, the Reason man consults must be infinite because it cannot be exhausted, and because it always has an answer for whatever is asked of it" (*Search*, Elucidation X: OC 3:130–31; LO 614).

The conclusion from these considerations regarding truth is that the Reason in which all human minds participate is itself universal, immutable, and infinite. But then, "if it is true that the Reason in which all men participate is universal, that it is infinite, that it is necessary and immutable, then it is certainly not different from God's own reason." Malebranche's strategy here is straightforward.

---

96. Malebranche here explicitly rejects Descartes's doctrine of the creation by God of the eternal truths. "Surely, if eternal laws and truths depended on God, if they had been established by a free volition of the creator, in short, if the Reason we consult were not necessary and independent, it seems evident to me that there would no longer be any true science" (*Search*, Elucidation X: OC 3:132; LO 615). See also *Réponse à Régis*, OC 17-1:308. For Descartes, the eternal truths depend on the will of God, which is identical with his understanding. For Malebranche, eternal truths depend on God's understanding but not on his will.

Truth exhibits certain evident characteristics, characteristics that can be derived only from the ideas in which it is grounded. But these same characteristics of the ideas, in fact, belong exclusively to God. Thus the ideas themselves must be in God. The vision in God is the only possible explanation for our universal knowledge of eternal, immutable truths.

Skepticism

Behind all the philosophical and theological arguments for the vision in God, and behind all the appeals to authority—the Augustinian pedigree—there lies what is clearly a significant motivation for Malebranche's commitment to this doctrine. The vision in God represents for Malebranche the strongest and most effective counterskeptical strategy available.

Skepticism can take two general forms. One regards the possibility of knowledge of mathematical and other necessary truths, as well as of knowledge of the *nature* of the external material world; the other form regards the possibility of knowledge about *existence* (of a material world, of other minds, of God). Malebranche is quite clear that the vision in God is useless in countering doubts about knowledge of the existence of material bodies[97] and other minds (although he does think that it affords a very elegant—indeed "the loftiest and most beautiful"—proof of the existence of God). None of the ideas we apprehend in God tell us anything about the existence per se of the objects they present. Thus the doctrine of vision in God can be of no help in dealing with skepticism about existence.[98]

The situation is different, however, with respect to skepticism about knowledge of eternal truths and of the nature of the world. In

97. See for example *Search*, Elucidation VI.
98. Does this mean that Malebranche gives in to skepticism about empirical existential knowledge? I do not think so. Rather, the (sensory) evidence we have for the existence of bodies, while not demonstrative and basically nonepistemic, is still sufficient to cause us to believe that they exist. As Malebranche puts it, while absolute certainty regarding the existence of the material world is not attainable, we nonetheless "have no reason to doubt" of its existence; see *Dialogues* VI.7: OC 12:141; D 139.

these cases the vision in God short-circuits the skeptic's gambit and guarantees the reality of knowledge. In the domain of mathematical knowledge and knowledge of eternal laws (including moral principles), the doctrine ensures that the ideas and truths we know are objective and independent of all human minds, and refutes any form of relativism or subjectivism.

> It is necessary, as St. Augustine says in five hundred places, that ideas be eternal, immutable, necessary, and common to all minds in order for there certainly to be truth and falsehood, the just and the unjust, and eternal truths and laws; and that our minds be illuminated by these same ideas in consequence of their union with this universal Reason that contains all [these ideas] in its substance. (RLA, OC 9:933)

The issue here is one of justification: how can we be sure that what we are compelled to believe—what appears certain to us when we clearly and distinctly perceive ideas and their relations—is in fact objectively and universally true? How do we know that what we have is knowledge and not just subjective conviction? Malebranche insists that unless the ideas we apprehend are mind-independent realities accessible to all knowers in a universal Reason, there can be no warrant for believing that what is clearly and distinctly perceived is also the truth. In particular, to insist that, on the contrary, ideas are only modifications of the soul is to open the door for skepticism, since all we would ever be in cognitive contact with would be fleeting (*passagères*) personal, subjective phenomena, mere perceptions. "To maintain that ideas . . . are only perceptions or momentary particular modifications of the mind, is to establish Pyrrhonism and to make room for the belief that what is moral or immoral is not necessarily so, which is the most dangerous error of all" (*Search*, Elucidation X: OC 3:140; LO 620). If the mathematical and moral ideas we perceive were not independent of our minds and accessible to all in God, then there would be no grounds for distinguishing in an objective, nonrelative way what is truly moral from what is immoral. Nor could we have any lasting confidence in our mathematical reasonings. All we could ever justifiably assert is that what we clearly and distinctly perceive to be contained, for example, in the idea of a circle or triangle can be affirmed to be contained in that idea—or, in other words, that we perceive what we perceive—and not that the thing is in itself such as we perceive it to be.[99]

In the case of knowledge of the nature of the material world, skepticism is forestalled because the ideas we apprehend are necessarily representative of bodies in that world (on the assumption, of course, that a material world exists). The idea of extension in general, and the particular ideas of extended bodies that are present to our minds, also serve and direct God in the creation of bodies. Thus they cannot fail to reveal the nature of extended things as they really are (qua extended), since it is inconceivable that God should fail to create bodies in complete agreement with the ideas he uses as archetypes.

> It is certain that things conform to the idea[s] which God has of them. For since God created them, He can only have made them according to the idea which He has of them. Now according to the view I maintain, the idea that I have of extension in length, breadth, and depth is not a modification of my soul: it is eternal, immutable, necessary, shared by [*commune à*] God and all intelligences, and this idea is the model for the created extension from which all bodies are formed. I can thus truthfully affirm of created extension what I see contained in this uncreated idea. (RLA, OC 9:925–26)

On the other hand, if ideas were, as Arnauld and others insist, merely modifications of the soul, there would be no justification for believing that what they represent about material bodies in the world really characterizes those bodies.

> For if our ideas were only our perceptions, if our modes were representative, how could we know that things correspond to our ideas, since God does not think, and consequently does not act, according to our perceptions but according to his own; and therefore he did not create the world according to our perceptions but in accordance with his ideas, on its eternal model that he finds in his essence (*Search* IV.11: OC 2:99; LO 320)

Malebranche elsewhere notes that Arnauld attempts to ground human knowledge on the evident Cartesian principle that "whatever is contained in the clear idea of a thing can be truthfully affirmed of the thing." But, Malebranche continues, Arnauld can never justify this principle.

99. See *Conversations chrétiennes* III, OC 4:71; and RLA, OC 9:932–33.

> The Author [Arnauld] thus establishes [a] ridiculous Pyrrhonism,
> since his principle can, and with good reason, be contested. Your
> principle is true, we can reply, if the thing conforms to the idea you
> have of it; but it is precisely this that is not certain. A creature
> necessarily conforms to the idea [in the mind of] whoever created it.
> I agree. But the idea that you have of it, you say, is nothing but a
> modification of your soul. And this modification is certainly not the
> Creator's idea on the basis of which he formed this creature. It is thus
> in no way certain that the thing conforms to your idea, but only that
> you think it does. Thus, your view establishes Pyrrhonism, but mine
> destroys it. (RLA, OC 9:925)

Only the vision in God, he argues, can warrant the principle in
question.

Malebranche's counterskeptical strategy is clearly a Cartesian
one in its employment of a divine guarantee that our clear and
distinct ideas are objectively true, although it represents an unorthodox (but Augustinian) transformation of Descartes's own epistemological use of God. In the *Meditations* Descartes undertakes to
prove that what we are subjectively certain of, what we clearly and
distinctly perceive to be true, is in fact true. He establishes this by
showing that a benevolent God exists, and that this God—who
cannot be a deceiver—created us with all our reasoning faculties.
Thus when we use these faculties properly and give our assent only
to what we clearly and distinctly perceive, we arrive at the truth. In
this way skepticism is defeated, since lasting knowledge has been
shown to be possible.

> I have perceived that God exists, and at the same time, I have
> understood that everything else depends on him, and that he is no
> deceiver; and I have drawn the conclusion that everything which I
> clearly and distinctly perceive is of necessity true. . . . Thus, I per-
> ceive plainly that the certainty and truth of all knowledge depends
> uniquely on my knowledge of the true God, to such an extent that I
> was incapable of perfect knowledge about anything else until I knew
> him. (*Meditations* V: AT 7:70–71; CSM 2:49)

For Malebranche, God also provides the guarantee of the truth of
our clear and distinct ideas. But God does so not because he stands
behind our reasoning faculty, but rather because our clear and
distinct ideas are God's own. "Our" mathematical ideas truly pre-

sent mathematical reality, and "our" idea of extension represents bodies as they really are, because in the first case we are in direct acquaintance with mathematical essences themselves, and in the second case we are in direct acquaintance with the divine model on which bodies were created. And we are in direct acquaintance with them only because God chooses to reveal them to us. For both Descartes and Malebranche, then, the proposition that God exists and relates in a certain way to our cognitive processes is central to the epistemological project. Justifying our beliefs in the face of the skeptical challenge involves knowing that, in one way or another, they have a divine origin.

Problems

Malebranche's doctrine naturally raises a particular question about the ontological status of ideas, a question similar to those raised in earlier chapters. We have seen that Malebranche's theory of ideas fails to answer two questions: (1) In the Cartesian framework, everything is either a substance or a modification of a substance; Malebranche's ideas are neither. So in what sense are ideas, as Malebranche claims, something "real"? What is their ontological status? (2) If ideas are neither minds nor modifications of minds, if they are not "mental" at all,[100] in what sense are they of the right ontological type to be present to the mind? And how can we explain this presence if not in terms of the way in which a mode belongs to a substance?

A related question is suggested by the doctrine of vision in God: In what sense are ideas *in* God? God, Malebranche says, is a mind or is mindlike (or at least, that is how *we* are limited to thinking about him).[101] But we are also told that ideas are *not* modifications of the divine substance: "the Infinite Being is incapable of modifications" (*Search*, Elucidation X: OC 3:149; LO 625), which rules out considering them as God's perceptions or thoughts. Or does it?

---

100. As Jolley notes, Malebranche de-psychologizes ideas; see *The Light of the Soul*.
101. In the *Search* (III.2.ix), Malebranche cautions against thinking of God as a mind or spirit as *we* conceive of minds or spirits. Rather, "we should term God a mind not so much to show positively what He is as to indicate that he is not material" (OC 1:473; LO 251).

They are certainly treated by Malebranche as the contents of the divine understanding.

In several contexts Malebranche suggests that representative ideas are the divine essence itself, insofar as it is "participable" by creatures. "Ideas are in God," he says, and explicates this (with a reference to St. Thomas) by claiming that "the divine ideas are only the divine essence in so far as creatures can imitate it or participate in it" (*Dialogues*, Preface, OC 12:12). Elsewhere he explains that by the idea of extension, or the archetype of all possible worlds, he means simply "the divine substance, not in itself, but as it is participable by the corporeal creature" (TL I, OC 6:201).

Yet by making ideas identical in some manner with the divine substance—and this must be without turning the ideas themselves into substances—Malebranche avoids one problem at the price of opening himself up to a host of others. If intelligible extension simply *is* God insofar as his essence is representative of extended creatures, does this not imply that God himself is really extended? How can extended bodies "imitate" God, even in their imperfect way, unless God is extended?[102] And this would appear to lead directly to Spinozism.[103]

Ultimately, Malebranche has no satisfactory answer to any of these ontological questions regarding ideas. Perhaps Jolley is correct when he suggests that Malebranche would have been better off breaking openly with the framework of Cartesian ontology. By giving up both dualism and the substance/modification picture—supposedly exhaustive categories, neither of which can accommodate Malebranche's ideas—he could have, Jolley believes, rendered his system more consistent.[104]

---

102. Arnauld raises this question in regard to Malebranche's claim that the idea of extension is in God, which he sees as tantamount to admitting extension formally in God; see VFI, chapter 11, and *Défense*, pp. 512ff. See Ndiaye, "Le Concept d'étendue intelligible: influences gassendistes sur Malebranche d'après Arnauld."
103. The question of Malebranche's alleged Spinozism can be raised in a number of different ways; see Dortuous de Mairan's letters to Malebranche in OC 19. Ndiaye ("Le Concept d'etendue intelligible") argues that Arnauld sees in Malebranche the threat not of Spinozism but of Gassendism and materialism: the infinite intelligible extension is perceived by Arnauld as a real, infinite, uncreated, necessary, incorporeal space or extension, distinct from the finite, created extension of matter.
104. See Jolley, *The Light of the Soul*, pp. 78–80.

Régis raises another question about the vision in God, focusing on Malebranche's claim that we apprehend ideas in God because we are in union with God: "If the soul sees bodies in God, this can only be because God is united to the soul. Now we can ask what precisely is this union between God and the soul? It must necessarily resemble either the union of two bodies, the union of two minds, or the union of a body and a mind." It cannot resemble the union of two bodies, nor the union of a body and a mind. But neither can it resemble the union of two minds, since such a union consists in the *mutual* dependence of thoughts and volitions between the two minds. And it is certain that God's thoughts and volitions do not depend on ours. Régis concludes that the only kind of union possible here is a *causal* one, whereby the effect depends ontologically on the cause that created and conserves it, with all its successive modifications (ideas).[105]

These, of course, are not the only problems that Malebranche's doctrine raises. In fact, it was to become one of the most highly criticized (and ridiculed) philosophical theories in the seventeenth and eighteenth centuries. It eventually attained the status of an "ism" and became a label which critics attached to systems which they sought to belittle.[106] One reason for this, I believe, is that the mechanics and details of Malebranche's theory have been greatly misunderstood.[107]

---

105. *Système général*, "Metaphysique" II.1.xiv, vol. 1, p. 185. For Malebranche's response, see the *Réponse à Régis*, OC 17-1:294–95.

106. Berkeley's system, for example, is frequently labeled by its critics as a kind of "Malebrancheism"; see Bracken, *The Early Reception of Berkeley's Immaterialism*.

107. Another reason, which I do not examine, is surely Malebranche's extreme theologization of knowledge. I do not think that Malebranche takes skepticism about God's existence as seriously as Descartes does. He admires and defends Descartes's proofs of God's existence (Malebranche claims they are "demonstrative": *Search* IV.6: OC 2:55–57; LO 293; see also IV.11). But for his own part, Malebranche is often satisfied simply to say that "there is nothing that does not prove the existence of God" (*Search* IV.2: OC 2:19; LO 270–71), or that we perceive God "by a direct and immediate perception" (*Search* III.2.vii: OC 1:449–50; LO 237), which, to the skeptic, will look like question-begging. On the other hand, his "argument from Truth" for the vision in God is very similar to Augustine's argument from Truth for God's existence in *On Free Will* (Book 2), and Malebranche certainly intends it to be seen in this way. In this case, demonstrating the vision in God is tantamount to proving God's existence.

5

Ideas, Knowledge,
and Perception

The vision in God serves in two related capacities in Malebranche's system, basically corresponding to the two roles ideas are required to play. On the one hand, it constitutes a theory of knowledge; on the other hand, it is the foundation of his account of our perceptual acquaintance with the world.[1] However, Malebranche's failure to distinguish carefully and consistently between these two contexts (one gets the sense that he is vague precisely when he needs and wants to be vague) has led to some confusion among critics and interpreters of his epistemology. In this last chapter I will concentrate on the various ways in which Malebranche's theory of perceptual acquaintance has been and can be read, and will show that it is a much more philosophically sophisticated and capable account than it has been made out to be.

In order to analyze and understand this theory, one must first distinguish the role ideas play in knowledge from the role they play in perception proper. The vision in God as a theory of pure understanding is an essential ingredient in Malebranche's account of perception of the material world, but it is not by itself intended to be an explanation of perceptual acquaintance.

---

1. When the vision in God is first introduced in the *Search*, it is clearly intended to explain how we come to perceive material bodies. But in the "Elucidations" and some later writings, it comes more and more to look like a theory of our knowledge of abstract and general truths. For a discussion of this change in Malebranche's theory, see Connell, *The Vision in God*, chapters 7 and 8; and Robinet, *Système et existence dans l'oeuvre de Malebranche*, pp. 233–39.

Ideas and Knowledge

Malebranche thoroughly accepts the Platonic–Augustinian conception of knowledge as necessarily something permanent, as a cognitive state that is not fleeting and subject to change as mere opinion or sensation are. And like Plato and Augustine, Malebranche believes that if human knowledge is to be objective and immutable, then it must have as its proper objects things that are themselves objective and immutable. For Plato, the objects of knowledge (*episteme, noesis*) are Forms or Ideas, eternal and universal essences not subject to change as are particular created beings. In a sense, in the Augustinian model that Malebranche adopts, these Ideas are simply placed in the divine understanding.

The vision in God, then, is first and foremost a theory of knowledge and understanding, an account of our nonsensory cognition of universals and essences and of the necessary and eternal truths based on them (e.g., mathematical principles). Only divine ideas have the immutability, universality, and eternality to be the objects of knowledge; particular created objects do not and thus, strictly speaking, are not "known" at all. Knowing truths about triangles, squares, numbers, space, being, time, and so on involves grasping certain essences and the relations between them. And the mind grasps these essences and relations, as I have shown in chapter 3, by means of what Malebranche calls "pure intellections" or "pure perceptions," operations of the pure understanding (l'entendement pur).

Take the case, for example, of geometric knowledge of triangles. The idea of the right triangle is simply the logical concept of right triangle. It both spells out in perfect detail the properties essential to a right triangle, and allows one to determine what is incompatible with being a right triangle (e.g., having all angles equal). On this basis we can formulate certain propositions or know particular truths about right triangles (e.g., the Pythagorean theorem). If we compare this concept with the idea of the circle, we can also determine what propositions can truthfully be asserted about the relationship between these two figures, for example, a theorem about the ratio between the area of a right triangle and the area of the circle in which it is inscribed. All this takes place at a purely rational or intellectual level. The senses have no role whatsoever to play here. Divine ideas, as abstract essences, are simply not the kinds of things of which one can have sensory awareness.

What this means is that our "perception" of ideas in God is not sense perception at all. In the seventeenth century the term 'perception' is used quite broadly to cover any kind of mental apprehension: rational, sensory, imaginative, mnemonic, and so forth.[2] Thus we find Malebranche saying that "the soul can *perceive* [*appercevoir*] things in three ways, by the pure understanding, by the imagination, and by the senses" (*Search* I.4: OC 1:66; LO 16; emphasis added). Descartes likewise uses 'perception' to refer both to the clear and distinct conception of essences and to the sensory apprehension of bodies. Malebranche's use of the word 'perceive', then, as well as of other perceptual terms ('see', 'regard', etc.), to describe the mind's relationship to ideas in God should not mislead us. The vision in God is not by itself an account of perception in the narrow meaning of the term. We do not perceive ideas in the ordinary sense in which we perceive the sun, trees, and meadows. The mind's relationship to ideas in God is cognitive and purely rational or intellectual; it is not perceptual. The vision in God gives us access only to abstract knowledge, not to sensory objects, since the ideas are not visual but logical or conceptual entities. Put differently, the faculty by means of which we apprehend divine ideas is the pure understanding, not vision or any of the other senses. The mental activity is a conceiving, not a perceiving. Malebranche's critics are not always clear about this. Arnauld, for example, in his critique of Malebranche's theory of ideas, slips easily back and forth between the broad and narrow senses of 'perception'.

The distinction is elucidated by Malebranche's discussion of the two ways in which we can apprehend extension. On the one hand, we can perceive the apparent extension of a body with our senses. Vision can convey into the mind images of figure and size, although the information obtained thereby is necessarily imperfect and limited. Our sensory apprehension of figure and size is always relative

2. 'Perception' is used broadly to describe the cognitive activity of one faculty of the mind—intellect or understanding in general—in order to distinguish it from the volitional activity of the other faculty, the will; see *Search* I.1. See also Descartes, *Meditations* V: AT 7:56–57; CSM 2:39–40.

to our body and perspective, and we should not use it as a basis for judgments about the truth of extended bodies: "Our sight, then, does not represent extension to us as it is in itself, but only as it is in relation to our body . . . it is clear that we must not rely on the testimony of our eyes to make judgments about size" (*Search* I.6: OC 1:84–85; LO 28). On the other hand, and in stark contrast with this explicitly visual or sensory apprehension of the (relative) extension of a body, there is the clear and distinct "perception" of the idea of extension in general and of the particular idea of an extended figure. These inform us truthfully and in a nonrelative way about the actual properties of bodies and about the extension of this particular body. This "perception" is not visual at all, but conceptual.[3]

Idealism

A failure to grasp the difference in Malebranche between visual, sensory perception and the purely intellectual "perception" of ideas in God, and the resulting tendency to treat the latter in terms of the former, can lead one into a serious (although tempting) misreading both of the doctrine of the vision in God and of Malebranche's theory of perceptual acquaintance.

Malebranche appears, prima facie, to have constructed a rather visionary theory of perception which, paradoxically, precludes perceptual contact of any kind with the material world. He seems, that is, to have surrounded the perceiving mind with what Arnauld calls a "palace of ideas." Not only are ideas, according to this interpretation, the proper objects of knowledge or of our purely intellectual apprehension, but once they have become particularized through

3. Malebranche does, at one point, insist that there is no distinction between the idea of extension I think of and the idea of extension I see—that "there are not two kinds of extension, nor two kinds of ideas representing them: one sensible, the other intellectual" (*Dialogues* II.11–12: OC 12:60; D 55). But what he means here is that, strictly speaking, the only *idea* of extension is the purely "intelligible" (i.e., intellectual) one. To be sure, in the *Search* (I.6) he does say that by vision we obtain a "sensible idea" of the extension of a body. But he is clearly using 'idea' here in a loose sense, particularly since he has not yet introduced the technical, Malebranchian sense of the term.

accompanying sensations (or alternatively, once a segment or subset of the infinite intelligible extension has become particularized by means of sensation), ideas are the sole objects of *perception* as well. Because of their representative character (and because their veracity is guaranteed by their divine nature), it is possible by inference to determine what the material world created by God is (or would be) like. But one never perceives this world. One perceives only representative, intelligible entities, not material bodies.[4] In sense perception the finite perceiving mind is in contact only with a world of divine ideas "colored" by senation. God, as the "place of finite minds," contains the objects of perception, in addition to the objects of knowledge.

On this reading, Malebranche's epistemological realism regarding ideas is extended and transformed (and, I argue, distorted) into a perceptual idealism, an extreme version of the kind of theory Berkeley is so concerned to combat. This is the reading Arnauld often gives to the *Search*. He insists that Malebranche

> suddenly transports us to unknown lands, where men do not have any true knowledge of one another, nor of their own bodies, nor of the sun and the stars which God has created; but where each sees, instead of the men toward whom he turns his eyes, only intelligible men; instead of the sun and the stars which God has created, only an intelligible sun and intelligible stars; and, instead of the material spaces which are between us and the sun, only intelligible spaces. (VFI 227–228)

> After much philosophizing on the nature of these representative entities, after having marched them around everywhere and having been able to place them only in God, the only fruit that he gathers from all this is not an explanation of how we see material things, which alone was what was sought, but rather the conclusion that our mind is incapable of perceiving them, and that we live in a perpetual illusion in believing that we see the material things that God has created when we look at them, that is to say when we turn our eyes toward them; and meanwhile seeing, instead of them, only intelligible bodies. (VFI 229)

---

4. In a sense we would still perceive "external objects," since Malebranche's ideas are objects as external to the mind as material bodies are, although unlike bodies they can be "present" to the mind.

Malebranche, according to Arnauld, holds that the mind knows and sees nothing, nor is it able to see anything, besides the intelligible entities intimately united with it. In chapter 11 of VFI, Arnauld accuses Malebranche of completely cutting the mind off from the material world that God intends it to perceive and know and act upon. "It is material food and material drink that I need to take through a material mouth in order to maintain the body which I animate . . . and not intelligible food and intelligible drink, which my mind would see being received by an intelligible mouth in an intelligible body" (VFI 231).

Locke, in his "Examination," offers a similar interpretation of Malebranche's theory of ideas. According to Malebranche, Locke notes, "we see nothing but God and ideas; and it is impossible for us to know that there is anything else in the universe; for since we see and can see nothing but God and ideas, how can we know there is anything else which we neither do nor can see."[5] Locke clearly has sense perception in mind here, for he says later that on Malebranche's view "we can by no means see or perceive [bodies] by our senses."[6] One never sees the sun, or any external body, but only the idea of the sun.[7]

On the Arnauld–Locke reading, Malebranche's doctrine of vision in God is a rather extreme version of the so-called "double object" view, or what Lovejoy calls "epistemological dualism."[8] There are two kinds of objects—bodies and ideas—both of which are independent of the human mind. Bodies are material, ideas are intelligible and representative of bodies. While our body may "causally" interact with other bodies (and even this is reduced to a kind of divinely maintained correspondence, given Malebranche's occasionalism), the mind's cognitive and sensory operations are directed only toward ideas. We do not (sense) perceive or know bodies at all. Both Arnauld and Locke believe that this consequence of Malebranche's theory of ideas constitutes an obvious and effective *reductio* of his doctrine. Such an account renders the material

5. "Examination," p. 239.
6. Ibid., p. 253.
7. Ibid., p. 221. See also Reid, *Essays on the Intellectual Powers of Man*, Essay II, chapter 7. Reid calls Malebranche's system "visionary." Berkeley labels it an "enthusiasm"; see *Three Dialogues*, Second Dialogue.
8. See Lovejoy, *The Revolt Against Dualism*.

world created by God superfluous and his creative act incomprehensible, even irrational: why would God create a world and surround our bodies with other bodies and yet not allow the soul to perceive those bodies?[9] Moreover, the vision in God not only fails to explain that which it is intended to explain (viz., how we perceive material bodies), but even proves the *explanandum* impossible.[10]

Admittedly, Malebranche himself often seems to furnish ample evidence to support this reading of his theory of ideas and perception. Among the ideas we perceive in God is the idea of extension, and material bodies are parcels of extension; thus the idea of extension, insofar as it undergoes limitation and configuration, includes the ideas of all bodies. "We do not see in God only numbers, figures, and all the speculative truths, but also the practical truths, eternal laws, and the immutable rules of Morality . . . we also see bodies in God" (*Dialogues*, Preface: OC 12:17–18). As Malebranche puts it, "we see *all things* in God," even material and corruptible things. And the manner in which Malebranche occasionally describes the structure of perceptual acquaintance fosters the impression that Arnauld and Locke are reading him correctly.

> When we close our eyes, we have present to the mind an extension without limits. And in this immaterial extension, which occupies no more place than the mind which sees it [*qui la voit*], as I have proven elsewhere, we can discover all kinds of figures, just as one can form a sphere or a cube from a block of marble. This extension and these figures are *intelligibles*, because they are in no way sensed. But when we open our eyes, this same extension becomes sensible in respect to us, simply by the fact that it touches us more strongly, and that it produces in our soul an infinitude of entirely different perceptions, which we call colors. (*Dialogues*, Preface: OC 12:19)[11]

It is easy to read this passage and others like it and conclude that in both conception and sense perception the only object before the mind is the idea of extension in God; that in conception we apprehend the idea by a purely intellectual act; and that in sense perception we perceive that idea (in the ordinary sense of 'perceive', i.e.,

9. See VFI 231–32; "Examination," 221.
10. See VFI 229; "Examination," 253.
11. See also *Entretiens sur la mort* II, OC 13:407–8.

with our senses). In fact, as we have seen, Malebranche occasionally claims that color sensation is simply a perception by means of which we sensibly perceive intelligible extension: "For, in fact, the perception of the soul in someone who sees or who feels an arm is only the perception, which is called color or pain, of the extension which composes the arm; that is, the immediate and direct perception of the ideal extension of the arm" (RLA, OC 9:961–62).

In and around the *Search* itself, Malebranche's language is very open to an idealist reading. He notes that "the material world we animate is not the one we see [*voyons*] when we look at [*regardons*] it, i.e., when we turn the body's eyes toward it. The body we see is an intelligible body and there are intelligible spaces between this intelligible body and the intelligible sun we see [*voyons*], just as there are material spaces between our body and the sun we look at [*regardons*]" (*Search*, Elucidation VI: OC 3:61; LO 572–73). "The objects we immediately see [*voit*] are very different from those we see externally, or rather from those we think we see or look at [*regarde*]; for in one sense it is true that we do not see these latter" (*Search* IV.11.iii: OC 2:99; LO 320). In the Tenth Elucidation Malebranche states that "the soul can only see [*l'ame ne peut voir que*] the sun to which it is immediately joined, only that sun that like it occupies no place" (OC 3:149; LO 625). In his first response to Arnauld, he speaks of the intelligible extension in God as "that which I see [*voi*] immediately and directly when I look at [*regarde*] bodies" (*Réponse*, OC 6:61). And in the *Conversations chrétiennes* (1677), Eraste insists that "when I look at [*regarde*] the stars, I see [*vois*] the stars; when I look at the stars of the material world, when I turn my body's eyes toward the sky, my mind sees the stars of the intelligible world" (OC 4:62).

In the later *Dialogues on Metaphysics* (1688), the same deliberately precise scheme seems to be at work: divine ideas appear to be the sole objects of sense perception as well as of intellection, with the material world beyond our sensory grasp. Theodore insists in his usual colorful way that "there is as much difference between the desk which I do see and the desk which you think you see as there is between your mind and body . . . while our bodies walk in a corporeal world, our minds for their part are unceasingly transported into an intelligible world which affects them and which thereby becomes sensible to them" (I.4–5: OC 12:36; D 29). Lest Aristes miss his point, he emphasizes that "it is in this [intelligible] world that we exist and live, though the body we animate lives and walks in another. It is this intelligible world which we contemplate, which we admire, which we sense. But the world we look at [*le monde que nous regardons*], or which we consider when we turn our heads on all sides, is simply matter, which is invisible in itself and which possesses nothing of all those beauties that we sense and admire when we look at it" (I.5: OC 12:38; D 31).

The distinction Malebranche is working with here rests on the difference between *voir*, to see or to perceive, and *regarder*, to look at or to turn one's eyes toward. In all the passages above, *voir* is used only with respect to intelligible entities, representative ideas. *Regarder*, on the other hand, always appears in conjunction with material bodies. Hence it seems as though the only objects of perception are ideas, that only intelligible entities are ever seen or perceived. One merely turns one's (bodily) attention toward, or looks at, bodies themselves. Those who believe that they are in perceptual contact of any kind with the external material world are mistaken; what is actually seen differs essentially from that toward which the eyes are turned ("Les corps qu'on voit ne sont nullement ceux qu'on regarde"). In other words, it would appear that ideas are perceived *instead of* bodies.

A Representative Theory

In spite of picturesque passages such as those just cited, it is clear that Malebranche does not intend to assert that there is no perception whatsoever of material things. In fact, there are good reasons for rejecting the Arnauld–Locke reading as simply a caricature and misinterpretation of Malebranche's theory. To be sure, Malebranche does allow Theodore his excursions into rhetorical excess for the purposes of laying down some essential points for the incredulous Aristes. But he also hints that we should not take these expressions of Malebranchian zeal too literally. We are told, for example, that while Theodore "upholds the side of truth," nevertheless "he overdoes things a bit [*il outre un peu les choses*]" (*Dialogues* VII.3: OC 12:152; D 149). Theodore himself admits that

"I exaggerate my way of speaking a bit so that it will impress you and you will not again forget what I tell you" (VII.1: OC 12:149; D 147). We should keep this in mind when we listen to his talk about the body living and walking in a world different from that in which the mind resides. Malebranche's vision in God doctrine is indeed a novelty in the seventeenth century (even if it does have fine ancestral roots in Augustine), and it would not be surprising if he likewise resorts in the *Search* to extreme expressions in order to convey to the reader the distinctions he needs.

In addition to this somewhat rhetorical evidence against the Arnauld–Locke reading, there is evidence of a more philosophical nature that Malebranche does not intend to preclude perceptual contact with the material world. In most contexts Malebranche is in fact emphatic that we *do* perceive bodies, but not in themselves ("non en eux-mêmes"). The passages just quoted need to be taken in conjunction with a distinction that, for Malebranche, parallels and works upon his usage of *voir* and *regarder*—the distinction, that is, between direct and indirect objects of perception. Malebranche often refers to ideas as the *direct* objects of perception and material bodies as the *indirect* objects of perception. Thus when Arnauld insists that on Malebranche's account we only look at (regarder) bodies and therefore do not perceive or see (voir) them at all, Malebranche sternly replies that we *do* see them, just not in themselves (*Réponse*, OC 6:101). He then distinguishes, for Arnauld's better comprehension, between "l'objet immédiat et direct" of the mind in perception, and the indirectly perceived "objet extérieur que l'idée représente (RLA, OC 9:910-11). In the *Search* he says that perception involves "two kinds of beings: those our soul sees immediately, and those it knows only by means of [*par le moyen de*] the former" (I.14.ii: OC 1:159; LO 69). Thus, although one always perceives directly (voir) ideas, and only looks at (regarder) external bodies, bodies are still, in perception, the mind's indirect and ultimate objects. This is accomplished by means of the representative character of ideas, which allows them to mediate between the mind of the perceiver and the material world. Malebranche tells Régis:

> With respect to my ideas, I believe that they only directly represent themselves, and that I only directly and immediately see what they contain. . . . But if God has created some being which corresponds to

my idea as to its archetype, I can say that my idea represents this being, and that in seeing [*voyant*] the idea directly I see [*voi*] it indirectly. (*Réponse à Régis*, OC 17-1:303)[12]

Note that here we see or perceive (voir) both ideas and bodies, although we perceive ideas directly and bodies only indirectly, by perceiving representative ideas.

Malebranche's use of the terms 'direct' and 'indirect' to characterize objects of perception appears to commit him to a representative theory of perception. His account, interpreted in such a way, would look something like this: Upon the presence of a material body to (or its contact with) the perceiver's body, God reveals to the perceiver's mind the idea (or a part of the infinite intelligible extension) representing that body, "colored" (or made particular) by the sensations God produces in the mind on the same occasion. This idea/ sensation complex is what is directly perceived by the mind, when the body's senses are turned toward a material body. (Or alternatively, the idea is itself "sensed" by the mind, since Malebranche sometimes speaks of color sensations as *perceptions* by which we apprehend intelligible extension.) Yet the material body is still "indirectly" perceived. The direct perceptual relationship (rapport direct) between the mind and a representative idea grounds and mediates an indirect perceptual relationship to *l'objet extérieur*.[13] And although Malebranche is rather vague on just how this indirect perceptual acquaintance is achieved, on the inferential (or other cognitive) processes that take place in the presence of a representative idea, he *is* clear in stating that an object indirectly perceived is still an object perceived.[14] In other words, while ideas, in nonreflec-

---

12. Instances of the phrase *perception directe* are more numerous in Malebranche's works than instances of *perception indirecte*; but see RLA, OC 9:962.
13. See RLA, OC 9:915.
14. In one context, Malebranche suggests that what mediates between the immediately perceived idea and the mediately perceived object (or alternatively, what is added to immediate perception to generate mediate perception) is a *judgment* of some kind: "There are two kinds of beings, those our soul sees immediately, and those it knows only by means of the former. For example, when I see the sun rise, I first perceive what I see immediately, and because I perceive this only because there is something outside me that produces certain motions in my eyes and brain, I judge that this first sun, which is in my soul, is external to me and that it exists" (*Search* I.14: OC 1:159; LO 69).

tive veridical perception, are claimed to be the direct and immediate objects of the mind, they are not claimed to be the *ultimate* objects of perception: "Bodies are seen [*on voit les corps*], but not in themselves immediately and directly. . . . It is not wrong to believe that they are seen; it is only wrong to believe that they are seen directly and in themselves: for they are often seen, but only indirectly" (RLA, OC 9:959). If the perception of a material body involves inference from ideal representative entities immediately perceived and "intimately united to our mind," it remains nonetheless the perception of a material body. On Malebranche's view, the (ultimate) object of perception is that which the idea represents, not the idea itself ("L'esprit apperçoit ce qui lui est representé": RLA, OC 9:920).

This representative or indirect realist reading of Malebranche not only has the virtue of avoiding the clearly distorted idealist picture that Arnauld and Locke draw of Malebranche's account of perceptual acquaintance,[15] but also has its own intrinsic plausibility: it makes good sense of much of what Malebranche says about ideas and perception. Many of his remarks do sound like what one would expect someone who holds a representative theory of perception to say: we directly perceive ideal entities and, by this means, indirectly perceive bodies. In fact, this is the interpretation favored by almost all recent commentators on Malebranche.[16] And yet, for reasons

15. It may be that Arnauld and Locke, in their interpretation, are not distorting Malebranche's doctrine, but rather are drawing attention to what they take to be the extreme idealist and skeptical consequences of such a representative theory.
16. See Church, *A Study in the Philosophy of Malebranche*, pp. 226–30; Connell, *The Vision in God*, p. 164; Gaonach, *La Théorie des idées dans la philosophie de Malebranche*; Gueroult, *Malebranche*, vol. 1, pp. 88–89; Jolley, *The Light of the Soul*, chapter 5; Lennon, "Philosophical Commentary," LO 795–96; Lovejoy, "Representative Ideas in Malebranche and Arnauld"; Matthews, "Locke, Malebranche, and the Representative Theory"; McRae, "'Idea' as a Philosophical Term in the Seventeenth Century"; Radner, *Malebranche*, pp. 13–14; and Rodis-Lewis, *Nicolas Malebranche*.
   Alquié (*Le Cartésianisme de Malebranche*, pp. 208–12) and Robinet *Système et existence dans l'oeuvre de Malebranche*, pp. 259–72) see Malebranche as moving away from the notion of the mind visually attending to inert ideas toward a theory of "efficacious ideas," whereby God's ideas are transformed from objects of perception into agents (via God) bringing about perception by modifying the mind (see chapter 3 in this study). Alquié thus suggests that Malebranche's doctrine ultimately substitutes "une vision par Dieu" for "une vision dans Dieu," and that "la considération de

which shall become clear, I do not think it is the correct interpretation of Malebranche's doctrine. It is in fact less satisfactory overall than the interpretation I offer in the next section. Its shortcomings become particularly evident when one tries to fill in the details of the representative theory.

All representative theories of perception involve the claim that whenever we perceive a material body (and in the illusory case, when we only *seem* to perceive a material body), we directly and immediately apprehend a nonmaterial object (an idea, sense datum, percept, etc.) which corresponds to (represents, resembles) the material body, and that *because* of this direct and immediate apprehension of the representative object, we perceive the body itself, but only mediately and indirectly. Or as it is sometimes expressed, in all cases we perceive bodies *by means of* perceiving ideas or sense data. Is this the theory Malebranche holds?

Partisans of the representative theory usually refer, in their less precise moments, simply to "direct" and "indirect" perception and to "direct" and "indirect" objects of perception. This suggests that when they claim we perceive ideas "directly" and bodies "indirectly," the verb 'perceive' (and the corresponding noun 'perception') is to be understood univocally and qualified as either "direct" or "indirect." And Malebranche certainly appears, on occasion, to treat the term this way: "I can say that my idea represents this being, and that in seeing [*voyant*] the idea directly I see [*voi*] it [the body] indirectly" (*Réponse à Régis*, OC 17-1:303). But first, I do not see that much sense can be made of the representative theory construed in this way. Direct perception cannot be only nominally different from indirect perception, since it necessarily involves a "face-to-face" confrontation with its object that indirect perception necessarily does not. Second, it is not clear that any representationalist in fact ever intends 'perception' to be understood univocally in the direct and indirect cases. Malebranche certainly does not think

---

la causalité et de l'efficace de l'idée remplace alors celle de son caractère visible" (p. 209). Yet both continue to read Malebranche's account as a representative theory. For Robinet, it remains an account according to which "l'esprit ne perçoit que [l'objet] ideal" (p. 274).

As far as I can tell, the only commentator who departs from a straightforward representationalist reading is Rome, *The Philosophy of Malebranche*.

that one "perceives" ideas in the *same* sense that one perceives bodies. Whatever the "perception" of ideas is, it is not sense perception, which *is* our mode of apprehending existing material bodies.[17] Representationalists, then, believe that there is an equivocation regarding the term 'perceive', depending upon whether it is used to refer to the apprehension of the representative object or to the apprehension of the material body. G. E. Moore, for example, distinguishes between "directly see" and the "common sense view of see"[18]; C. D. Broad similarly discriminates between, on the one hand, "direct awareness" or "sensing," and on the other hand, "sense perception" or "perceiving."[19] 'Directly see', 'direct awareness', and 'sensing' are properly used of sense data, and 'sense perception' and 'perception' of material objects. As Broad notes, "words like 'seeing'. . . are ambiguous. They stand sometimes for acts of sensing, whose objects are sensa, and sometimes for acts of perceiving, whose objects are supposed to be bits of matter and their sensible qualities."[20] Thus on the representative view, the *perception* of a material object involves as a constituent the direct awareness or sensing of an idea/sense-datum/and so forth, along with some element of interpretation or judgment or inference which carries one beyond the intermediary.

It might appear that this kind of theory is precisely what Malebranche has in mind. He says that ideas are directly perceived and material bodies are indirectly perceived. Moreover, Malebranche occasionally describes the kind of direct awareness we have of ideas in perception as a *sensing*. In chapter 3 I have shown that the difference between conception and perception, at least as Malebranche describes it in some contexts, is that while in conception a finite subset of intelligible extension (the idea of an extended body) is apprehended by a *perception pure*, in perception we apprehend a

17. This is clear from the fact the Malebranche constantly says that the sense perception of bodies *includes* (but is not *of*) ideas; see *Search* III.2.vi: OC 1:445; LO 234. A contrary reading is offered by some commentators, who say that to (sense) perceive the idea directly is to (sense) perceive the body indirectly; see for example Radner, who consistently insists that for Malebranche we see or perceive ideas *instead of* bodies (*Malebranche*, pp. 13–14, 106–7).
18. Moore, "Visual Sense-Data."
19. Broad, "The Theory of Sensa."
20. "The Theory of Sensa," p. 97.

part of the intelligible extension by a sensation or *perception sensible* such as color. In the *Conversations chrétiennes*, Malebranche describes this by saying that in sense perception "the mind sees or senses [*voit ou sent*]" the idea of extension (III: OC 4:75–76). Finally, one of Malebranche's arguments for ideas is strikingly similar to the argument from hallucination that sense-data theorists offer for their brand of indirect realism. In cases of hallucination and less extreme illusion, where one seems to, but in fact does not, perceive a material body, some (ideal) object still must be apprehended by the mind to account for the qualitative character of the perceptual experience, to explain why one seems to perceive an *x* instead of a *y*.[21] The only differences would be that for most recent representative theories, the directly apprehended object is mental and private, while for Malebranche it is a mind-independent and publicly accessible idea.[22]

Thus it is very tempting to read Malebranche's account of perceptual acquaintance as a representative theory. On the whole, it is a plausible interpretation of the way in which ideas function in the perception of material bodies. Many passages and elements in Malebranche readily lend themselves to such a reading—in fact, some appear to be incomprehensible on any other reading. Yet ultimately I believe this interpretation fails in at least one very crucial respect: it misconstrues the nature of representative ideas for Malebranche. In order for ideas to do the kind of work they would have to do in a representative theory, they cannot be anything but visual-like, sensible data (like sense data), and our apprehension of them cannot be anything but visual-like or perceptual. Ideas would, in other words, have to be like the entities all other representative theories employ to mediate our perceptual consciousness of bodies, and our awareness of them would have to be like the "direct awareness" those theories employ to explain our apprehension of their intermediary entities.

Now Malebranche's ideas necessarily cannot be like sense data in respect to presenting secondary qualities like color and heat, since

---

21. Lennon picks up on the apparent similarity in argumentation: "Representationalists have often argued, as did Malebranche, from examples of existential error like hallucination" ("Philosophical Commentary," LO 796).
22. See Jolley, *The Light of the Soul*, pp. 85–88, for a comparison of the standard and the Malebranchian versions of the representative theory.

ideas present only quantitative properties. But this representation-alist interpretation would still have Malebranchian ideas be picture-like images which we sense or of which we are sensibly "directly aware." Ideas of extension would pictorially present colorless, visual figures (triangles, squares, circles) which, when "filled in" by colors, become the ideas of particular material bodies. In the perception of the sun, we would be directly aware of an immaterial picture image of a circular figure (the idea) rendered yellow (by sensation). I do not see any other way of understanding Malebranche's account, if it is read as a representative theory. But we then lose the distinguishing and essential feature of Malebranche's ideas, for, as I have shown in chapter 2, they are not visual-like at all—they are logical or conceptual in nature. A Malebranchian idea does not present its content as a pictorial image presents its content (nor, therefore, as a sense datum presents its content). Thus any interpretation of Malebranche's account of perception that involves treating ideas as visual-like data, and our apprehension of them as perceptual,[23] simply does not do justice to his theory of ideas. If we want to preserve ideas as abstract logical or conceptual entities, as essences or definitions—and I believe that doing so is of the utmost importance in understanding Malebranche's system, particularly in comprehending the vision in God as a theory of knowledge—then we must reject the claim that Malebranche holds a representative theory of perception.

Ideas and Perception

Malebranche's language in describing the role of ideas in perception is not always so picturesque and visionary as it is in the passages which appear to support the idealist reading (and he admits to using "extreme" expressions for rhetorical purposes). In fact, very often Malebranche does not speak of ideas as objects of perception at all, and the visual model that he occasionally employs to describe the relationship between the mind and ideas gives way to a different

---

23. For example, Lennon claims that for Malebranche "to *directly* perceive an idea is already to *indirectly* perceive a physical object" ("Philosophical Commentary," LO 795). Jolley similarly insists that Malebranche holds that "directly we perceive ideas, and indirectly we perceive the physical world" (*The Light of the Soul*, p. 85).

picture. On this basis it is possible to construct a more accurate, intelligible, and consistent reading of Malebranche's theory than the idealist or representationalist readings. His considered account of perceptual acquaintance is not an idealism of the sort Arnauld and Locke attribute to him; nor is it a representative theory, as most recent commentators insist. For Malebranche, we perceive (in the ordinary sense of the term) external, material bodies such as trees, chairs, rocks, and the sun. To be sure, ideas play an essential role in perception, and the mind still "perceives" ideas in the broad seventeenth-century sense of the term, by means of a purely intellectual grasp. But we can now dispense with the readings of Malebranche according to which he surrounds the mind with an impenetrable veil of ideas.

Let us first look at some passages that are important not just for what they say, but also for what they do not say. Malebranche, in the midst of his central argument for the vision in God, remarks in the *Search* (III.2.vi) that

> it might be said that we do not so much see [*voit*] the ideas of things as the things themselves [*les choses mêmes*] that are represented by ideas, for when we see a square, for example, we do not say that we see the idea of the square, which is joined to the mind, but *only* [*seulement*] the square that is external to it. (OC 1:439; LO 231; emphasis added)[24]

It is crucial to note carefully his language here. Can one read him as saying once again that, although one perceives or sees only ideas, one still looks at or turns one's attention toward the material body? Or that ultimately it *is* the material body which one perceives, but only indirectly by means of perceiving an idea? No. The verb he uses in the passage with regard to *les choses*, the things themselves, is 'see [*voir*]', not 'look at [*regarder*]'. And, as my emphasis indicates, the word 'see' or *voir* is properly used *only* with respect to external bodies. We see material things, bodies, not ideas.

In his discussion of the understanding in *Search* I.1.i, Malebranche asserts that "it is the same thing for the soul to perceive [*appercevoir*] an object as to receive the idea that represents the object" (OC 1:43; LO 3). In response to Arnauld, he notes that

24. Connell, referring to this passage, admits that "Malebranche, at least in the *Recherche*, is not above using the language of direct realism"; see *The Vision in God*, pp. 164–65.

"it is evident that it is by means of perceptions that objects are perceived [*apperçus*]; but they are perceived only because they are rendered present to the mind by the ideas which represent them and which are the necessary conditions for the perception we have of them" (RLA, OC 9:923). Taking issue with Arnauld's accusation that on his view we see only God and not at all the creatures he has surrounded us with, Malebranche insists that "we certainly do see [*voit*] the created beings, when their ideas are present to our minds" (*Réponse*, OC 6:135).

There is evident here and in other contexts an important difference from the passages cited earlier in Malebranche's language in his description of the role ideas play in perception. Consider the following well-known passage from *Search* III.2.i:

> I think everyone agrees that we do not perceive objects external to us by themselves. We see the sun, the stars, and an infinity of objects external to us; and it is not likely that the soul should leave the body to stroll about the heavens, as it were, in order to behold all these objects. Thus, it does not see them by themselves, and our mind's immediate object when it sees the sun, for example, is not the sun, but something that is intimately united to our soul, and this is what I call an *idea*. Thus, by the word *idea*, I mean here nothing other than the immediate object, or *the object closest to the mind, when it perceives something* [i.e., that which affects and modifies the mind with *the perception it has of an object*.] It should be carefully noted that *for the mind to perceive an object*, it is absolutely necessary for the idea of that object to be actually present to it. (OC 1:413; LO 217; emphases added. The bracketed phrase was added in the fifth (1700) edition.)

There are two things to be noted about all these passages. First, nowhere are the words 'see' or 'perceive' used with respect to anything other than external material things. We see or perceive bodies (or "objects"), not the ideas of bodies. I do not believe that Malebranche is simply speaking loosely here; he is not just drawing broad strokes that will be filled in later by the *voir/regarder* distinction. On the contrary, as the passage from *Search* III.2.vi suggests, this is how the terms are to be used strictly and properly. Moreover, the words 'see [*voir*]', 'perceive [*appercevoir*]' and 'perception', used to describe only the mind's relationship to material things, are never qualified as "indirect."

Second, the visual or perceptual model that Malebranche elsewhere employs to describe the mind's relationship to ideas is not present here. Thus while ideas are still spoken of as "the immediate object[s] of the mind," this phrase is given a somewhat different, almost spatial meaning in the last passage. To be the immediate object of the mind is to be "the object closest [*le plus proche*] to the mind." We thus see Malebranche referring to entities immediately in the mind, entities the presence of which to the mind allows the mind to perceive material things external to itself: "We see beings [*les êtres*] because God wills that what in Him represent[s] them should be revealed to us" (*Search* III.2.vi: OC 1:439; LO 231).

What Malebranche is claiming in these passages is that the "presence" of an intelligible representative entity—an idea—to the mind is a necessary condition for the perception of a material body. But such an entity is not itself the object of perception (although it is the object of an act of intellection). In other words, every *perception* of a material body must include some intelligible or cognitive component. Otherwise, all that would be taking place is mere sensory awareness. Before laying out in detail what I take to be Malebranche's theory, however, I must make some brief general remarks on the nature of perception.

There are certain facts about perception—or more particularly, our perceptual acquaintance with the material world—that any theory of perception must take into account. For the sake of labeling, I refer to them as 'discrimination', 'recognition', and 'anticipation' or 'expectation'.

Discrimination. When I perceive an object (or a collection of objects), I identify it as a unity and as discrete from other objects in the environment or in my visual field. I perceive a chair, and immediately discriminate between that chair and the desk in front of it and the floor below it. This is done by means of shape—the object begins and ends with its figural or geometrical outline. Boundaries between objects, and thus my discrimination of them, are a function of my grasp of their different shapes.[25]

Recognition. The perception of an object includes an element of recognition of that object. This need not, of course, involve a fully

---

25. It is plausible to suggest that discrimination of different shapes is itself a function of color: for example, I could not discriminate the shape of the chair from the shape of the table, if each did not have a color to make its shape visible, discrete, and identifiable. This, at least, is a point Malebranche makes; see *Réponse*, OC 6:61. Still, even if color makes such discrimination possible, it is still ultimately done on the basis of shape.

articulated knowledge of what the object is. I can perceive a tree and not know what species of tree it is, just as I can see a person and not recognize who that person is. But even in these cases there are certain things about the object I do recognize and grasp. I perceive that it is a tree, and I perceive that it is a human being walking toward me. Or at an even lower level, I perceive that something is tree- or human-shaped. For the sake of argument we can even dispense with all generic labels. What we then perceive is that something *x* is shaped in such and such a manner, without recognizing what kind of thing it is or what kind of shape it has. Even in this extreme case, I grasp in perception the geometrical nature of the object , even if I cannot label it. Likewise when I perceive *x*, I notice that it has the color it has, even if I cannot identify that color as "chartreuse." And this holds for other properties of objects. This very minimal recognition, that something is shaped (or colored, etc.) in such and such a manner (or alternately, that it has the shape it does), nevertheless constitutes quite a significant cognitive step and represents perhaps the most important difference between perceptual awareness and mere sensing.

Anticipation. The actual perceptual awareness of an object, while it is an event limited to the present (I can perceive only objects actually present to me and to which I am now attending), nonetheless involves implicit reference to the future in the form of anticipated appearances. When I perceive a square object, for example, I am at any given moment really apprehending only one partial aspect of it, perhaps a side face-on. But if I perceive that it is a square (and this would be the kind of recognition just discussed), then I also expect certain perceptual appearances to be forthcoming as I change my vantage point. When I perceive a human being from the front, I do so with the implicit belief that were I to walk around the person I would have such and such appearances. Of course such anticipations may remain unfulfilled.

The point of this discussion is that perception is essentially a cognitive activity; this is what distinguishes it from mere sensation. Perception is more than a bare sensory reaction to one's environment, more than the passive reception of stimuli and raw sensuous data. At the very least, perception includes some kind of judgment or belief. To perceive *x* involves grasping that it is discrete from other objects surrounding it and has the shape, color, size, and so on, that it has (or at least appears to have), while at the same time anticipating further perceptions of the same object. Another way of putting all this is to say that perception is fundamentally epistemic.[26]

One means of accounting for this cognitive aspect of perception, for the beliefs necessarily accompanying any perceptual experience, is by way of concepts. On this view, perception involves bringing incoming sensory data under concepts. The application of concepts is what explains, for example, the recognitional component ("that x is cube-shaped") and whatever expectations of forthcoming perceptions are present (presumably, the concept of cube would inform one as to what lies beyond the single side one is currently apprehending). Without this conceptual element, all that would be taking place is sensation.[27] Such concepts might themselves be the product of earlier perceptual experiences, empirically acquired notions subject to modification over time, or some might be innate in the mind, part of its original constitution (Malebranche rejects both these options).

Thomas Reid incorporates this theory of concept-informed perception in his *Essays on the Intellectual Powers of Man* (1785). Reid notes that in perception proper, something in addition to a sensory impression is present: "It is impossible to perceive an object without having some notion or conception of that which we perceive. We may indeed conceive an object which we do not perceive; but when we perceive the object, we must have some conception of it at the same time."[28] Now it may make perfect sense to say that, on this view, concepts "mediate" perception, and perhaps even that, with concepts, our perception of material bodies is thus mediate and indirect. This is in fact what Malebranche is claiming. But to say that perception is *informed* by concepts in the manner just discussed is not per se to commit oneself to a representative theory of

---

26. See Heil, *Perception and Cognition*, chapter 4. For various discussions of the epistemic nature of perception, see also Armstrong, *Belief, Truth, and Knowledge*; Pitcher, *A Theory of Perception*; and Dretske, *Seeing and Knowing*.

27. See Heil, who insists that "[p]erception is cognitive. . . . It must include what I have elected to call . . . the application of concepts. It may well be the presence (or absence) of this conceptual dimension that distinguishes the categories of perception and sensation" (*Perception and Cognition*, p. 42).

28. Essay II, chapter 5, p. 112.

perception or indirect realism. In the meaning of the phrase as it is ordinarily understood by philosophers, objects are, on the account under consideration, still "directly perceived." If concepts are required in perception, it does not follow that these concepts are directly apprehended, immaterial objects standing between perceivers and external bodies.[29]

I now return to Malebranche. I argue that something like the above account, where perception is essentially cognitive and involves the use of concepts, is precisely what Malebranche has in mind, with the novel modification that the concepts that inform perception are not abstracted from particulars. In fact, these concepts are not empirically acquired at all, nor are they innate in the mind. Rather, they are the ideas in the divine understanding that God reveals to finite minds.

When Arnauld accuses Malebranche of cutting us off perceptually from the material world, Malebranche responds by insisting that he never denied that we perceive material bodies; in fact, it is his project to show how we do so.[30] We *do* perceive bodies, he insists, only not by themselves (en eux-mêmes). And what he means by this is that we cannot perceive bodies without ideas, that an immaterial representative entity—a concept—distinct from the material body (and from the perceiver's mind) is required to render that body intelligible to the mind: "In order for the mind to perceive an object, it is absolutely necessary for the idea of that object to be actually present to it" (*Réponse*, OC 6:94). In the *Search* he says that "[w]hen we perceive something sensible, two things are found in our perception: *sensation* and pure *idea*" (III.2.vi: OC 1:445; LO 234). One cannot perceive an external material body without an idea. But this is not to say that the idea is perceived *instead of* the body itself. Rather, it is only to claim that in order for the activity in question to be the *perception* of a material body, as opposed to being just a *sensing* of it, an idea representing the essence of the object qua extended body must be present to the mind. That is, there must be some conceptual element involved.

29. See Heil, *Perception and Cognition*, pp. 100–102.
30. "J'ai dit qu'on voyait les corps: j'ai voulu expliquer cette vérité" (*Réponse*, OC 6:101).

Thus for Malebranche ideas are "present" in perception without themselves being the direct objects of perception. When he claims that we "perceive" ideas, he does not have in mind 'perception' in the ordinary sense of the term. Ideas are apprehended by a purely intellectual intuition. They are logical concepts, essences—not visual data. Our "perception" of them *must* be of a purely intellectual nature, and cannot be the kind of sensory "direct awareness" that sense data theorists claim for their mental intermediaries. It follows, then, that included within and partly constitutive of the perceptual awareness of a material body is the intellectual apprehension of an idea. But note that it is the *body* that is perceived.[31]

Another way of considering this is to compare conception, sensation, and perception. In conception, Malebranche claims, the mind apprehends an idea by means of an act of the understanding, a "pure intuition" free of any sensory component. In sensation a mental event of a purely sensuous nature, devoid of any understanding, is occasioned in the mind by the external, material world affecting the body. What happens in perception is that both these elements—a conceiving and a sensing, each of which can otherwise occur by itself—are present. The conceiving introduces into sense perception those clear and distinct elements that distinguish it from mere sensing. In particular, the conceiving informs the perceptual experience with a knowledge of the properties of the body qua extended. The sensation, on the other hand, signals the body's existence and introduces sensuous components like color and pain.

---

31. Yolton is on the right track when he claims that, for Malebranche, the sense perception ("what [Malebranche] calls bodily seeing") of an object "has to be assisted and guided by the intellectual understanding of the mind"; see *Perceptual Acquaintance*, p. 44. He concludes that Malebranche's theory of perception is essentially no different "from many other accounts that combined cognition with sensation in our awareness of objects" (p. 55). See also Rome, *The Philosophy of Malebranche*: "Sense perception is a complex activity: it involves the act of conception, or pure intuition, and also sensation. Conception presents a universal meaning clearly and distinctly. The same meaning is present in perception" (p. 291). Rome's interpretation is important because of her stress on the central role of conception, or the pure intuition of ideas, in Malebranche's epistemology and in his account of perception in particular. My reading of Malebranche's theory is, I believe, similar in some respects to Rome's. But if I understand Rome correctly, on her reading ideas for Malebranche are still what are "directly apprehended" in sense perception, although they are apprehended as "immanent" in objects or "as being in the external world" (p. 60).

> There is always a clear idea and a confused sensation in the view we have of sensible objects, the idea representing their essence, the sensation informing us of their existence. The idea makes known to us their nature, their properties, the relations they have, or can have, to one another, in short, the truth; the sensation, on the other hand, makes us sense the difference among them and the relation they have to the convenience and preservation of life. (*Dialogues* V.2: OC 12:113; D 107)[32]

One can perform an act of conceiving with one's eyes closed, and thereby intellectually apprehend a pure idea of extension undistracted by any (visual) sensations. When one opens one's eyes, the act of conceiving, which formerly took place by itself, now becomes, along with the onrushing flood of sensations, an element in our perceptual consciousness of the objects in the world around us.[33] On the other hand, one can have sensations without any ideas present, without attending to any intelligible representations, and thus without any conceptual elements involved. In this case the understanding plays no role in the process. As Malebranche puts it, one is then looking without seeing or perceiving (*Réponse*, OC 6:137).

An example may clarify this, and demonstrate exactly what the idea contributes to the perception of an object. In perceiving a penny, I am at least sensibly conscious of a certain bronze color shaped in a certain way (remember that for Malebranche there is a sensory apprehension of the *relative* shape of a body). But if my activity is to qualify as a *perception* of the penny, not only must I sense the object's roundness, but also I must see *that* it is round (or

32. Jolley sees the importance of distinguishing between the ways the two "heterogeneous elements" in Malebranche's theory of perception operate, and his account of the relationship between conceiving and perceiving is helpful and accurate; see *The Light of the Soul*, pp. 108–10. He also recognizes that ideas, for Malebranche, are logical or conceptual entities. Nevertheless he accepts, apparently without any argumentation, the traditional view that Malebranche holds a representative theory of perception (p. 85f.), although he also suggests that Malebranche "gives a new twist to the representative theory of perception; indeed, his uncompromising insistence that ideas are not psychological entities transforms that theory almost beyond recognition" (p. 87). But as Bertrand Russell insists, one need not hold sense data to be mental items.
33. See *Dialogues*, Preface, OC 12:19.

at least *that* is has such and such a shape). Thus the idea, first of all, makes possible the element of recognition necessary to perception. For Malebranche, the idea is necessary if one is to see *that* the object has the particular geometric features it has. This is because the ideas of bodies are pure intelligible extension: essences of figures and nothing more. Moreover, if I see that the penny is round, I am also thereby led to anticipate further possible appearances of the penny. For example, while perceiving it straight on, I also expect that, were I to perceive it at an oblique angle, it would appear ovoid. This anticipation, too, is made possible by the presence of the idea or concept of circle in my perception of the penny, since such an idea would inform me as to the various properties of the circular penny qua circular. The idea also allows me to grasp precisely the relationship in which this particular extended figure stands to other figures in my perceptual field, for example, the size relationship between the penny and the quarter next to it. In general, whatever beliefs or epistemic elements accompany and are essential to perception are a function of the idea(s) present therein.[34]

Malebranche is quite clear, however, that the only information the idea infuses into the perceptual awareness of a body is information regarding its extension. He uses the example of a marble column:

> There is thus a clear idea and a confused sensation in the perception one has of a marble column. I say a clear idea of the extension and not of the marble. For I know the nature and properties of the extension; but I do not know the internal configuration of the parts of the marble, that which makes the marble what it is rather than a brick or lead. (*Réponse*, OC 6:98)

Nor do I know, from the idea, whether or not the material object I perceive exists.

For Malebranche, then, what we perceive are material bodies, although in doing so we at the same time (as a component of the same complex activity) intellectually apprehend an idea. This is because Malebranche sees perception as essentially including an

---

34. An exception should be made for those "natural judgments" that are an immediate part of sensation itself; see earlier in chapter 2.

intelligible content, a knowledge of the essence of the object perceived insofar as it is an extended body. Perception is thus a relationship between the perceiving mind and the material body and is "informed" by divine ideas.

I have hesitated so far to give a lable to Malebranche's theory of perception. In many essential respects it might be proper to call it a direct realism. But what about his many references to "direct" perception (of ideas) and "indirect" perception (of bodies)? Or his claims that ideas are perceived immediately and bodies only mediately? Can such representationalist-like talk be reconciled with the nonrepresentationalist reading of Malebranche that I am advocating?

If one keeps in mind that the "perception" of an idea is really a case of a nonsensory, purely intellectual intuition of a logical concept, one can accommodate these *façons de parler*. On the one hand, to claim that our perception of ideas is "direct" and "immediate" is just to claim that our intuitive grasp of them is straightforward and nonmediated, a simple rational apprehension by the mind of a clear and distinct content that is intelligible on its own. On the other hand, to claim that bodies are perceived "indirectly" or "mediately" is simply one way of saying that our perceptual acquaintance with them is (and must be) mediated by concepts. The perception of bodies cannot be "direct" because, without the idea to contribute the cognitive element, a body is *inintelligible*.[35] The activity in question, without the idea, would not have the epistemic qualifications of perception proper. But as I have shown earlier, the perception of a body can be mediated by concepts and thus be "indirect" in this sense, without implying that it is "indirect" in the representationalist's sense.

It is clear from this explanation that when Malebranche claims we perceive ideas "directly" and bodies "indirectly," there is an ambiguity in his use of the word 'perceive': we "perceive" (i.e., intellectually intuit) ideas directly, and we perceive (i.e., perceive in the ordinary sense of the term) bodies indirectly. Similarly, when Malebranche claims (as he frequently does) that "we do not perceive bodies by themselves [*en eux-mêmes*]," he does not mean that we do not perceive bodies but some other things (ideas) instead;

---

35. See RLA, OC 9:915.

rather, he means that in perception our sensory apprehension of a body must necessarily be combined with conception, with the coincident intellectual apprehension of an idea.[36]

Another apparent complication for my reading of Malebranche's account of perception stems from his arguments that ideas are necessary in perception. One such argument seems to work like the argument from hallucination offered by sense data theorists: we can have perception of objects that do not really exist (or are not actually present) only because the ideas of the objects are present before the perceiving mind. Does not such an argument require ideas to be themselves the objects of perception? It would seem that ideas can account for why we have a perception of x when x does not exist, only because we nonetheless perceive an immaterial x (or representation of x). Malebranche's use of this argument appears to be evidence that he holds a representative theory of perception.

But hallucinations and the kinds of perceptual illusions Malebranche employs in his arguments are in fact simply erroneous cases of "seeing that . . ."—instances of having, in the face of certain sensory experiences, justified perceptual beliefs that do not happen to have any existing material body present corresponding to them. The hallucinatory experience of seeing a large purple pyramid on Fifth Avenue can be explained in terms of a certain stimulation of the sense organs that in this abnormal case results in the same sensuous appearances as would ordinarily be occasioned by the object itself (color, for instance, appearing in a pyramid shape—and again, the shape appearance would, for Malebranche, also be at the level of sensation). These sensuous elements must also be accompanied by the relevant beliefs: that this is a pyramid (recognition); that if I walked around it I would experience such and such perceptual appearances (anticipation); and so forth. Malebranche's arguments are intended to explain why I believe I see a pyramid when there is none before me—in other words, why I have such and such perceptual beliefs on this particular occasion. The answer is because the idea of a pyramid is currently present in my mind—along with the abnormally occasioned sensuous elements—informing this perceptual experience with whatever epistemic ele-

36. As Yolton suggests, the phrase "by themselves" simply means "without ideas"; see *Perceptual Acquaintance*, p. 49.

ments (especially beliefs) are required. There is no need here to take Malebranche's ideas as visual picture-like representations in order to make sense of his argument.

A proponent of the representationalist reading of Malebranche might next turn to Malebranche's well-known skepticism regarding knowledge of the existence of the external material world to support his or her interpretation. Malebranche insists that "an exact demonstration," with perfect geometric rigor, of the existence of the material world is not possible. And the evidence of sense perception, independent of faith in God as a nondeceiver and revelation of what he has willed, is not by itself sufficient to establish with absolute certainty its existence (although sensation does lead us nonepistemically to believe that there are bodies really out there[37]). As Malebranche puts it, "it is very difficult to prove that there are bodies," and we are wrong to think that we have but to open our eyes to be assured that the bodies we see actually exist.[38]

Now surely, it might be argued, this kind of skepticism can result only from holding a representative theory of perception. Only one who believes that we perceive ideas instead of bodies would be led to demand (and also doubt the efficacy of) arguments to the effect that bodies exist. In fact, it has been suggested that skepticism of this variety can only be the result of having surrounded the mind with a "veil of ideas" and then wondering whether, beyond those ideas, there is a real, material world. Thus Reid claims not only that Malebranche's skepticism here is a result of his maintaining "the common theory of ideas" (i.e., a representative theory of perception),[39] but also that Malebranche at least deserves some credit for

---

37. Malebranche puts it in causal terms: the sensations excited in us by God on the occasion of the presence of an object to our body "makes us judge that it exists" (*Search,* Elucidation X: OC 3:143; LO 621).

38. See *Search*, Elucidation VI.

39. If a philosopher should think "that the existence of external objects of sense requires proof," Reid takes this as evidence that he holds "ideas to be the immediate objects of perception" and "that we do not really perceive the external object"; see *Essays on the Intellectual Powers of Man* II.7, p. 125. Radner also believes that Malebranche's alleged representationalism is, at least in part, the source of his skepticism; see *Malebranche*, pp. 61–63.

his honesty in acknowledging the insoluble doubts to which that theory must inevitably lead.[40] This is, in essence, the standard objection usually raised against any representative theory: if we perceive only ideas, how can we ever know that there are material objects?

But raising the skeptical question about the possibility of certain knowledge of the existence of the external material world is not, by itself, evidence that one holds a representative theory of perception. A direct realist must, as much as a representationalist, acknowledge the force of the skeptic's challenge here. Whether one claims that we are able directly and immediately to perceive bodies or only ideas, one must admit that sometimes our perceptions are nonveridical, and that what perceptually appears to exist may not in fact exist. Doubts about the existence of the material world should be able to occur as easily on one philosophical account of perception as on the other.[41] Thus Arnauld, who holds a direct realist theory of perception, does not take issue with Malebranche's belief that the existence of the material world is something that requires proof; he contends only that, contrary to Malebranche, such a proof is possible.[42] But if raising the skeptical question cannot be evidence that one holds a representative theory, then neither can a negative answer such as Malebranche gives. To be sure, a direct realist does indeed believe that there is an external world; otherwise, his or her direct realism about the perception of bodies would reduce to a merely hypothetical claim. But then, Malebranche also believes that there is a material world, not because there are epistemically compelling or "invincible" reasons to do so, but rather because "I

---

40. "It is obvious that the system of Malebranche leaves no evidence of the existence of a material world, from what we perceive by our senses; for the Divine Ideas, which are the objects immediately perceived, were the same before the world was created. Malebranche was too acute not to discern this consequence of his system, and too candid not to acknowledge it" (*Essays on the Intellectual Powers of Man* II.7, p. 130).

41. As Lennon puts it, "the question as to whether we ever perceive physical objects is logically prior to any theory of perception"; see "Philosophical Commentary," LO 795. See also Bolton, "A Defense of Locke and the Representative Theory of Perception"; Nadler, *Arnauld and the Cartesian Philosophy of Ideas*, pp. 131–34; and Jackson, *Perception: A Representative Theory*, pp. 148–49.

42. See VFI, chapter 28.

do not see that there can be any good reason here for doubting the existence of bodies in general" (*Dialogues* VI.7: OC 12:141; D 139). And it is perfectly consistent to claim both that we perceive bodies and also that demonstrably certain, geometrically rigorous knowledge of the existence of bodies is not attainable.

Finally, there seems to be some difficulty in reconciling my nonrepresentationalist reading of Malebranche with what he says in several contexts about color sensations. Malebranche on occasion speaks of color sensations as "perceptions" of the intelligible extension in God: "The perception of the soul in someone who sees or feels an arm is only the perception, which is called either color or pain, of the extension composing the arm; that is, the immediate and direct perception of the ideal extension of the arm" (RLA, OC 9:961–61). This certainly seems to suggest that the idea ("l'étendue idéale du bras") is the object of sense perception for Malebranche, very much in the way a sense datum is the object of a sensory "direct awareness." And this would make it very hard to sustain the nonrepresentationalist reading I am offering.

If we are to take such talk literally, and as Malebranche's considered view, then I must admit that I do not know what to make of Malebranche's position. I do not see how to reconcile this account of sensing ideas with everything else I have claimed about the nature of Malebranchian ideas and their role in knowledge and perception. My only suggestion is that we not take such talk literally, just as I have argued earlier that we take not literally, but rhetorically, claims such as this: "the material world we animate is not the one we see when we look at it." In the *Search* itself there are no references to color sensations as *perceptions* of ideas. Rather, ideas are there described as "found in conjunction with," "accompanying," and "joined to" sensations,[43] and sensations are clearly means of apprehending "things," "objects," or "bodies," but not ideas.[44] This suggests that the *perception* account of sensation just noted is not an integral or essential part of Malebranche's doctrine. Moreover—and this bears repeating—Malebranche's ideas simply are not the kinds of things that *can* be sensed. They are logical concepts, not colorless visual-like data. Thus we should reject any

43. See, for example, III.2.vi: OC 1:445; LO 234.
44. See Elucidation X: OC 3:141–42; LO 621.

interpretation that would reduce ideas to images that can be sensibly apprehended.

To sum up, the perception of an external material object involves conceptual thought. On Malebranche's view it is distinguished from mere sensation by the presence of a conception of the object perceived qua extended body. Objects *en eux-mêmes* are unintelligible and thus unperceivable. The idea is what renders them intelligible to the mind. Ideas, on this reading of Malebranche, are not the direct objects of perception in any literal sense, but they do "inform" the perceptual consciousness of a body. They are objects of consciousness in the sense that in perception one is aware of its cognitive content (at least, this is Malebranche's point). But the way in which a concept is present in the perceptual consciousness of a body differs from the way in which a sense datum or representative idea has traditionally been understood by indirect realists to be present to the mind.

Appendix:
The Arnauld–Malebranche Debate

My interpretation of Malebranche's account of perceptual acquaintance, and particularly of the role of ideas in that account, provides a new perspective on what is at issue in the philosophical (as opposed to the theological) side of the Arnauld–Malebranche debate over ideas.

At one time the debate was regarded as being between two representationalists, each of whom believes that ideas are proxy objects perceived in place of bodies. Lovejoy, for example, insists that both Arnauld and Malebranche accept what he calls "epistemological dualism," according to which representative ideas stand between the perceiving mind and the material world and are the primary objects of perceptual apprehension. The only difference between their respective accounts, he claims, is that for Arnauld ideas are mental entities, while for Malebranche they are ontologically distinct from the human mind. "The theory of mediate perception which [Arnauld] is criticizing is, then, still that which would introduce, not a *tertium* but a *quartum quid.* . . . An immediatism [by which Lovejoy apparently means a direct realism] which should dispense with ideas and percepts altogether was not within Arnauld's intellectual horizon."[1]

Recently, however, the debate has, with greater plausibility, been characterized as being between a direct realist (Arnauld) and a representationalist (Malebranche). Arnauld's ideas are, on this interpretation, mental acts directed toward external bodies, and they acquire their intentionality by virtue of their representational con-

---

1. "'Representative Ideas' in Malebranche and Arnauld," p. 459. See also Church, *A Study in the Philosophy of Malebranche,* pp. 154–55.

tent. Malebranche's ideas, on the other hand, are still regarded as somehow interposed between us and the world, as being immaterial objects directly perceived instead of bodies (although we still perceive the latter "indirectly" and "mediately").[2] There is no question that this is how Arnauld sees what is at issue between himself and Malebranche. This is particularly clear from the kinds of criticisms he levels against Malebranche's theory.

But Malebranche himself offers a different, somewhat narrower explanation of the debate. The sole issue, he insists, is whether representative ideas are modifications of the soul or not.

> What is the issue at hand? Mr. Arnauld insists that the modalities of the soul are essentially representative of objects distinct from the soul; and I maintain that these modalities are nothing but sensations, which do not represent to the soul anything different from itself. (*Réponse*, OC 6:50)

> It is true, I have denied this proposition ["It is clear to anyone who reflects upon his own mind that our perceptions are essentially representative"] perhaps five hundred times. I have always declared to M. Arnauld that if this proposition were true, then he would be right and I would be wrong on the question of ideas. . . . The entire debate between us with respect to ideas depends upon this matter. (RLA, OC 9:902)

Cook argues that Malebranche's statement of the disagreement is "misleading and inaccurate," mainly because Malebranche ignores the direct realism/representationalism issue.[3] But in fact, if my reading of Malebranche's account of perceptual acquaintance is correct, then Malebranche's characterization is accurate and the debate (whether or not Arnauld realizes it) really is solely over the ontological status of ideas—over whether the ideas that enter into perception are themselves mental (acts) or are representations dis-

---

2. See Cook, "Arnauld's Alleged Representationalism" and "Malebranche versus Arnauld," where he argues explicitly for reading Malebranche as a representationalist. This is how I characterize the debate in *Arnauld and the Cartesian Philosophy of Ideas*. My main purpose there is to present Arnauld's theory. Jolley's claim that Malebranche "receives rather less than his due" in that book is correct (see his review of *Arnauld*). I intend for this present study to fill that gap.

3. "Arnauld's Alleged Representationalism," p. 54.

tinct from the mind—and *not* over whether we perceive bodies or ideas.

> I have contended that an idea is necessary to see [the stars]. . . . I have only contended that something distinct from the sun is required to represent it to the soul. Whether this is a modality of the soul, according to the sentiment of Mr. Arnauld . . . or intelligible extension rendered sensible by color or light, according to my opinion, this I leave to be examined later. (*Réponse*, OC 6:95–96)

Both Malebranche and Arnauld believe that we perceive bodies. And Malebranche's own description of the debate should alert us to the fact that he, at least, does not see it as a direct realism/representationalism conflict. This of course makes understanding the debate even more complicated, for now Arnauld and Malebranche differ not only over the nature of ideas, but also over what their disagreement is about in the first place.

Bibliography

Historical Sources

Ambrosius Victor (André Martin). *Philosophia christiana.* 5 vols. 2nd ed. Paris, 1667.

Arnauld, Antoine. *Oeuvres de Messire Antoine Arnauld, docteur de la maison et société de Sorbonne.* 43 vols. Paris, 1775.

Arnauld, Antoine, and Pierre Nicole. *La Logique, ou l'Art de penser.* 1662; Paris: Flammarion, 1970.

Berkeley, George. *The Works of George Berkeley, Bishop of Cloyne.* 9 vols. Ed. A. A. Luce and T. E. Jessop. London: Nelson, 1948–57.

Charleton, Walter. *Physiologia Epicuro-Gassendo-Charltoniana.* 1654; New York: Johnson Reprint, 1966.

Commentarii in tres libros de Anima Aristotelis. Conimbricae [Coimbra], 1598.

Cordemoy, Géraud de. *Oeuvres philosophiques.* Ed. P. Clair and F. Girbal. Paris: Presses Universitaires de France, 1968.

Cureau de la Chambre, Marin. *Systeme de l'ame.* Paris, 1664.

Descartes, René. *Oeuvres de Descartes.* 12 vols. Ed. C. Adam and P. Tannery. Paris: J. Vrin, 1974–83.

———. *The Philosophical Writings of Descartes.* 2 vols. Ed. and trans. J. Cottingham, R. Stoothoff, and D. Murdoch. Cambridge: Cambridge University Press, 1985.

Desgabets, Dom Robert. *Critique de la Critique de la Recherche de la vérité.* Paris, 1675.

Eustacius a Sancto Paulo. *Summa philosophica quadripartita.* Paris, 1609.

Foucher, Simon. *Critique de la Recherche de la vérité.* Paris, 1675.

———. *Réponse à la Critique de la Critique de la Recherche de la vérité.* Paris, 1676.

———. *Réponse pour la Critique à la Préface du second volume de la Recherche de la vérité.* Paris, 1676.

Galilei, Galileo. *Discoveries and Opinions of Galileo*. Trans. S. Drake. New York: Anchor Books, 1957.

Gassendi, Pierre. *Petri Gassendi opera omnia*. 6 vols. Lyons, 1658.

La Forge, Louis de. *Oeuvres philosophiques*. Ed. P. Clair. Paris: Presses Universitaires de France, 1974.

Leibniz, Gottfried Wilhelm. *Die philosophischen Schriften von Gottfried Wilhelm Leibniz*. 7 vols. Ed. C. J. Gerhardt. Hildesheim: Georg Olms, 1960–62.

——. *New Essays on Human Understanding*. Trans. P. Remnant and J. Bennett. Cambridge: Cambridge University Press, 1981.

——. *Philosophical Essays*. Trans. D. Garber and R. Ariew. Indianapolis: Hackett, 1989.

Locke, John. *The Works of John Locke*. 10 vols. London, 1823.

Malebranche, Nicolas. *Dialogues on Metaphysics*. Trans. W. Doney. New York: Abaris Books, 1980.

——. *Dialogues on Metaphysics and Religion*. Trans. M. Ginsberg. New York: Macmillan, 1923.

——. *Oeuvres complètes de Malebranche*. 20 vols. Ed. A. Robinet. Paris: J. Vrin, 1959–66.

——. *The Search After Truth*. Trans. T. M. Lennon and P. J. Olscamp. Columbus: Ohio State University Press, 1980.

Ockham, William. *Opera philosophica et theologica*. 9 vols. St. Bonaventure, N.Y.: Franciscan Institute, 1970.

Régis, Pierre Sylvain. *Cours entier de philosophie, ou Système général selon les principes de M. Descartes*. 3 vols. Amsterdam, 1691; New York: Johnson Reprint, 1970.

Regius, Henricus. *Philosophia naturalis*. 2nd ed. Amsterdam, 1654.

Reid, Thomas. *Essays on the Intellectual Powers of Man*. Ed. B. Brody. 1785; Cambridge, Mass.: MIT Press, 1969.

Toletus, Franciscus. *Opera omnia philosophica*. Hildesheim: Georg Olms, 1985.

Voltaire, François Marie Arouet de. *Lettres philosophiques*. Ed. H. Labroue. Paris: n.p., 1910.

Secondary Sources

Aaron, Richard. *John Locke*. 2nd ed. Oxford: Oxford University Press, 1955.

Adams, Marilyn McCord. "Ockham's Nominalism and Unreal Entities." *The Philosophical Review* 84 (1977): 144–76.

——. "Universals in the Early Fourteenth Century." In Norman Kretzmann et al. eds., *The Cambridge History of Later Medieval Philosophy*, 411–39.

Alquié, Ferdinand. *Le Cartésianisme de Malebranche*. Paris: J. Vrin, 1974.

Armstrong, D. M. *Belief, Truth, and Knowledge*. Cambridge: Cambridge University Press, 1973.

Ayers, M. R. "Mechanism, Superaddition, and the Proofs for God's Existence in Locke's *Essay*." *The Philosophical Review* 90 (1981): 210–51.

Balz, Albert G. A. *Cartesian Studies*. New York: Columbia University Press, 1951.

Bergmann, Gustav. "Some Remarks on the Philosophy of Malebranche." *The Review of Metaphysics* 10 (1956): 207–26.

Boas, G. *Dominant Themes of Modern Philosophy*. New York: Ronald Press, 1957.

Böhner, Philothenus. "The Realistic Conceptualism of William Ockham." *Traditio* 4 (1946): 307–35.

Bolton, Martha Brandt. "A Defense of Locke and the Representative Theory of Perception." *New Essays on Rationalism and Empiricism*, *Canadian Journal of Philosophy*, suppl. vol. 4 (1975): 101–20.

Bracken, Harry. "The Arnauld–Malebranche Debate: Philosophical or Ideological?" In Stuart Brown, ed. *Nicolas Malebranche*, 35–48.

———. "Berkeley and Malebranche on Ideas." *The Modern Schoolman* 41 (1963): 1–15.

———. *The Early Reception of Berkeley's Immaterialism*. The Hague: Martinus Nijhoff, 1965.

Bréhier, Emile. "Les 'jugements naturels' chez Malebranche." *Revue philosophique de France et de l'étranger* 125 (1938): 142–50.

Brentano, Franz. *Psychology from an Empirical Standpoint*. Trans. A. C. Rancurello, D. B. Terrell, and L. McAlister. London: Routledge and Kegan Paul, 1973.

Broad, C. D. "The Theory of Sensa." In Robert J. Swartz, ed., *Perceiving, Sensing, and Knowing*, 29–48.

Brown, Stuart, ed. *Nicolas Malebranche: His Philosophical Critics and Successors*. Assen: Van Gorcum, 1991.

Chisholm, Roderick, "The Theory of Appearing." In Robert J. Swartz, ed., *Perceiving, Sensing, and Knowing*, 168–86.

Church, Ralph W. *A Study in the Philosophy of Malebranche*. London: George Allen and Unwin, 1931.

Clark, Desmond. *Occult Powers and Hypotheses: Cartesian Natural Philosophy Under Louis XIV*. Oxford: Clarendon Press, 1989.

Connell, Desmond. "Cureau de la Chambre, source de Malebranche." *Recherches sur le XVIIᵉ siècle* 2 (1978): 158–72.

———. *The Vision in God: Malebranche's Scholastic Sources.* Paris and Louvain: Nauwelaerts, 1967.

Cook, Monte. "Arnauld's Alleged Representationalism." *Journal of the History of Philosophy* 12 (1974): 53–64.

———. "Malebranche versus Arnauld." *Journal of the History of Philosophy* 29 (1991): 183–99.

Copleston, Frederick. *A History of Philosophy.* Vol. 4, *Descartes to Leibniz.* London: Burns Oates & Washburn, 1958.

Costa, Michael J. "What Cartesian Ideas Are Not." *Journal of the History of Philosophy* 21 (1983): 537–49.

Doney, Willis, ed. *Descartes: A Collection of Critical Essays.* Notre Dame, Ind.: University of Notre Dame Press, 1967.

Dretske, Fred. *Seeing and Knowing.* London: Routledge and Kegan Paul, 1969.

Dreyfus, Ginette. *La Volonté selon Malebranche.* Paris: J. Vrin, 1958.

Farfara, Richard. "The Notion of the 'Idée Efficace' in the Philosophy of Malebranche." Ph.D. diss., University of Toronto, 1975.

Findlay, J. N. *Meinong's Theory of Objects and Values.* Oxford: Clarendon Press, 1963.

Firth, Roderick. "Sense-Data and the Percept Theory." In Robert J. Swartz, ed., *Perceiving, Sensing, and Knowing,* 204–70.

Gaonach, J.-M. *La Théorie des idées dans la philosophie de Malebranche.* 1908; New York: Slatkine Reprints, 1970.

Gay, Peter. *John Locke on Education.* New York: Columbia University Press, 1964.

Gilson, Etienne. *The Christian Philosophy of St. Augustine.* New York: Random House, 1967.

———. *Etudes sur le rôle de la pensée médiévale dans la formation du système cartésien.* Paris: J. Vrin, 1930.

———. *Index scolastico-cartésien.* 2nd ed. Paris: J. Vrin, 1979.

Gouhier, Henri. *La Philosophie de Malebranche et son expérience religieuse.* Paris: J. Vrin, 1948.

Gueroult, Martial. *Malebranche.* 3 vols. Paris: Aubier, 1955.

Hatfield, Gary C., and William Epstein. "The Sensory Core and the Medieval Foundations of Early Modern Perceptual Theory." *Isis* 70 (1979): 363–84.

Heil, John. *Perception and Cognition.* Berkeley: University of California Press, 1983.

Hessen, Johannes. *Augustins Metaphysik der Erkenntnis.* Leiden: E. J. Brill, 1960.

———. "Malebranches Verhältnis zu Augustin." *Philosophisches Jahrbuch* 33 (1920): 52–62.

Jackson, Frank. *Perception: A Representative Theory.* Cambridge: Cambridge University Press, 1977.

Jolley, Nicholas. "Leibniz and Malebranche on Innate Ideas." *The Philosophical Review* 97 (1988): 71–91.

———. *The Light of the Soul: Theories of Ideas in Leibniz, Malebranche, and Descartes.* Oxford: Oxford University Press, 1990.

———. Review of Steven Nadler, *Arnauld and the Cartesian Philosophy of Ideas.* In Oxford Studies in the History of Philosophy, vol. 2. Forthcoming.

Kenny, Anthony. "Descartes on Ideas." In Willis Doney, ed. *Descartes,* 277–49.

Kretzmann, Norman, Anthony Kenny, and Jan Pinborg, eds. *The Cambridge History of Later Medieval Philosophy.* Cambridge: Cambridge University Press, 1982.

Laporte, Jean. *Etudes d'histoire de la philosophie française au XVIIᵉ siècle.* Paris: J. Vrin, 1951.

Lennon, Thomas. "Angelus Domini: Malebranche's Argument for Ideas." Paper presented at the conference "Ideas: Sensory Experience, Thought, Knowledge, and Their Objects in 17th and 18th Century Philosophy," University of Iowa, April 1989.

———. "Philosophical Commentary." In Nicolas Malebranche, *The Search After Truth,* 755–848.

Lovejoy, A. O. "Representative Ideas in Malebranche and Arnauld." *Mind* 32 (1923): 449–61.

———. *The Revolt Against Dualism.* LaSalle, Ill.: Open Court, 1930.

Luce, A. A. *Berkeley and Malebranche.* Oxford: Oxford University Press, 1934.

Matthews, H. E. "Locke, Malebranche, and the Representative Theory." In I. C. Tipton, ed., *Locke on Human Understanding,* 55–61. Oxford: Oxford University Press, 1977.

Maurant, John A., ed. *Introduction to the Philosophy of St. Augustine: Selected Readings and Commentaries.* University Park: Pennsylvania State University Press, 1964.

McCracken, Charles. *Malebranche and British Philosophy.* Oxford: Oxford University Press, 1983.

McRae, Robert. "'Idea' as a Philosophical Term in the Seventeenth Century." *Journal of the History of Ideas* 26 (1965): 175–84.

Meinong, Alexius. "The Theory of Objects." Trans. I. Levi, D. B. Terrell, and R. Chisholm. In R. Chisholm, ed., *Realism and the Background of Phenomenology,* 76–117. Glencoe, Ill.: Free Press, 1961.

Michael, Emily, and Fred S. Michael. "Corporeal Ideas in Seventeenth-

Century Psychology." *Journal of the History of Ideas* 50 (1988): 31–48.

Moore, G. E. "Visual Sense-Data." In Robert J. Swartz, ed., *Perceiving, Sensing, and Knowing*, 130–37.

Moreau, Joseph. "Le Réalisme de Malebranche et la fonction de l'idée." *Revue de métaphysique et de morale* 51 (1946): 97–141.

Nadler, Steven. *Arnauld and the Cartesian Philosophy of Ideas*. Princeton, N.J.: Princeton University Press, 1989.

———. "Cartesianism and Port-Royal." *The Monist* 71 (1988): 573–84.

———. "Ideas and Perception in Malebranche." *Studies in Early Modern Philosophy* 2 (1988): 41–60.

———. "Intentionality in the Arnauld–Malebranche Debate." Forthcoming.

———. "Occasionalism and the Mind–Body Problem." In Oxford Studies in the History of Philosophy, vol. 2. Forthcoming.

Ndiaye, Aloyse-Raymond. "Le Concept d'étendue intelligible: influences gassendistes sur Malebranche d'après Arnauld." *Recherches sur le XVIIᵉ siècle* 4 (1980): 99–113.

Pitcher, George. *A Theory of Perception*. Princeton, N.J.: Princeton University Press, 1971.

Price, H. H. *Perception*. London: Methuen, 1932.

Prior, A. N. "Intentional Attitudes and Relations." In P. T. Geach and A. Kenny, eds., *Objects of Thought*, 111–30. Oxford: Oxford University Press, 1971.

Radner, Daisie. *Malebranche: A Study of a Cartesian System*. Assen: Van Gorcum, 1978.

Riley, Patrick. *The General Will Before Rousseau*. Princeton, N.J.: Princeton University Press, 1986.

Robinet, André. *Malebranche et Leibniz: relations personelles*. Paris: J. Vrin, 1955.

———. *Système et existence dans l'oeuvre de Malebranche*. Paris: J. Vrin, 1965.

Rodis-Lewis, Geneviève. "L'Arrière-plan platonicien du débat sur les idées: de Descartes à Leibniz." In *Permanence de la philosophie: mélanges offerts à J. Moreau*, 221–40. Neuchâtel: La Bacconière et Payot, 1977.

———. "La Connaissance par idée chez Malebranche." In *Idées et vérités éternelles chez Descartes et ses successeurs*, 63–88. Paris: J. Vrin, 1985.

———. *Nicolas Malebranche*. Paris: Presses Universitaires de France, 1963.

Rome, Beatrice. *The Philosophy of Malebranche*. Chicago: Henry Regnery, 1963.

Smith, Norman Kemp. *Studies in the Cartesian Philosophy.* New York: Russell and Russell, 1902.

Stewart, M. A. "Locke's Mental Atomism and the Classification of Ideas." *The Locke Newsletter* 10 (1979): 53–82; 11 (1980), 25–75.

Swartz, Robert J., ed. *Perceiving, Sensing, and Knowing.* Berkeley: University of California Press, 1965.

Walton, Craig. "Malebranche's Ontology." *Journal of the History of Philosophy* 7 (1969): 143–61.

Watson, Richard A. *The Breakdown of Cartesian Metaphysics.* Atlantic Highlands, N.J.: Humanities Press, 1987.

Williams, Bernard. *Descartes: The Project of Pure Enquiry.* Harmondsworth: Penguin, 1978.

Wilson, Margaret. *Descartes.* London: Routledge and Kegan Paul, 1978.

Yolton, John. "Ideas and Knowledge in Seventeenth-Century Philosophy." *Journal of the History of Philosophy* 13 (1975): 145–66.

———. *John Locke and the Way of Ideas.* Oxford: Clarendon Press, 1956.

———. *Perceptual Acquaintance from Descartes to Reid.* Minneapolis: University of Minnesota Press, 1984.

———. "Representation and Realism: Some Reflections on the Way of Ideas." *Mind* 96 (1987): 318–30.

Index